FINDING LOST

SEASON 5

NIKKI STAFFORD

ECW Press

For Sydney and Liam

Copyright © Nikki Stafford, 2009

Published by ECW PRESS
2120 Queen Street East, Suite 200, Toronto, Ontario, Canada M4E 1E2
416-694-3348 / info@ecwpress.com

LIBRARY AND ARCHIVES CANADA CATALOGUING IN PUBLICATION

Stafford, Nikki, 1973–
Finding Lost, season 5: the unofficial guide / Nikki Stafford.

ISBN 978-1-55022-891-5

1. Lost (Television program). I. Title. II. Title: Finding Lost, season five.

PN1992.77.L67S735 2009   791.45'72   C2009-902550-7

Developing editor: Crissy Boylan
Cover concept: Barry Johnson
Cover and text design: Tania Craan
Typesetting: Gail Nina
Front cover photo: (island) © Scott Mead Photography
Printing: Transcontinental   2   3   4   5

The publication of *Finding Lost, Season 5* has been generously supported by the Ontario Arts Council, by the Government of Ontario through Ontario Book Publishing Tax Credit, by the OMDC Book Fund, an initiative of the Ontario Media Development Corporation, and by the Government of Canada through the Book Publishing Industry Development Program (BPIDP).

Canadä   ONTARIO ARTS COUNCIL
             CONSEIL DES ARTS DE L'ONTARIO

PRINTED AND BOUND IN CANADA

ECW PRESS
ecwpress.com

Table of Contents

A Few Words From the Readers

Like many *Lost* fans, I share an unhealthy obsession with any and all Oceanic 815–related lore. Also, like many of the fans below, I enjoy the fan movement just as much as the show itself. Through her *Finding Lost* guides, Nikki Stafford has become a hub for that movement and a voice for fans.

For her fifth season guide of *Finding Lost*, I suggested to Nikki that the fans be given the chance to praise *her* for her work. She accepted with grudging modesty, and thus this page was born.

Being the first, I want to say how awesome it is sharing and theorizing together on Nikki's blog, Nik at Nite (nikkistafford.blogspot.com). I often feel like Hurley doing a cannonball, just thinking about sharing my half-cooked musings about every detail of the show.

Finding Lost, being the big-book translation of that blog, gives fans an excellent on-hand reference to every hot theory, cast bio, and book on Sawyer's shelf. Intelligent analysis? Check. Thorough research? Check. Sassy and stylish writing? Whoa, *big* check. *Finding Lost* has it all. Nikki works hard to feed our flame, so on behalf of all the *Lost* fans reading this: a real thank-you to Nikki. Please continue to be our compass for finding *Lost*.   — Matthew Dykstra

Marlene Dietrich once said of Orson Welles, "When I have talked with him, I feel like a plant that has been watered." And those, like me, who read her work, books, or blog know the same can be said of Ms. Stafford. Her passion and knowledge come across in such a wonderfully casual way that can only come from someone who loves what she does. And we certainly love what she does! More water, please.
    — Michael L. Holland

If you want to know your Benjamin Linuses from your Henry Gales or your John Lockes from your Jeremy Benthams, let Nikki Stafford be your constant. Her writing reflects the insightfulness, passion, and humor of both the show and its fans.
    — Steve "The Shout" Dandy

Nikki plunges headlong into the dense, sometimes byzantine, jungles of *Lost*, leading her readers with a torch of keen insight in one hand and a machete of cutting analysis in the other. We emerge on the other side, wiser and more entertained.

— Austin "Teebore" Gorton

In the universe of *Lost*, there are scores of fans, bloggers, and commentators offering their take on the myth and meaning of the pop phenomenon spawned by the show. None offer such accessible and comprehensive analysis on the series' multi-layered and innovative storytelling as Nikki Stafford. The arrival of the latest installment in Stafford's *Finding Lost* series is met with a resounding cheer by her ginormous (and growing) fan base. Her in-depth analysis of the relationships, storytelling, and mythology of the show proves the popular theory that *Lost* is best enjoyed and understood by sifting through the minutiae of the show and its ever-expanding universe in the company of like-minded obsessives. Nikki lays it all out in comprehensive detail: story arcs, literary references, inside jokes, and mind-blowing narrative. The truth may be Out There, but we are all in *here*, turning the pages and delighting in Nikki's meticulous research and engaging writing style. Now, if only I could find a Frozen Donkey Wheel, I could go back and read her books again, for the first time.

— humanebean

Nikki's blog is, quite simply, addictive. Her love of all things *Lost* is surpassed only by her talent for writing about the show intelligently, in a way that speaks both to us uber-fans as well as the casual viewer. Her blog attracts thousands of readers, many of whom contribute comments, which, along with Nikki's responses, make for the most illuminating, stimulating, and, quite frankly, fun *Lost* discussions on the web.

— Batcabbage

The insights Nikki offers in her books and in her blog are incredibly thought-provoking and the intelligent, open, and often hilarious discussions always have me coming back for more. The *Lost* experience is definitely richer and more enjoyable for me thanks to her.

— Rebecca "SonshineMusic" Thompson

Nikki always helps find a deeper understanding for the show's twist and turns, and really knows her stuff. Her commentaries are insightful, thought-provoking, and often laugh-out-loud hilarious. If you love *Lost*, you'll love what she has to say.

— Jeff Heimbuch

Enlightening, engrossing, and just plain entertaining, Nikki's is the definitive guide; it's like watching *Lost* with a friend who misses nothing and who shares her insights with passion, humor, and an irresistibly down-to-earth perspective. No one should get *Lost* without her; the perfect guide to a near-perfect show!

— Lisa Mallette

Nikki Stafford's *Finding Lost* books give both the casual viewer and *Lost* devotees better reasons for finding *Lost*.   — Bob "Hutch" Hutchinson

Nikki Stafford's writing has allowed true fans of *Lost* (those of us who faithfully gather with like-minded souls the morning after an episode to dissect every minute detail of the show) access to a light-hearted yet in-depth analysis of the show. Her words allow us flashes of insight into not only the characters and events that leave us breathless, but also the overarching ideas and recurring themes presented by the writers. The *Finding Lost* series is a perfect partner for *Lost* — both easily captivate their audiences and both demand a second . . . or third . . . or fourth examination just to make sure we found everything we were looking for.

— Sharon Johnson

My first stop after watching an episode of *Lost* is Nikki's blog. I love the way she helps tie together the new episodes with things from the past. Nikki's insight into the books mentioned on *Lost* alone is just tremendous and saves me so much time. Not only does she take the time to recap the book itself, but then goes the extra mile to explain how the book ties into the series. I'd be "lost" without Nikki!

— sirputtsalot

Nikki's *Finding Lost* series and blog make watching *Lost* even more amazing than the show on its own. Her articulate and analytical books outline each episode in detail: Hurley's numbers, character wounds, Easter eggs, production errors, music, philosophy, and everything else that makes *Lost* the best show on television. She discusses Egyptian gods and goddesses, the psychology of romance, nosebleeds, Jack's beard, and my favorite — summaries of novels on the show and how they relate to the storyline. Her writing is a definite treat for Losties.

— Tammy Najarian

Of all the online *Lost* communities, Nikki Stafford's blog has consistently been the most welcoming, as well as one of the most enlightening. Her writing on *Lost* helps tie loose pieces of the show together that could have been otherwise overlooked by viewers, and then the tightly knit community she fosters helps elucidate even the most complicated of plots. Her work brings the hardcore fan and the casual fan together where both feel equally welcome as well as a constructive part of the discussion.   — B.J. Keeton

Thanks to Nikki Stafford I've got more time to watch *Lost*, as I don't have to read the more than a thousand pages of *Ulysses* myself.

— mgkoeln (Cologne, Germany)

Finding Lost is the must-have companion to each *Lost* season.

— Jim Drews

Nikki's *Finding Lost* series is informative, witty, entertaining, and loaded with so much interesting information it'll make your head spin. A definite must-read for casual *Lost* fans, hardcore 815 followers, and every Other in between.

— Andrew "The Question Mark" Fantasia

Nik at Nite is the first blog that I check after a new episode of *Lost*. Nikki Stafford just has this great way of being able to bring out new information from the show that you might have missed without telling you in a condescending way, just like you're talking to your super smart friend.   — Ashlie Hawkins

Watching *Lost* without Nikki's books is like mashing potatoes with a toothpick. Nikki's books add a little knob of butter and a giant masher to smooth out the complex *Lost* story — well done, Nikki!   — Matt Ede

As a Whedon Studies scholar, I initially read Nikki's blog after meeting her at a conference, where I had heard and thoroughly enjoyed her keynote address. I admired her rhetorical style and wit so much that I returned repeatedly to her blog and found myself reading far beyond the Whedonverses therein. Though I had quit watching *Lost* a few years earlier, her enthusiasm for the series and her ability to convince me of its value as quality television led me to watch and relish season 5. Thank you, Nikki.   — Cynthea Masson

From the first reading of Nikki Stafford's blog through all of her *Lost* books thus far, I have become and remained a huge fan. There is so much going on in the series that I need someone to help organize my own thoughts and present new ideas that I haven't even thought of. Nikki is that someone. Her *Finding Lost* books are an invaluable guide for both obsessed fans like me and casual observers. Along with that, they are also just plain fun to read. Nikki's style of writing is never overbearing. It is as if she is talking to you and actually reminds me of one of my favorite teachers — never preachy, just fun to hear.

— Michele in Newfoundland

With *Lost* it is easy for fans to get pulled into a world of smoke monsters, time travel, and mysterious hatches, but even the most devoted fan, such as myself, can use some help unraveling the mysteries of the island and its castaways. With the help of Nikki Stafford's books and blogs, fans are treated to her unique insight, witty humor, and a perspective that shines a light on *Lost*'s darkest mysteries.

— Chris Temple

I've long enjoyed episode guides to the likes of *Star Trek, Buffy*, and *The X-Files*. What makes Nikki's *Finding Lost* volumes stand out among such efforts is that they're not just about ferreting out nitpicks and Easter eggs. Her analysis helps the show's creative team make this intricate fiction more than what you see on the screen, and I wouldn't rewatch *Lost* without it.

— Brian Saner Lamken, blamken.blogspot.com

Finding Lost is the perfect companion for casual viewers and die-hard fans alike. Nikki thoroughly explains what newbies need to know to follow along, while exploring the minute details of the series' dense mythology for hardcore enthusiasts. A must-read!

— fb

It is no wonder that Nikki is an editor in her other life — she has the editor's keen eye for detail and a mind that makes tracking disparate plot points across multiple storylines seem effortless. All of which combine to make her a pretty much perfect *Lost* tour guide, never thinking for you but masterful in nudging you toward fascinating new paths through the jungle.

— Joshua Winstead

Lost can be an overwhelming series and Nikki Stafford provides clarity with her books, breaking the show down into delicious bite-sized pieces. Nikki highlights events of interest, brings up questions to ponder, and helps explain what is going on around the island (time travel and a smoke monster, oh my!). Fun to read while still being very thorough (hard to do!), Nikki packs in plenty of in-depth information for the avid *Lost* fan and lots of quick bits for the casual viewer.

— Abigail

Stafford's writing, whether in her brilliant and thought-provoking *Finding Lost* books, or on her captivating Nik at Nite blog, always points out details and concepts that I would have otherwise missed, and generates fascinating conversation, on the blog or among friends who also enjoy *Lost*. Always impartial about character preferences (except for Desmond, of course) and ready to tear through any book that the *Lost* writers throw her way, Nikki sheds light into the darkest corners of The Island, and brings *Lost*'s amazing stories to new heights with a knowledgeable perspective that helps cultivate the best ideas in each of her readers.

— Barry Johnson

How Not to Get Lost – **Season 5**

Go to any area of the Lostverse online, and you'll probably find the same resounding note regarding season 5: "This was my favorite season yet!" Season 4 was amazing, but season 5 stepped things up to a level that was breathtaking; by that same token, the plot entered a level of complexity that probably left many viewers a little lost (pardon the pun). But unlike season 3, where people got tired of polar bear cages and didn't get enough of the verbal sparring between Jack and Locke or Hurley and Sawyer, fans didn't walk away from season 5. More casual fans than ever were jumping online and trying to find the answers to the mysteries on the show. There were a few concepts that were difficult to get our heads around — the time traveling alone had people reeling — but the story was *so* good people wanted to stay. Week after week audiences felt like they had run a marathon at the end of the episode, and couldn't wait for the following week. For the first time in the show's run, fans began lamenting the ever-looming series finale that was an entire year away, and yet seemed too soon. What will we do without these characters week after week? How many years will fans be debating the central themes of the show? How many questions will "Darlton" (the fan name for Damon Lindelof and Carlton Cuse, the two main showrunners) ultimately answer?

To recap: season 1 was about trying to get off the island, season 2 was about the Losties learning to live with each other, season 3 was about dealing with the native people of the island, and season 4 was about the invasion of the outside world into the microcosm of the island. Season 5 was about getting off the island — *and coming back*. Where the writers had come up with new ways to show a character's story (we'd seen real flashbacks, what-if flashbacks, and even flashforwards) this season came up with an even more inventive form of the "flashback" . . . and it was groovy, baby. The end of season 5 was more jaw-dropping than any other finale before it, putting characters we thought we knew in an entirely new light.

As I've written in the introduction to my previous *Finding Lost* books, this book is intended to be read alongside the episodes. You can watch the entire season and then read through the book, or you could watch an episode and read the corresponding guide to it. What I strive for in these guides is not plot summaries (if you're looking for plot summaries so you don't actually have to watch the series, this isn't the book for you) but instead analytical, detailed, in-depth readings of each episode that will help you sort out the clues, work through the mysteries, and figure out all that time travel that happened to be a big part of season 5.

Aside from writing these books, I keep a blog called Nik at Nite (nikkistafford.blogspot.com) where, during the season, I analyze each episode the night of the show and my readers and I discuss the episodes at length for the next week. In season 5 there was a *lot* to discuss, and many of the blog entries had over 200 comments (the finale alone had over 400). I owe a lot to the regular commentators on that blog who show up day after day to discuss their favorite TV show.

Finding Lost is *not* a substitute for watching the show. You will not understand what I'm writing about if you haven't watched (or aren't watching along as you read) these episodes. This book will provide a deeper understanding of the characters, the events, and the mysteries, but it will not be a replacement for *Lost* itself. No book could ever hope to do that.

The book is formatted episode by episode. Almost every guide is accompanied by some tidbit of information, such as a small sidebar of interest, or a larger chapter on the historical significance of something. Much like the plot of life on the island is interrupted by flashbacks of the characters, so too will the episode guide be broken up by these sections. You can come back to them later and just focus on the guide in the beginning, or read through them to get a better understanding of the references in the episodes.

Since season 1, several characters have been seen reading books — initially Sawyer was the bookworm on the beach, and since then Ben has become the island's chief bibliophile. The writers have said that any book seen on screen is actually a clue to the island's mysteries, so whenever a book is featured prominently on screen, I will provide a book summary chapter for it. In each book summary, I will give a brief rundown of the plot, and point out the deeper meaning in each book (the book chapters contain no spoilers for any episode past the one where I've placed them), and then offer some suggestions concerning the importance the book has on the show, and why it may have been chosen by the writers. Four of the books analyzed — *Ulysses*, *Y: The Last Man*, *A Separate Reality*, and *Everything That Rises Must Converge* — were seen on screen being read by characters on the show, while a fifth — *The Little Prince* — was hinted at through an episode title and subtle references within the show.

Some of the sections will touch on historical explanations of allusions on the show, such as what the U.S. Army's "Operation Castle" had to do with the third episode of the season, or which Egyptian gods are candidates for the statue on the island. Others will take a facet of the episode and explore it more closely than you might have seen on the show, and still others will look outside the show to things like the DharmaWantsYou alternate reality game (ARG). Much of season 5 refers back to earlier seasons, so some sections in this book will link together ongoing motifs, like Geronimo Jackson or the smoke monster.

The guides to the individual episodes will contain some spoilers for that particular episode, so I urge you to watch the episodes before reading each one. Because I am a severe spoilerphobe, I've been careful not to spoil any episodes beyond the one you're reading about, so if you watch an episode, and then read the corresponding guide to it, you will be pretty safe from being ruined for any future surprises. The episode guide will feature a brief summary of the episode followed by an analysis. After each analysis, you'll find special notes of interest, and they require some explanation:

Highlight: A moment in the show that was either really funny or left an impression on me.

Did You Notice?: A list of small moments in the episode that you might have missed, but are either important clues to later mysteries, or were just really cool.

Interesting Facts: These are little tidbits of information that are outside the show's canon, explaining allusions, references, or offering behind-the-scenes material.

Nitpicks: Little things in the episode that bugged me. I've put these things in nitpicks because I couldn't come up with a rational explanation myself — but maybe you have an explanation, and if so, I'd love to hear it. What makes the Nitpicks section difficult is that what appears to be an inconsistency on this show could be a deliberate plot point by the writers that will take on massive significance later. So I'm prepared for several of these to be debunked by the show. Please read these knowing that I nitpick only to point things out, but not to suggest the writers aren't on their game. These are meant to be fun.

Oops: These are mistakes that I don't think could be explained away by anything.

4 8 15 16 23 42: In the late–season 1 episode, "Numbers," Hurley reveals a set of numbers that have had an impact in his life, and it turns out those numbers have popped up everywhere, on the island and in the characters' lives before the crash. This section will try to catalog them.

It's Just a Flesh Wound: This is a list of all of the wounds incurred by the characters on the show.

Lost in Translation: Whenever a character speaks in another language that is not translated for us or we see something written that's not immediately decipherable, this section will provide a translation wherever I could find one. Thanks to all of the fans who have provided these to the English speakers like me.

Any Questions?: At the end of each episode, I've provided a list of questions that I think viewers should be asking themselves at that point. Some questions will be answered in later episodes, but because these guides are meant to be read as one goes through the season episode-by-episode, these questions are meant to be the ones you *should* be asking yourself at the end of each hour.

Ashes to Ashes: Whenever a character on the show dies, this section will provide their very brief obituary.

Music/Bands: This is a list of the popular music we hear on the show. In most cases I've provided in italics the name of the CD where you could find the song, but if I haven't, it's because it's a song that is featured on several compilations.

And there you have it, a guide to the guide. I hope you enjoy the book, and I welcome any corrections, nitpicks, praise (please? just a little?), and discussion at my email address, nikki_stafford@yahoo.com, or come on over to my blog. I cannot stress this strongly enough, however: the opinions in the following pages are completely my own, and if anyone out there has contrary opinions, I respect those. I don't expect everyone to have the same views as I do. What makes *Lost* so much fun to watch and discuss is how many possibilities it presents to us. Ten fans can come away with ten different interpretations of what they just saw, and that's what makes a show great, in my opinion.

Nikki Stafford
nikki_stafford@yahoo.com
nikkistafford.blogspot.com
July 2009

"We Have to Go Back!": Season 5

At the end of season 3, Darlton had been given the assurance by ABC that *Lost* would be given 48 more episodes (and would not be canceled, regardless of ratings), allowing them to piece the remaining bits together to unfold their mystery the way they wanted to. The result was a tightly woven, beautifully written fourth season that won back many of the fans they'd lost the year before. With the end of season 4 answering the big question from the end of season 3 — *Locke* was the guy in the coffin — fans got their big bombshell cliffhanger . . . and then had to wait another eight months to see anything more.

Season 4, by far the shortest of the show's history due to a smaller scheduled number of episodes and an unscheduled writers' strike, was about the outside world invading the island and what happens when you get the very thing you'd wished for. It was about the rescue of the survivors; well, some of them, anyway. We saw the Oceanic 6 — Kate, Jack, Hurley, Sayid, Sun, and Aaron — taken off the island with Frank and Desmond. But through flashforwards, that handy-dandy plot device the writers added at the end of season 3, we saw how their happiness at being rescued quickly dissipated as they succumbed to guilt, personal demons, and destiny. Kate and Jack settled down to play house with Aaron, even going so far as to get engaged. But Jack's obsessions got in the way, and he became an alcoholic and drug addict, driving his loved ones away from him. He sees Locke's obituary in the newspaper and heads to the funeral home, where Ben confronts him and tells him he needs to return to the island. Kate remains fiercely protective of Aaron, and never wants to return to the island. Hurley ends up back at the mental institution after seeing the late Charlie standing in a convenience store. Sayid briefly finds love with Nadia, but when she's killed, he turns into a soulless hitman, working for his nemesis Ben Linus. Sun, devastated by Jin's death, gives birth to Ji Yeon on her own, separates herself from everyone else, and becomes vengeful, reaching out to Widmore.

And now, they're about to go back. How will everyone get back to the island? Will Jack be able to convince everyone? If Sun is working against everyone else, why would she willingly return? Would Kate bring Aaron with her? Will some of the Oceanic 6 have to be returned against their will? And how did Locke end up in that coffin? These were the questions that kept fans talking through the *very* long summer, fall, and winter that preceded season 5.

Ha ha ha! Oh, this island is so much fun it's easy to forget about the deaths and murders and kidnappings and disappearances and . . . (© MARIO PEREZ/ABC/RETNA LTD.)

In July, Darlton appeared at the San Diego Comic-Con, the event where they've been teasing viewers and spilling secrets since the show's first season. They answered questions about season 4, and hinted at spoilers for season 5 (which I won't include here). As in other years, however, the audience had to take everything they said with a grain of salt (these are the guys who promised an explanation of the four-toed statue in season 3 and a Rousseau flashback in season 4), but even when these guys are just pulling our legs, they're still a lot of fun to watch. They talked about time travel and how they were going to try to do it differently than other movies and TV shows (see page 169). They showed some of the extras that would appear on the upcoming season 4 DVDs. They held up a Jack action figure and argued about whether or not it actually looked like Jack, only for Matthew Fox to suddenly appear unannounced to answer the question once and for all. And then they showed the orientation video for season 5.

The video opens with a fanboy who is at the Dharma orientation booth at Comic-Con. He's about to go into a room where he'll be shown a classified video,

Thousands of fans lined up for a season 5 open casting call for extras on *Lost*. (RYAN OZAWA)

and he's got a hidden camera on him so he can record the information he sees inside the booth. We see Hans Van Eeghen (see page 128), head of Dharma Recruitment, talking to him in advance, and he's the one who introduces the video we're about to see. The video opens with the Asian man we see at the beginning of all the Dharma orientation videos, who says his real name is Pierre Chang and he's a professor of theoretical astrophysics at Ann Arbor, Michigan. He says he knows the people watching this video are seeing it roughly 30 years from the moment he's speaking, and gives key indicators to prove he's aware of what the world will be like in the future. He says all of his people will be killed in a purge that they are powerless to stop. He says his information is coming from a trustworthy source, and at that moment you can hear Daniel Faraday's voice behind the camera, telling him all of this information is irrelevant and that he needs to get to the point. Chang tells the viewer that the island has special properties, and urges anyone watching to please continue the research because maybe they can come back in time and prevent the cataclysmic events from happening and save all of them. At that point, Daniel gives up, frustrated, and says no one is ever going to watch the video. Chang jumps up, pleading with him to let him continue, and the video shuts off. At that point Hans steps over, sees the hidden camera that's been recording the whole time, and shouts for security. The fanboy runs out of the booth, exclaiming that he "got it" and keeps running until a multi-colored test pattern covers the screen, and it's over (to watch the video, go to lostpedia.wikia.com/wiki/Dharma_booth_video).

Fans speculated for months about the significance of the scene. Chang is wearing sweatpants in a 1970s-style, which would make sense because that's the era he is from, but why is Daniel in the video? Did he travel back in time to Chang? Were they somehow able to stop the Purge?

The Dharma video led fans outside to the Dharma recruitment booth, where they could sign up as new Dharma recruits and take a series of tests. This game was the beginning of the new *Lost* alternate reality game (ARG) that kept fans busy for a few weeks in the summer (see page 128).

At the same Comic-Con, the opening scene of J.J. Abrams' new fall series, *Fringe*, was shown to eager audiences, who immediately jumped onto blogs and other networking devices to reveal that the scene featured people on a plane . . . that hits turbulence . . . and they all crash to earth, with no survivors. Was it just déjà vu? A colossal joke? Or was J.J. just giving a not-so-subtle wink to the show's predecessor, showing audiences that *Fringe* would keep them glued to their seats in the same way *Lost* did, filled with little mysteries that viewers would have to piece together? (*Fringe* debuted in September to stellar ratings, which quickly fell when the first few episodes didn't live up to the hype; by the end of the season, the series had redeemed itself, appearing at the top of critics' year-end best-of lists and proving J.J. had another enigmatic hit on his hands.)

Throughout the hiatus, *Lost* was recognized in several awards ceremonies, and shut out of others. The show was nominated for Best Drama at the Emmy Awards, with Michael Emerson receiving a nod for Best Supporting Actor (Drama). Jorge Garcia won an ALMA (American Latino Media Award) for Best Supporting Actor in a TV Series, Drama. Later in fall 2008, the show was shut out of the Golden Globe and Screen Actors Guild awards, but was nominated for a Writers Guild and Producers Guild award.

In August, the cast quietly began renegotiating their contracts with ABC. Most of them were making $80–90,000 per episode, with Matthew Fox (who is considered the lead) making $150,000. Fox was given a raise to $225,000 per episode, and the other stars negotiated their raises separately.

At the beginning of September, the new casting announcements began. Zuleikha Robinson was cast in the part of Ilana, a role described in the casting call as "a European female in her late 20s to early 30s who possesses great intelligence, but who's also dangerous as all get out. She's alluring and apparently used to getting her own way." The deal was for a recurring part in season 5, with the possibility of becoming a regular cast member in the final season. Robinson is a British actress who also appeared in *Hidalgo*, as well as *The Namesake*, the ill-fated FOX series *New Amsterdam*, the *X-Files* spinoff *The Lone Gunmen*, and as the strong-willed Gaia on the HBO series *Rome*.

The following week, Robinson was joined by Saïd Taghmaoui. A French actor who was originally a professional boxer, his move to Hollywood began in screenwriting, where he cowrote the screenplay for the French film *La haine*, with director Mathieu Kassovitz, who won the Best Director prize at Cannes for it. It's a remarkable film about three men in Paris, angered by the recent police assault on an Arab, who are eventually questioned in the case. The film starred Vincent Cassel, Taghmaoui, and Hubert Koundé. Since that film Taghmaoui has become a star in France, though to North American audiences he may only be recognized from appearances in a handful of episodes of *The West Wing* and the films *Three Kings*, *Hidalgo*, *The Kite Runner*, and *Vantage Point* with Matthew Fox. When the casting call went out for the part of Caesar, it read, in part, that he would be "a dangerous, physical, and extremely intelligent male between the ages of 35 and 45. Although his intentions are unclear, this much is certain: he's as skillful at charming people as he is at killing them. He also has a dark past . . ."

In October, while completing *Star Trek*, J.J. Abrams hinted in an interview that a *Lost* movie was a faint possibility. His emphasis was on the word "faint," but the media picked up on "possibility," quoting the section of the interview where he said, "The one thing that makes you think maybe there could be [a movie] . . . is that ABC agreed to end the series after six years. Which is a gift, because you know you won't have years seven and eight where you're thinking 'they should've ended at year six,' and you know how to pace yourself so that you know how to end the series." They seemed to leave out the part where he added, "My gut is it would never happen."

Just to clarify, a few days after this interview made waves, Lindelof insisted there would not be a movie, which came as a relief to most fans for the very reasons

Fans were recruited for the Dharma Initiative at the 2008 San Diego Comic-Con as part of an online game. (RYAN OZAWA)

he outlined: "People have been so patient with the show and to basically say that we're going to end the TV show but we're going to leave some questions unanswered so that you can pay $14 and go see it in the theater? . . . You never say never but what we are saying is that when the final episode of *Lost* airs, that will be very conclusive. There will not be a question mark at the end of the words 'THE END.'"

At the end of October, ABC began airing promos for season 5, which caused a flurry of excitement among fans. With the season tagline, "Destiny Calls," the trailer showed various quick cuts of scenes from season 5, causing blogs to light up with questions and speculation ("Why is someone holding a gun to Charlotte's head?" "Who locked Sun in that room and why is she banging on the door?" "Is Hurley holding a *gun*?!"). The second trailer began airing at the end of November, and it announced the new season would begin in January, not February as previously assumed.

In November, it was announced that series composer Michael Giacchino, who had also written scores for movies such as *Speed Racer*, *Mission Impossible III*, *The Incredibles*, *Ratatouille* (for which he was nominated for an Oscar), and most recently *Up*, would be conducting the orchestra at the following February's Academy Awards. Said the producers in a joint statement, "Michael is an extraordinarily talented and versatile musical artist. . . . We couldn't be happier that he is game to come onboard."

As the promo for the new season ramped up, *Lost*'s fourth season began showing up on year-end best-of polls, appearing in *TV Guide*'s top shows of the years, as well as AFI's list of best shows on television. In December ABC began running a new, longer promo for the fifth season as a mini-video for The Fray's new single, "You Found Me," which subsequently became a hit for the band.

Through the ongoing Dharma ARG, fans were given sneak peeks of full scenes from the first episode of season 5, and ABC released a promotional photo of the cast. Each member had been individually shot against a green screen, and then Photoshopped into a picture, making it look like they were sitting in an apartment building surrounded by paraphernalia from the first four seasons of *Lost*. Fans who took a close look at the picture noticed that Daniel's foot was missing, as were Juliet's toes. Could it be a sign? Did this mean Daniel had one foot in the grave? Could Juliet's days be numbered? The producers released a statement saying no, in fact, it was just really shoddy Photoshop work.

As the date of the show's premiere — January 21, 2009 — loomed, and fans caught up on season 4 through the newly released DVD set, the producers began hinting at the season that was to come, promising time travel, many surprises, and one character in particular coming to the forefront. "We really feel it's the year of Sawyer," Lindelof said in an interview. "He's really stepping up in a major way." For a guy who didn't even get his own episode in season 4, this was a big deal. How would Sawyer be stepping up? Would he and Kate be reunited? Would both of them end up with other people?

The fans would have to wait and see . . .

SEASON 5 – January–May 2009

Cast: Matthew Fox (Jack Shephard), Evangeline Lilly (Kate Austen), Terry O'Quinn (John Locke), Josh Holloway (James "Sawyer" Ford), Jorge Garcia (Hugo "Hurley" Reyes), Naveen Andrews (Sayid Jarrah), Yunjin Kim (Sun Kwon), Daniel Dae Kim (Jin Kwon), Henry Ian Cusick (Desmond Hume), Michael Emerson (Benjamin Linus), Elizabeth Mitchell (Juliet Burke), Jeremy Davies (Daniel Faraday), Ken Leung (Miles Straume), Rebecca Mader (Charlotte Lewis)

Recurring characters: Alan Dale (Charles Widmore), Jeff Fahey (Frank Lapidus), John Terry (Christian Shephard), Nestor Carbonell (Richard Alpert), François Chau (Pierre Chang, always uncredited), Sonya Walger (Penelope Widmore), William Blanchette (Aaron), Sam Anderson (Bernard), L. Scott Caldwell (Rose), Zuleikha Robinson (Ilana), Saïd Taghmaoui (Caesar), Patrick Fischler (Phil), Reiko Aylesworth (Amy), Doug Hutchison (Horace Goodspeed), Sterling Beaumon (Young Ben), Eric Lange (Radzinsky), Brad William Henke (Bram), Jon Gries (Roger Linus)

5.1   Because You Left

Original air date: January 21, 2009
Written by: Damon Lindelof, Carlton Cuse
Directed by: Stephen Williams
Guest cast: Tom Irwin (Dan Norton), William Mapother (Ethan Rom), Sean Whalen (Neil "Frogurt"), Brad Berryhill (Anxious Guy), Chantal Boom'la (Counter Girl), Michael Dempsey (Foreman), Leslie Ishii (Woman), Sven Lindstrom (Crew Member), Cindy Paliracio (Reporter/TV Anchor), Stefanie Smart (Ticket Agent)

Focus: Everyone

It's been three years since the Oceanic 6 were rescued, and Ben and Jack are trying to figure out how to round up the others to return to the island. Sayid has helped Hurley escape the hospital, Kate is faced with lawyers demanding something she won't give them, and Sun is stuck at an airport with another key player in the island mystery.

Meanwhile, three years earlier on the island, a record is skipping, tossing the survivors from one time period to another.

A woman we don't know shakes a man awake and tells him to tend to the baby we hear crying in the background. He puts on a record from a few decades ago and gets the baby ready for the day before heading to work. We realize he's the man from the orientation videos, the time period probably some point in the '70s. Suddenly he's rushed from his tranquil day to an emergency at some construction site. As he yells at one of the workers about the intricacies of time travel, he bumps into . . . Daniel Faraday, looking the same in the '70s as he did in 2004. It's a jarring opening that is completely baffling.

Welcome to another season of *Lost*.

We left our favorite castaways in precarious positions at the end of season 4. The island had disappeared when Ben turned the Frozen Donkey Wheel. Dan and a bunch of redshirts were in a Zodiac boat in the water when it happened, and the Oceanic 6, plus Frank and Desmond, were in a helicopter. The latter group saw the island disappear, but we didn't know what would become of the people on, or near, the island. Through flashforwards we knew the Oceanic 6 would get home, go through their own trials and tribulations — discovering parenthood, becoming assassins, having birthday parties, growing terrible beards — and wherever they went, the island would follow them in one way or another. We also knew that in 2004 Locke was on the island, but by 2007 he was off the island . . . in a coffin.

The Oceanic 6 have come a long way since their rescue . . . and not necessarily in a good way. They seem evenly split between those who want to return, and those who refuse to do so. At the end of season 4, Sayid killed a man while breaking into the Santa Rosa Mental Institute, and Hurley's first words to him were, "We're not going back, are we?" as if that was the last thing he wanted to do. But the moment they were outside, in this episode, Hurley says, "We never should have left the island," as if he's suddenly realized the truth.

On the island Hurley was tricked, his girlfriend was killed, he was pursued by Others, almost eaten by polar bears, and had, um, regularity issues, but at least he wasn't cooped up in a mental hospital talking to dead people. All Hurley has ever wanted is peace. He won the lottery, and his friends abandoned him, his father used him, his mother bought golden messiahs, and wherever he went he was in the spotlight. Yet it wasn't the tabloid pressure that got to him, it was his inner turmoil. He was convinced that the very lottery numbers that had won him millions of dollars were cursed, and he had doomed not only himself, but everyone around him. Since the crash, his greatest fear is losing his mind, and while he projects a jolly demeanor, inside he is filled with confusion and misery. Fans love Hurley, and we want to see him happy. Will season 5 bring him the happiness he deserves?

Just as Hurley says they never should have left, Sayid shoots back that if he ever runs into Ben, do the opposite of whatever he asks. Sayid divulges that he's been working for Ben for two years, so whatever emotional pain Hurley is in, Sayid's is probably even worse. We know that in the last three years he's lost Nadia, he's been turned into Ben's hitman, and he's been knocking off the people working for Widmore one by one. Now he appears to be no longer working for Ben, so something has happened between them, and whatever it was has turned Sayid even more deeply against Ben than he was before. Sayid does not want to return to the island under any circumstances. When he was there last, he at least had a faint glimmer of hope that Nadia might be out there somewhere. Now he knows she's gone, and there's nothing left for him to hope for. What sort of man will Sayid be now? (Other than a crazy-ninja-move, tranquilizer-filled Iraqi–James Bond sort of man, of course.)

Ben obviously wants to return to the island — it is everything to him. He's convinced Jack, but if there's one thing we all know about Ben, it's that practically everything that comes out of his mouth is a lie. That makes it difficult to watch the scene of him chatting with Jack in the hotel room without raising one eyebrow and questioning everything. If Sayid is right, and whatever Ben says, the opposite is actually true, then maybe Ben has actually seen Locke since the island; that he does know what happened to the survivors after the island moved; and that everything happening on the island right now has nothing to do with the Oceanic 6 leaving. Ben is just trying to get them back there to fit his own agenda. Or, if Sayid is mistaken, then Ben is telling the truth. (I think I'll go with door number one.)

Unlike Sayid, Jack has been pulled in not only by what Ben has told him, but by his own guilt. Since the flashforward that ended season 3 in "Through the Looking Glass," we've seen how leaving the island has reduced Jack to a shell of his former self. Now, as he shaves off the "Jeard" (and fans everywhere cheer loudly), he seems to have a renewed purpose. If he can help Ben get everyone back to the island, he can stop the craziness happening there, and he can fix things. Again. Or, as we at home see it, he will not fix things, as usual, and he'll

Matthew Fox — sans beard, the way we like him — greets fans warmly at the San Diego Comic-Con in 2008. (JENN ELLIS)

be in a worse spot than he was before. Watch Matthew Fox throughout this season — his performance is a tour de force that rivals that of any other actor on this show.

When the Oceanic 6 first left the island, they made a perfect show of solidarity; with the exception of Sun (who was unavailable largely due to distance), they attended Hurley's birthday party and Christian Shephard's memorial service, and no doubt kept in touch regularly. But then it became apparent that Sun's distance wasn't just physical, it was emotional. Hurley is the only one who comes to see Ji Yeon, and both he and Sun are happy that no one else does. Soon after, Nadia is killed, and when Sayid joins forces with Ben, it breaks him away from the others. Hurley is the next to separate himself, when he happily commits himself to an institution after a chat with the now-dead Charlie. Jack, Kate, and

Aaron play happy family for a while before Jack begins his downward spiral, and Kate orders him out. At that point, the split is complete, with only Kate and Aaron staying together.

Kate is strongly attached to Aaron, but when two lawyers show up on her doorstep and tell her they want a blood sample to confirm she is his mother, Kate does the one thing she does best — she runs. Being a mother to Aaron has given Kate a new lease on life, and given her a reason to stay put for once. Before the Flight 815 crash, Kate bounced between fathers while growing up and then bounced between towns and countries while on the run from the law. The one time she thought she could settle down with a husband, she was wrong, and was again on the run within months. But even then, there was a moment when she took a pregnancy test, as if telling herself that if she's pregnant, she will stay with her husband and have the baby. When the test was negative, she broke down and cried, knowing she'd leave him.

Now she has Aaron, the baby that has allowed her to settle down, but an outside threat forces Aaron into a carseat and both of them to be on the run. This time, she finds it's not easy to run away when you have a child with you. And more than the threat itself is the mystery of it: who is asking for a blood sample? Who has figured out that Aaron is not hers? Kate is the last person who would want to return to the island, but it seems to be haunting her still.

And finally, Sun breaks with the Oceanic 6 by aligning herself with Charles Widmore and declaring her intention to kill Ben Linus. In the season 4 finale, "There's No Place Like Home, Part 3," Sun approaches Widmore and offers him a business card and the proposition that they work together to achieve the same goal. Widmore, clearly angry that this underling has approached him as an equal (and apparently not aware of just how powerful Sun can be), is at the same time intrigued. Is she lying to him? Does she really want to kill Ben or is it all part of some larger plot to lure Widmore into danger? Upon her return, Sun staged a coup at Paik Industries and when she confronted her father, she said two people were responsible for her husband's death, Paik being one of them. The question is, who is the other person she holds responsible? Since Widmore is the man who sent the freighter that caused his death, could it be him? Or is it really Ben, the man who caused the ship to explode?

On the island, things are even more confusing than they are off. When Ben "moved the island," he appeared to have flipped a switch that has unmoored the survivors in time, and now they are jumping helplessly from one time period to another. In one time period, their camp is gone, because they've gone back in time and it hasn't been built yet. In another, the Swan station has exploded, but in the next, it's intact again. The time jumping is a literal fact, and a symbolic description of how each of them feels removed from the moment. Sawyer's thoughts aren't on the island, but on the helicopter that just left with Kate on it (or, as he fears, that exploded along with the freighter). When he snarls at Daniel that everybody he cares about just blew up on the boat, it's possibly the most poignant moment for Sawyer yet. In seasons 1 and 2, he was the cad who sat on the beach and bogarted the supplies, put the "I" in "team," and gave everyone clever nicknames. After cavorting with Kate in a polar bear cage (only on *Lost* could that line not sound ridiculous), he became more serious, as if Kate had given him something more to live for. But he believed her feelings were for Jack, and he turned away from her. When Locke put him face to face with the man who'd destroyed his life, Sawyer went down a dark path that has haunted him ever since. In season 4 he became a leader, as if he no longer had to hunt or be hunted by the man known as Sawyer. People refer to him as James more often these days, and when he leapt from a helicopter in "There's No Place Like Home," he secured his place as the hero of the show. But now that he thinks Kate is gone (along with his chance of ever being rescued), he's struggling to see the point in life.

Like Sawyer, Dan's thoughts are elsewhere, usually in his journal, and he somehow knows more than the rest of them. When Dan realizes that the raft time-jumped with the island, he says, "We must have been inside the radius," as if he knew the island was jumping through time. How does he know what the island is doing? How did he know it was going to happen at that moment? Last season when he realized Ben and Locke were heading for the Orchid, he made a mad dash to get everyone off the island, as if he knew everything that was about to happen. The answers seem to be in his journal, but it's not clear how that information got in there.

Juliet remains quiet throughout the episode. For three years she's been trapped on this island against her will, and Ben Linus promised her numerous times that she would soon get to leave. But every opportunity for freedom has been thwarted, and when she realized Ben was obsessed with her, her hopes of ever leaving the island were dashed. He promised her a sub ride off, and then Locke blew up the sub. She was moments away from being taken to the freighter, and that blew up, too. Juliet stands apart from the rest of the survivors: they don't know if they can trust her, despite the fact she wants to leave the island as much as (if not more than) they do.

Meanwhile, one man is doing his own thing, as usual.

From the moment Flight 815 crashed into the island, John Locke has been on his own. To Jack's eternal annoyance, Locke believes he has a destiny, and the curing of his paralysis was the miracle that convinced him of it. In season 1, he disappeared into the jungle, found the hatch, and tried to open it. The one time he enlisted someone's help with his scheme (Boone), the person ended up dead. In season 2, he often visited Ben in his cell alone, and again was on his own spiritual journey, trying to figure out if this "Henry Gale" person was really telling the truth, and whether he should continue to push the button. Locke was the man of faith on the island, but when that faith started to waver — helped along generously by Benry — he stopped pushing the button, which resulted in a catastrophe. In season 3, he again embarked on a personal journey, beginning in the sweat lodge where he had a hallucination, continuing as he led people across the island, doing weird things along the way, and ultimately coming to a point where once again, he broke away from the group. He joined up with Richard Alpert, who told him the truth about Sawyer's past, and Locke lured Sawyer into another scheme, where Sawyer emerged still alive, but broken. From there, Locke continued his journey on his own, almost dying in a pit of corpses before lurching from the jungle long enough to plant a knife in someone's back and then slinking away into the jungle once again. In season 4, Locke convinced half the survivors to come with him, so Locke was no longer alone. But even surrounded by people, Locke kept to himself, made decisions for everyone, and, once again, he broke away from them, following his own agenda. As Ben turned the wheel, Locke was joining "his people," becoming the leader of the Others and turning his back on the survivors once and for all.

But now, the island is skipping through time and Locke is alone. While the other survivors try to understand what is happening on their own, Locke is once again confused, afraid, and trying to negotiate with his situation and with those — like Ethan and Richard — who enter into it. If the island is controlling the time jumps, it appears to be orchestrating them so John can discover his mission.

Despite being a loner, Locke has always obeyed what he believes are the rules of the island. He's following his own path to find his destiny. But according to Dan, there are overriding rules at work here. Rules are a major theme of this episode, and have been throughout the series. One of the standout lines of season

4 followed the heartbreaking moment where Alex was killed by Keamy, and Ben, standing by the window and completely shattered, mumbles, "He changed the rules." By "he" Ben meant Widmore, and ever since that iconic line, fans have been wondering: what rules?

From the beginning of season 1, we've seen several characters playing games. Locke loves backgammon. Ben prefers chess. Hurley, Locke, and Sawyer attempt world domination in a game of Risk. All of these games require cunning, planning, and a fierce strategy. But when it comes to the rules of the island, it's a different game altogether.

Daniel explains to the group that what is happening to them is similar to a record skipping. If the island and its inhabitants are the record, then they are the needle, bouncing around to various grooves on the record, going backward and forward. In each time period, they can be seen and can interact with those who are currently on a linear path. What he doesn't explain is why some people are jumping through time while some aren't (like the Others, who disappear when Locke time-jumps).

Time travel is one of the cornerstones of science fiction. We've had several mentions of it on *Lost*. (There were references to Stephen Hawking throughout season 3, and Desmond appeared to go back in time in "Flashes Before Your Eyes." In season 4, Desmond had a consciousness time-traveling moment in "The Constant.") But Daniel insists that despite the oft-used conceit of going back in time "to kill Hitler" (which has been used in several sci-fi stories, often with disastrous results), you cannot actually do anything to change how things turn out. So when Sawyer begins banging on the hatch hoping to be let in, Daniel begs him to stop, saying they can't see him because they weren't supposed to meet yet. Similarly, Ms. Hawking in "Flashes Before Your Eyes" (the white-haired lady who explains to Desmond that he cannot become engaged to Penny because he's not supposed to) espouses these very same rules. At the beginning of this episode, Pierre Chang tells a worker that "there are rules" to time travel, and one assumes he's referring to the same ones listed off by Dan and Ms. Hawking.

And yet, just as Locke has always been separate from the other survivors, there appears to be someone who operates outside of these rules: Desmond. He might have been discouraged by Ms. Hawking from changing the rules when he wanted to get married to Penny and never go to the island, but in "The Constant," Daniel sends him back in time to tell a 1996 Daniel the very coordinates that he wouldn't have discovered yet. Is that not tinkering with past events? Despite

Daniel spouting these rules, he's the very person who broke them. And when he looks at his journal at the end of this episode — the same journal that featured the line, "If anything ever happens to me, Desmond Hume will be my constant" — he sees something in there that changes his mind. Faced with a crazed, HAZMAT-wearing, rifle-wielding Desmond, Daniel tells the Scot that he is different, that "the rules don't apply to you. You're special. You're uniquely and miraculously special." In other words, unlike everyone else, Desmond *can* go back in time and change things. He can manipulate past or future events. If, for everyone else, the rule is "whatever happened, happened," Desmond stands apart from that. And if Desmond can do it, is it possible anyone else can?

Highlight: Richard's response when Locke asks him what the compass does: "It . . . points north, John."

Did You Notice?:

- This is the second season premiere in a row that is titled after a line Ben says.
- The opening was the same as the openings of seasons 2 and 3 — we are in a house that appears to be older, watching people we don't know, listening to a song from a few decades ago, and it always turns out that we're still on the island.
- Until now, we referred to the guy in the orientation videos using the only names we knew: Dr. Marvin Candle, Dr. Mark Wickmund, and Dr. Edgar Halliwax. This is the first time we hear his real name: Pierre Chang.
- The opening sequence was hinted at by the video that Darlton showed at the 2008 Comic-Con (see page xvi). We saw Chang filming a video and saying they were going to die. You hear a baby crying in the background, and Chang tells his wife to take him outside.
- This is also the first time we find out what the purpose of the Arrow station was. Chang says "this station's primary purpose is to develop defensive strategies and gather intelligence on the island's hostile indigenous people." The Arrow station is the one where the Tailies were living in season 2, and by that time it seemed to hold only a chest of some kind that had a few artifacts in it, but there was no video equipment or televisions, so it's unclear how anyone who had once worked there could have gathered any intelligence.
- As we see in this episode, the Orchid station looked originally like it was

going to be rather state-of-the-art. Compared to the decrepit wooden shell of a place we saw at the end of last season, this building looked like it was the beginning of something big.

- In the center of the sonogram taken of the Orchid's construction site is the Frozen Donkey Wheel. The fact that they have a sonogram immediately makes one think of the fertility issues on the island.
- The man who has been injured is suffering from a nosebleed, just like Minkowski and Desmond were in "The Constant."
- When Ben brings the gurney into the funeral home, there's a poster behind him that says, "Safety First: Don't try to lift more than you are able," which could be interpreted as a symbolic comment on the huge emotional burden they're all bearing.
- Again, when Ben recalls his last meeting with Locke, he tells Jack that he'd apologized to Locke for making his life difficult, as if he's had a hand in every miserable moment of Locke's life, and not just those in the past three months.
- Frogurt is on the raft with Daniel. Frogurt was first mentioned in the season 2 episode, "S.O.S.," where Bernard was building the S.O.S. sign on the beach with large rocks. He asks Hurley if the "frogurt guy" is coming, and clarifies that he used to make frozen yogurt. Hurley corrects him, saying his name is Neil. He appeared in the season 4 mobisode, "The Adventures of Hurley and Frogurt" (see *Finding Lost — Season 4*, page 132), so maybe fans enjoyed it enough that the writers thought it would be funny to insert him into this episode.
- In case you're wondering why Sawyer doesn't know Daniel, Sawyer was in New Otherton when Daniel was around, and never actually met him.
- When we first see Kate and Aaron, Aaron is watching cartoons, and a train goes into a tunnel. He says to Kate, "Choo-choo tunnel," and Kate laughs and teases him, saying he knows that if he goes into the tunnel he's never coming out. This seemingly innocuous line suggests Kate's underlying fear that once she's been to the island, she'll never be rid of it. Or, if she returns to the island, she's never coming back.
- As Kate and Aaron leave her house, there's a photo of Jack holding Aaron sitting on a writing desk near the door. They've used a different child actor, because it's a picture of a much younger Aaron, and it's clearly not William Blanchette in the photo.

- Sawyer asks Daniel for his shirt, even though Daniel is probably 40 pounds lighter than he is, as if this is his way of asserting his superiority over Daniel.
- Daniel mentions the island is skipping like a record, just like the Willie Nelson song starts skipping at the beginning of the episode.
- When the Beechcraft (Eko's drug-smuggling plane) is hurtling toward the island, it's trailed by black smoke, which is obviously the engine conking out, but it also looked a little bit like Smokey.
- The way Locke ducks as the plane comes in close above him is reminiscent of the famous scene with Cary Grant in Alfred Hitchcock's *North by Northwest.* The movie is about an innocent man who is being followed by agents who believe that he has a microfilm. It could be a comment on how Locke is an innocent person caught in the middle of the island's larger purpose.
- Sun's passport says it was issued on May 31, 2001. Some fans thought this was a production error (and considering the history of them on the show, it might well be) because Sun would have lost her passport during the crash. However, the passport she was traveling on Flight 815 with was made for her in 2004 by the woman who was helping her make her great escape. Perhaps she had a previous passport (the one she's using here) that she left at home, and the one she would have used for Flight 815 might have had a different issuing number and different identity on it.
- When Widmore and Sun are in the holding cell at the airport, the time on the clock is 9:22. That's the date of the original Oceanic crash.
- Hurley and Sayid grab some fast food at the Rainbow Drive-in. The restaurant name is yet another reference to the film *The Wizard of Oz,* and Dorothy's song, "Somewhere Over the Rainbow."
- Sayid clearly anticipates the men being at the safehouse, because *no one* loads a dishwasher with the chef's knives positioned sharp end up.
- Daniel seems far less jittery and more lucid in this episode than ever before. Suddenly he's talking about the Dharma Initiative and what he knows, and he remembers everything. This is the guy who couldn't remember three playing cards moments after seeing them in "Eggtown."
- Richard Alpert hands John a "constant" in the form of the compass, as if this object will keep him grounded as he jumps through time, and tells him he won't recognize him in the past, the same way Daniel told Desmond to mention "Eloise" to convince him of his sincerity in "The Constant."

- In the flashback of season 4's "Cabin Fever," Richard visits Locke when John is only five, and he lays six objects in front of him: a baseball glove, a vial of sand, The Book of Laws, a comic book, a knife, and the compass that he hands to John in this scene.
- Charlotte's nose is bleeding like Minkowski's and Desmond's did before Minkowski died and Desmond almost did.
- Desmond asks, "Are you him?" which is the first thing he asks Locke in season 2's "Man of Science, Man of Faith." Desmond also asks Daniel, "Do I know you?" as if he's suddenly recognizing the man he'd met at Oxford in 1996.
- After this episode, some fans speculated that maybe the whispers we hear in the jungle are actually people unstuck in time and talking in an adjacent time period.

Nitpicks: Sayid pushes Hurley against the wall, pressing his sandwich against him, which would have smeared some ketchup on him. But when Hurley stands against the railing holding the gun, he looks as if Sayid's squeezed a quarter of a bottle of ketchup onto his shirt. And just before Alpert emerges from the jungle to patch up John Locke, Locke enters the plane. There is moss growing all over the top of it, so it's clear we're in a time period later than when the survivors were on the island. But in "The 23rd Psalm," Eko lit the plane on fire. Why weren't the bodies reduced to ash? Why isn't there the tiniest bit of charcoal on the Virgin Mary statues? Why is the very flammable *straw* in which they were packed still intact? Is it possible that something really did change in the past and Eko never actually set the plane on fire, or is this simply a continuity error?

Oops: At the end of season 4, when the island moved, we got a flash of the Zodiac boat and all its passengers — Frogurt was definitely not in it.

4 8 15 16 23 42: The clock at the beginning said **8:15**, which are not only two of Hurley's numbers, but also the Oceanic flight number that started this whole mess. When the construction worker hands Chang a sonogram of the cave, the Frozen Donkey Wheel is located between **15** and **17** feet in. When Sun is in the airport, a voice on the loudspeaker says Flight **23** to Paris is now boarding at Gate **15**. The address of the safehouse is **1818**.

It's Just a Flesh Wound: Sawyer slaps Daniel, and threatens to do the same to Charlotte. Locke is shot in the leg by Ethan; Richard pulls the bullet out. Sayid throws an assassin off the balcony at the safehouse and kills him. Sayid is punched a few times by another assassin in the safehouse, and Sayid turns the fight around and impales the man on kitchen knives. Sayid is shot with three tranquilizer darts.

Any Questions?:

- What is Chang's backstory? How did he know about the energy on the island? Why does everyone show him so much respect?

- If everyone in the Dharma Initiative knows Chang, and the videos are intended for new recruits who will no doubt also know him, then why bother with the pseudonyms? Why not just say he's Pierre Chang?

- Did Daniel travel back in time to the island to see Chang?

- Ben asks Jack if Locke told him what happened after the island moved, and Jack says no. Ben responds, "Then I guess we'll never know." But they're about to go back to the island. Couldn't they just ask them? Does Ben know something that Jack doesn't? Does he assume they're all dead and there's no way they'll be able to ask them what happened?

The *Lost* production crew sets up the shots from a hotel balcony, complete with stacks of boxes the stuntman will land on as the "assassin" is thrown over the edge. (RYAN OZAWA)

- The island itself is staying constant, like a record, while the survivors on it are jumping around, like the needle. So why did the island actually disappear at the end of season 3? Is there a suggestion that somewhere along the line while they're jumping through time, they are going to obliterate the island and it will no longer exist in 2004? Or did Ben move the island physically as well as temporally? Why aren't the Others jumping? Are they an organic part of the island?

- Who are the people from the law firm called Agostini and Norton? Who sent them and wanted blood samples from Kate and Aaron? Widmore? Jack? Ben?

- Why is Sayid no longer working for Ben?
- Who were the men waiting for Sayid in his safehouse? Why was he able to keep fighting so hard despite all the tranquilizer darts in him? Had he some sort of immunity to them, like Westley built up immunity to the poison in *The Princess Bride?*
- Daniel asks Sawyer if all of their people are accounted for, and Sawyer says not everyone, remembering Locke. What about Claire? Has he decided she's dead? And why are they leaving Rose, Bernard, and the redshirts behind on the beach? Shouldn't they all stick together in such a precarious situation, when one never knows when they'll be jumping through time again?
- Why did Locke go back to the time when the Beechcraft crashed onto the island? Is there a reason?
- If Widmore was called because Sun swiped her passport for an Oceanic flight, does that mean he actually owns Oceanic Airlines? It would make sense, since he used an Oceanic plane in his ruse — staging a fake Flight 815 crash at the bottom of the ocean — and if he'd wanted the passengers to find the island for him, he might have orchestrated the original 815 flight.
- Daniel says you're not supposed to meet people in the past you didn't meet before. So did Locke break the rules by meeting Ethan? Was the gunshot wound retribution for him breaking those rules? Does that mean Ethan should have recognized Locke in season 1, since this scene would have taken place in Ethan's past?
- Miles comments that it took Widmore 20 years to find the island the first time. When the freighter folk arrived, they seemed to know very little about their mission. How would he know how long Widmore had been looking for the island? Had he been briefed by Widmore's people?
- Daniel says he knows about everything because his journal contains everything he ever learned about the Dharma Initiative. That's new . . . what was he doing studying the Dharma Initiative? Why has he wasted so much time sitting around the island doing weird experiments instead of actually trying to visit each of the Dharma stations?
- How did Richard Alpert know what was going to happen next with John Locke? How far in the future are they in this scene?

- In the last time jump, the hatch is still intact. If Locke hadn't yet found it, did Juliet just help him do so? She pulled all the vines and foliage off it, which might have helped him see it later.
- Juliet nonchalantly tells Miles there was a man in the hatch pushing a button every 108 minutes, and chuckles. Why is she so dismissive of Desmond, knowing the Sisyphean task he was forced to perform and what that did to him? Was she not also trapped on the island for three years, like him, held prisoner and unable to leave?
- Why is Charlotte's nose bleeding while no one else's is? Will they all start suffering these effects and she's the first to get it?
- What did Daniel see in his journal that made him go and knock on the door?
- When does this final time jump take place? It would seem that Desmond is alone in the hatch, and asks Dan specifically if he is "my" replacement, not "our" replacement. Kelvin Inman, the man who was originally in the hatch with Desmond, never let Desmond outside of the hatch in the suit, as we discovered in the season 2 finale, "Live Together, Die Alone." If Inman had been in the hatch, he would have answered the door. So one could argue that this must take place after Inman's death and before Locke finds the hatch. But the same day Inman dies, Desmond realizes there's nothing to fear in the air; in which case Desmond, when Dan knocked, wouldn't have bothered getting suited up. Inman suggests there's only one suit in the hatch. And if Desmond looks a little off when Locke first meets him it's because he's completely stir-crazy, which suggests he never leaves the hatch. Maybe there really was another suit in the station, and Desmond found it and answered the door when Inman was out fixing the boat (unbeknownst to Desmond). Or maybe this is all a big continuity error.
- What does Daniel mean about Desmond being special? Why is Desmond special? What made him the way he is?
- At the end of the episode, Desmond suddenly had a memory that wasn't there before. Why would it only occur to him now? If the event of Dan delivering the message happened in 2004 and changed the future, would Desmond be on a new timeline where he always had spoken to Daniel and had always had that message, or is there a particular way the time jumping is happening, which made the memory jump for the first time into Desmond's 2007 brain?

Music/Bands: Chang plays Willie Nelson's "Shotgun Willie," the first track on his album of the same name, released in 1973. The record gets stuck on the line, "You can't make a record if . . ." and we don't hear "you ain't got nothin' to say."

5.2   The Lie

Original air date: January 21, 2009
Written by: Edward Kitsis, Adam Horowitz
Directed by: Jack Bender
Guest cast: Michelle Rodriguez (Ana Lucia), Lillian Hurst (Carmen Reyes), Mary Mara (Jill), Cheech Marin (David Reyes), Sean Whalen (Neil "Frogurt"), Matthew Alan (Cunningham), Tom Connolly (British Guy), James Jeremiah (Detective), Dana Sorman (Darlene)

Focus: Hurley

As Hurley rushes to save Sayid's life, we flash back to see what happened in the first days after the rescue, and how Jack got everyone to lie about what had really happened on the island.

In many ways, *Lost* is a parable about what happens when a group of people fails to communicate. If they're not simply withholding important information from each other, the survivors are outwardly lying or performing long cons on people they should be aligning themselves with in the name of survival. How many times in the first three seasons did fans wish they would just *talk* around the fire? So after seeing the title of this episode, a fan wouldn't be blamed for asking *which* lie the title is referring to.

Many of the characters on the show live by lying to others (and to themselves). Sawyer is a professional con artist, yet he is also the most easily conned. Despite reinventing himself as the man he's spent a lifetime hunting down and performing the very same cons on other couples that the original Sawyer committed against his parents, James is also the most gullible, most easily tricked, and the last person to pick out another con artist in a lineup. Juliet has lied about many things. We've seen her in cahoots with Ben while pretending to be aligned with the people on the beach. But she's also helping the people on the beach while deceiving Ben. She comes across as sweet and innocent, but below that smiling, dimpled exterior lies a woman who knows a *lot* more than she is letting on. Every time the survivors discover something new, she shrugs and tells them everything she knows about it, surprising everyone (including the viewers). There's a lot more to Juliet than meets the eye. Daniel, Charlotte, and Miles are all keeping secrets — no one seems to know about Miles's special skill, Charlotte seems to be more familiar with the island than she's letting on, and Daniel's been keeping some history of the Dharma Initiative in his journal and not telling anyone about it. While Dan comes off as the one

Jorge Garcia attends the premiere of J.J. Abrams's *Star Trek* (a.k.a. "The Boss's New Flick"). (AL ORTEGA)

who is probably the most sincere, the way he casually walks out of the jungle and lies about having been lost for the past two hours makes us wonder what else he's been keeping from everyone.

But the biggest liars have all left the island, and the Oceanic 6 maintain the titular lie of this episode. Kate has lived a life of pseudonyms and phony backstories, but there's an innocence about her, that, like Sawyer, makes it easy for people to see through her. She doesn't enjoy making up names and stories and rarely makes eye contact when she's lying. But now that she's off the island, she's no longer lying for herself: she's lying for Aaron. She has someone who means more to her than anyone ever has, and he's worth the lie. She maintains the lie about what really happened after the crash (and who his mother is) with more conviction than she's ever shown for anything else, because of what would happen should she let her guard down.

Sayid has always been honest about who he is and what he did before coming to the island. When Hurley first asks him which battalion he fought with in Iraq, Sayid looks him dead in the eye and says, "The Republican Guard." He's explained to others that he was a torturer, and his skills have served him well on the island. But we've also discovered, through flashforwards of his time after the island, that he is a master of deceit. While working for Ben, as we saw in "The Economist," he could convince anyone of anything. As such, unlike Sawyer, Sayid can also see through anyone else, and has a built-in lie detector — he was the first to see that "Henry Gale" was lying, and he never wavered from his conviction. But the thing about Sayid is, his heart can get in the way. Just as he was about to successfully pull off his mission in "The Economist," he realized he'd fallen in love with his target, and almost died as a result. He tries to be hard and cold-blooded, but he's not. Perhaps his greatest lie is convincing everyone around him that he is not haunted by the atrocities he committed for so many years. In this episode he resolutely supports Jack in his decision to lie.

Jack is not so much a liar as a withholder of information. While on the island, he never told people about seeing his dead father walking around in the jungle, or why he was in Sydney in the first place. When he discovered new information he often kept it from the others, deciding that he alone should bear the burden of that knowledge. Jack's motivation for lying is the same as his motivation for everything else: he wants to fix things. If he can keep the truth from other people, then he can figure out how to fix the situation on his own without anyone getting in his way, and *voila*, everyone will be safe. In the case of the colossal lie, Jack is the one who creates it, and he needs the others to help him maintain it. But as we've seen, three years into the future, Jack's resolve will crumble, as it always does. Like Sayid, deep down Jack cares too much, and that's what hurts him. The lie becomes too big for him to carry around any longer, and he needs a new tactic, so he joins forces with Ben to see if he can take the next step: go back to the island and save everyone himself.

Sun lied to Jin when she was planning on leaving him. Quiet and submissive when she first came to the island, Sun soon showed us that she truly is Paik's daughter. As she gained her confidence after the crash, she was able to tell her husband the truth, and Jin and Sun became the favorite couple on the show. Now, off the island, she's not really upholding the lie the way the others are. We saw her go along with everyone at the press conference, and she's probably continued the ruse with her parents, but if the entire reason to lie in the first place was to keep the truth from Widmore, Sun is the weak link. Because the one person she's told the truth to . . . is Widmore. Now, face to face with Kate, Sun isn't so much a liar as fiercely passive-aggressive, telling Kate she doesn't blame her for Jin's death while reminding Kate — in detail — of those fateful last moments on the freighter deck. Sun knows exactly what she's doing, and how to hurt someone with an apparently innocent comment.

Hurley is unique. While he could never be trusted to keep anyone else's secrets, he never let one of his own slip. He didn't tell the other survivors that he was a millionaire, because in his mind, being on a deserted island, he wasn't a millionaire any longer, and they didn't need to know. Hurley is *too* sincere; in fact, the rest of the survivors quickly learned that if you need information, go and trick Hurley into giving it to you. The guy cannot tell a lie. So when Jack urges him to get on board with the rest of them, Hurley is the only one who doesn't want to lie about what happened after the plane crashed, and who doesn't think lying is necessary anyway. Worse than being a millionaire to Hurley is the fact that he was once in a mental institution. Jack suggests to Hurley that if he alone tells the truth while the rest of them are telling a different story, people will think he's crazy. Just saying that word cuts to the heart of Hurley's deepest fear, and Hurley reluctantly agrees to go along with it. Where Kate will lie to protect Aaron, Hurley will lie so people won't think he's crazy again. But when you have someone as frank and genuine as Hurley walking around with the enormity of this lie, something bad is bound to happen.

And then there's Ben. I'd considered including a sidebar of all of Ben's lies, but realized I'd need a long chapter instead . . . which would pretty much consist of every line Ben's ever uttered on the show. Ben is the king of the lying liars. He lies so much, it's like a chronic condition with him. He could insist he's a vegetarian *while* eating a steak, and could probably convince half the room he's telling the truth.

Ben has convinced Jack, the most skeptical of the bunch, that he needs to return to the island. He convinced Sayid to become his personal hitman. Now he faces Hurley, the one who might be the most easily swayed, but who has also been instructed by Sayid to not fall for anything Ben says. Ben knows exactly what makes each person tick, and he uses their flaws against them. Knowing the inner turmoil Hurley has been facing since he's left the island, Ben offers him a tranquil life of peace and coconuts, coming off as a cult leader promising Hurley a new life with a new religion: "Come with me and you won't ever have to lie again." It doesn't work, and Ben narrowly avoids getting covered in burning hot pizza sauce. Ben won't give up.

The reason Ben is the most fascinating of all of the liars, however, is that the audience never knows *when* he's lying. When one of the other main characters is lying about something, we know they're lying because we've seen their backstory, even if the other characters are oblivious to it. But in the case of Ben, we just don't know what is true and what is a lie. When he goes into the butcher shop, most of his conversation with Jill is enigmatic, and his brief defense of Jack comes out of the blue. Did Ben just stick up for Jack and admit Jack's had a rough time? Where is *that* coming from? And who is this Jill person, anyway? Ben makes the show fun to watch; he's the one who keeps us guessing in every scene.

For now, Hurley is out of Ben's clutches, but Ben has a pretty good idea of what makes Hurley tick, and what he can use to get him back to the island. Jack's guilt comes from his inability to fix the situation. Hurley's comes from the burden of the enormous lie he's been telling. In one of my favorite scenes in season 5, Hurley finally comes clean to his "Ma," who listens as Hurley unleashes a torrent of craziness about what *really* happened on that island — the Others, a smoke monster, some button they had to push, the Dharma Initiative, someone's girlfriend's father sending a freighter of mercenaries. While Carmen's eyes go wide and the music switches from sad to loopy to indicate a comic moment, she does the one thing that no one else on the show ever seems to do: listen. Hurley communicates the truth to her, and she listens to every word without ever cutting in. And at the end, when she sees her son's resolve and the pain he's going through holding on to all of this ridiculous stuff, she leans forward and says, "I believe you." These are the three most powerful words anyone could say to Hurley, and to hear them from his beloved Ma means more to him than anything.

Hurley could hold onto his convictions to stay behind, or he could return to the island. But if he returns, he knows that at least one person in the outside world will know where he went, and why. And she'll understand.

Highlight: There were several highlights in this episode, from every scene Carmen Reyes was in to Locke emerging from the jungle and casually saying hello to Juliet and Sawyer. But the best moment is when Hurley throws the Hot Pocket at Ben and it hits the wall. Officially a *Lost* comedy classic.

Did You Notice?:

In Kaimuki, the *Lost* crew sets up the shot of Kate's car pulling into the gas station just as Hurley leaves. The gas prices on the sign were dropped way down to as low as $3.22, causing excitement among motorists, but the 3s were promptly switched back to 4s as soon as they were finished shooting. (RYAN OZAWA)

- The island doesn't bloop the survivors into a different time in this episode, as if some of the bloops last longer than others.
- Jorge Garcia puts in a stunning performance in this episode, and a lot of it is simply in his facial expressions: from the subtle way his face changes when Jack tells him people will think he's crazy if he tells the truth, to the pain on his face as he sits before his mother and struggles internally with whether or not to tell her, to the comic timing of the way he delivers the truth to her, to the way he returns to the seriousness of the moment in telling her there are still people on that island, to the mental struggle he endures trying to decide whether or not to trust Ben. Characterized as just the funny guy, Garcia is underrated as an actor.
- "Ana Lucia" tells Hurley *not* to get arrested, but he does the opposite. If she

and the other dead people who communicate with him are manifestations of the island, then it's clear the island wants them all back.

- Maybe "Ana Lucia" meant it as a nice thing to say, but the throwaway line, "Oh yeah, Libby says hi," was *harsh*.
- Wouldn't Bernard know how to start a fire without any matches? He was one of the Tailies, a group who had no supplies and somehow survived for 48 days.
- Jack tells Ben he was looking for his pills to flush them down the toilet. It seems even being in the same vicinity as Ben brings out the liar in everyone.
- When Ben tells Jack to pack a suitcase, he instructs him to bring anything "in this life" that he wants, as if he's not merely taking him back to the island, but giving him a rebirth.
- Ben tells Jack that they're going to the island and never coming back. Jack accepts this as truth, and yet he still wants Sun to return to the island, knowing she'd never see her daughter again.
- Ben doesn't answer Jack when he asks if Locke is really dead.
- Papa Reyes is watching *Exposé*, the show Nikki guest-starred in. In the show's dialogue, you can hear references to the Scorpion, the Cobra, the Tsunami, and Dragon Lady, all things that have to do with a tropical island or a desert, two places that feature prominently on *Lost*. (I'm counting Nikki as the Dragon Lady.)
- Hurley's father is everything his mother is not, and vice versa. The guy had nothing to do with his family for 17 years, but is now living high on the hog while his son is wasting away in a mental institution. He doesn't seem concerned or worried about Hurley at all as he eats his caviar sandwich in front of the TV; he only cares about the money that his son has left behind for him to spend. When Hurley arrives and tells his father the absolute truth, Papa Reyes just looks at him and says either he's crazy or a liar. Hurley is neither, but his father doesn't see it. The frantic scenes between Hurley and his father are a perfect contrast to the quiet one with Hurley's mother.
- The casual way Kate jokes and plays with Aaron as she gets out of the elevator with him shows what a great mom she is.
- Charlotte is forgetting things the same way Daniel did.
- Rose tells Frogurt that he needs a time out. In the previous episode, as Dan was hurrying the group to the Swan station, Sawyer stopped and said they all needed to take a time out. It's an interesting choice of words for both of

them, considering they're all currently out of the regular time-space they would normally be living in.

- Miles can talk to animal ghosts as well as human ones, since the dead boar has "told" him it's been dead three hours.
- Neil refers to Bernard as "Bernie the dentist," a reference to the Christmas children's TV classic, *Rudolph the Red-Nosed Reindeer*.
- Frogurt is around for two episodes, ranting and raving and being the epitome of *annoying*. And then he dies a glorious, flamey death. His death was very much like that of Leslie Arzt from season 1, who annoyed the hell out of us (and the survivors) for two episodes before exploding.
- Hurley manages to sum up the entire series in about 30 seconds . . . *that* is a feat in itself.
- The whooshing noise the pendulum makes sounds a lot like the whoosh we get before a flashback or flashforward.
- The woman we see at the end of the episode in the room with the pendulum is Ms. Hawking from "Flashes Before Your Eyes." This is the woman who told Desmond that he couldn't change the future or everyone would die. In "Catch-22" when Desmond was a "bruthah" in a monastery, there was a photo of Ms. Hawking standing with Brother Campbell sitting on Campbell's desk.

Interesting Facts: The beer Lapidus was carrying at the beginning of the episode was called Jekyll Island Red Ale. Jekyll Island is a vacation spot in Georgia. The beer doesn't actually exist; it's a beer label made by a company called Independent Studio Services that provides props to television and movie productions. The beer was previously seen in an episode of *Dexter* and the film *The Rules of Attraction*. The name of the beer is apt in this episode, because of the two-faced nature of Dr. Jekyll and Mr. Hyde, and the duplicity of the Oceanic 6.

Hurley tells his dad that "they'll find us at the hospital, like in *The Godfather*." He's referring to the scene where Michael Corleone goes to see his father, Vito, and a man in black enters the hospital with a gun to get rid of both of them. When Michael first comes into the hospital, you can hear a record skipping in the background, making this reference an interesting nod to Daniel's analogy from the previous episode.

Nitpicks: I must admit, I'm with Hurley in the opening scene. What good will it do to lie about what really happened? Jack says that the main reason to lie is to protect the survivors from Widmore. But Widmore knows they're lying. He knows several people survived that plane crash, and that some people are still alive on the island they'd crashed onto. He already found it once, and he'll probably find it again. In fact, Sun seems to be helping him do just that. So why keep the secret? If they lied because no one would believe them, that would make a lot more sense.

While, admittedly, the line "Why is there a dead Pakistani on my couch?" is laugh-out-loud hilarious (I adore Lillian Hurst), why doesn't Mrs. Reyes recognize Sayid? He's one of the Oceanic 6. He was definitely at Hurley's house for Hurley's birthday party. Knowing Carmen, she would have cut out every single mention of the Oceanic 6 from every newspaper and magazine imaginable. So she would have known it was Sayid on the couch, and not a dead Pakistani. (Still, I'm glad she says it, for the chuckle I get every time I watch it.)

4 8 15 16 23 42: When Hurley is in the convenience store, he sees a story about him on Action **8** News. Jack's phone number is 323-555-0156. The first three numbers add up to **8**, the next three add up to **15**, and the final set adds up to 12, or **8** + **4**. Sun's hotel room is on the 31st floor (3 + 1 = **4**). Ben pulls number **342** at the butcher shop. Jack puts an oxygen mask on Sayid and the meter on it goes up to **15**. Hurley says he killed **4** people, before correcting the number to 3.

It's Just a Flesh Wound: Several people are hit with flaming arrows. Juliet and Sawyer are handled roughly by three men in uniform. Sayid grabs Jack by the throat. Both Jones and the man holding the machete to Juliet's wrist are hit in the head with rocks, and Sawyer punches Cunningham. Locke stabs the man who'd been holding the machete.

Any Questions?:

- Hurley has now seen Ana Lucia, Eko, Charlie, and Libby. Is he really crazy, or is the island projecting these people to him? Eko also saw Ana Lucia after she died, and both Locke and Jack have seen Christian, so Hurley isn't the only one who's communicated with the island's dead. Is it possible Hurley isn't crazy, but special in the way Miles is?
- What exactly was Ben storing in that vent? He handles it very carefully when putting it into his suitcase. Is it a travel-sized Frozen Donkey Wheel?
- Who are Jill (the woman in the butcher shop), Gabriel, and Jeff? Are they Others who are working off the island? If Ben can't find his way back, how can they? Are they aligned with Ms. Hawking and helping her pinpoint the way back to the island? What do they know about Locke?
- Why isn't the island jumping around in time anymore?
- Why has Sun come to see Kate? Was it really just to tell her she didn't blame

Rather than have Naveen Andrews sit in a hot car all day, the scene of Hurley in the gas station was filmed with a Sayid mannequin sitting in the passenger seat. (MICHAEL ROBLES)

her, or is this part of her quest to find Ben — find Kate first, then find Jack, and he'll be with Ben?

- One of the people Ben mentions to Jill in the butcher shop is "Gabriel." In Judeo-Christian and Muslim faiths, Gabriel is one of God's archangels, and an important messenger. He is the one who tells Mary that she is pregnant with Jesus, and similarly announces the birth of John the Baptist. In Islam, Gabriel revealed the Qu'ran to Muhammed. Does this Gabriel have a similar function? Is he an important messenger in some way? Or are the writers just teasing us?

- Who shoots the flaming arrows into the group? Is it the same men who grab Juliet and Sawyer at the end of the episode? Are they the original members of the Dharma Initiative? Are they Others?

- In "Through the Looking Glass" it appeared Jack's addiction to pills got

The Foucault Pendulum

The giant pendulum that is swinging in the basement of the church is an example of a Foucault Pendulum. The pendulum was originally discovered by Léon Foucault, who was experimenting with ways to prove that the earth was rotating on its axis. He discovered that when a heavy weight (or bob) was suspended by a strong wire, and was pushed to begin swinging, the pendulum would gradually change direction over the course of the day, turning in a complete circle, and that 24 hours later it was back where it started. It proved that if the pendulum was swinging freely but the mark on the floor below it was turning, then the building, and therefore the Earth, was turning, and the pendulum was holding its place.

Because it was difficult for the naked eye to see the pendulum moving, Foucault came up with the idea of placing a circle around the pendulum that contained lightweight pins. As the pendulum would swing, it would knock the pins down one by one, showing that the pins were, in fact, turning. Unfortunately, due to outside circumstances, a Foucault Pendulum cannot swing indefinitely. It often stops and needs a good push to get started again. As well, various electromagnetic energies or other outside interference can alter the bob's path. Therefore it generally isn't in exactly the same position every 24 hours, and doesn't act as a reliable time-piece. But it does effectively prove that the Earth is indeed spinning on its axis. When Foucault first showed off the pendulum in 1851, the news made immediate waves through the scientific community, and he won many awards and accolades for his work. Today there are Foucault Pendula around the world, the most famous being in the Panthéon in Paris.

him fired from the hospital. So how is he getting into a hospital room to treat Sayid?

- How is Mrs. Hawking trying to find the island? What was that pendulum setup supposed to be telling her?
- Why does she give Ben 70 hours? What will happen if they don't make it back?
- Ms. Hawking's final line — "God help us all" — is an echo of the same line uttered by Pierre Chang in the opening of "Because You Left."

Ashes to Ashes: Bye-bye, Frogurt. Neil used to be in the frozen yogurt business, and was better known to his frenemies as "Frogurt." A whiny loser who considered himself a bit of a ladies' man, Neil pretty much got what was coming to him. He died by a flaming arrow to the chest (immediately followed by another one), possibly several years before he was actually born. A few other background socks (extras) also die flaming deaths.

Music/Bands: When Hurley is in the convenience store, you can hear Cheap

Trick's "The Dream Police," from the album of the same name. The song is told from the point of view of someone who can't fall asleep for fear the dream police will find him and know what he's been up to. It's a song about paranoia and mental instability, and in one of the lines, he sings that he can't tell lies because the dream police will know he's lying.

5.3   Jughead

Original air date: January 28, 2009
Written by: Elizabeth Sarnoff, Paul Zbyszewski
Directed by: Rod Holcomb
Guest cast: Imelda Corcoran (Abigail Spencer), Sarah Farooqui (Theresa Spencer), Matthew Alan (Cunningham), Tom Connolly (British Guy/Jones), Dan Hildebrand (Custodian), Alexandra Krosney (Ellie), Raymond Ma (Salonga), Tuli Roy-Kirwan (Secretary), Mary Ann Taheny (Moira)

Focus: Desmond

As Desmond tries to find Daniel's mother to deliver his message to her, he discovers a frightening link between himself and Daniel. Meanwhile, on the island, the group has traveled back to 1954 and find themselves face to face with more than one familiar person — and a hydrogen bomb.

Ever since the season 4 episode, "The Constant," the lives of Desmond and Daniel seem to become more and more intertwined. In that episode, Desmond's consciousness time traveled back to 1996 while his body remained in 2004, and he was distraught and confused, not knowing where he was or who any of the people around him were. It was Daniel who talked him through the moment, sending him on a mission to go and visit Daniel in 1996, where he was a professor at Oxford hell-bent on sending a rat's consciousness back in time. Desmond gave Dan the coordinates he needed to make the machine work, and in doing so, changed the future; or rather, maintained a future wherein Desmond had always traveled back to that point to give Dan the coordinates.

Just two episodes ago, Dan broke the time traveling rules once again by visiting Desmond in the past — three years before he was supposed to have met him for the first time — to once again send him to another time period to deliver a

The Jughead tower was built specifically for this episode, and sat in Kualoa Ranch in Oahu, where many of the "clearing" scenes are filmed on *Lost*. (ALLISON JIRSA)

message. In "The Constant" Daniel sends Desmond back in time to find a past version of himself, but in "Because You Left," Dan gives a message to past-Desmond to pass on to someone in the future. The mission is moving in the opposite direction temporally, but to the same end.

Why have Dan and Desmond been so inextricably linked? Both of them show unique attributes relating to time travel. After he turned the key in the base of the Swan station, Desmond experienced a zap to his consciousness that left him with the ability to see the future. But this ability was given to him, it appears, only to one end: to warn Charlie that he was going to die and to watch Charlie follow through with his "destiny." Since Charlie's death, we haven't seen Desmond have any more flashes of the future. Instead, his consciousness has traveled to the past, and now to the future. Meanwhile, in the last couple of episodes, it's Daniel who seems to have some sort of foreknowledge of events. He checks his journal obsessively, and it's unclear why information about things Dan shouldn't know anything about would be in there, but it is. He seems confident in the scenes in Richard Alpert's camp (Ye Olde Otherton?) but then again, we know he's a genius and has spent a lifetime using his powers of deduction, so he uses the scant evidence he has — dead bodies of soldiers, a bomb, the dated look of the clothing — and plays along.

A fascinating thing about Dan and Desmond is that they've had virtually no contact in the present. When Dan was conducting his experiments near the helicopter in "The Economist" and Desmond showed up, there was no dialogue between the two of them. Instead, Desmond spoke to Frank before getting on the helicopter and leaving Dan behind. Desmond remains on the freighter for the rest of the season, while Dan stays on the island. In "There's No Place Like Home, Part 1," Dan begins ferrying the survivors from the island over to the freighter, and Desmond is standing on the deck of the freighter helping them off. The two look at each other and nod, but no words are exchanged between them.

In many ways the two men are being set up as symbolic brothers. Desmond is rushing around trying to find Daniel's mother in this episode. Widmore has funded Daniel's research like some surrogate father, and he is Desmond's father-in-law (for better or worse). At the beginning of season 5, picking up from the clues of seasons 3 and 4, it would appear that time travel will become a vital part of the show. And the only two characters moving through time before the island started blooping are Daniel and Desmond. Will the series come down to them in some way? The big shock of this episode is when Alpert refers to The Man Formerly Known as Jones as "Widmore," causing audience jaws to drop simultaneously. If this is Charles Widmore, on the island in 1954, then he has a connection with Daniel long before he has one with Desmond. The two don't say much to each other, but the connection has been made nonetheless.

If this is an episode focusing on The Special Ones, we can't leave out John Locke. The climax of the episode is Locke's meeting with Richard Alpert in 1954, where he tells Richard that he is his leader, and to come and visit him in 1956 to see his birth. It's an interesting scene that calls into question everything we know about Locke: We've seen Alpert at Locke's birth and witnessed him giving Locke the "specialness test" when Locke is five ("Cabin Fever"). Now we see how Alpert knew enough about Locke to follow him right from the beginning. But does that mean Locke *isn't* actually special, and that Alpert only believes Locke is special because Locke told him so? Think back to the scene where Alpert gives five-year-old Locke the test. He places before him a vial of sand, a compass, The Book of Laws, a knife, a baseball glove, and a comic book, and says the enigmatic words, "Tell me what already belongs to you." Now, of course, those words make perfect sense to us. Richard met a time-traveling Locke seven years before this moment, and Locke claimed to be the leader of the island (hence the vial of sand) and handed Richard a compass — the very compass Richard now puts on the table before five-year-old Locke. Young John takes the vial of sand and the compass, and then pauses. Richard Alpert smiles, and waits . . . and when John takes the knife, Richard, confused and frustrated, says no, packs up quickly, and leaves. To him, John didn't make the right choice — in fact, the way Alpert's face lights up when John glances at The Book of Laws suggests the book was the correct one. But if that scene is now supposed to reflect the scene in Richard's tent in 1954, the other object he *did* have on him was none other than the knife. In other words, that already belonged to him, and young Locke did make the correct choice. Why would Richard have said it was wrong? Perhaps he didn't realize Locke had a knife on him (Locke usually has them well hidden on his person) and instead was going by John's assertion that he'd been sent there by Jacob. Perhaps The Book of Laws is a sort of Jacobean Bible, and Jacob's followers know it inside and out, and that is the thing that should have already belonged to Locke.

Or maybe Alpert meant something else. In season 2's "What Kate Did," Eko tells Locke the story of Josiah, whose kingdom's temple was in ruin. Josiah decided to rebuild the temple using gold, but instead his people found an ancient book, which was called "The Book of Law," or what is now known as the Old Testament. "And it was with that ancient book," Eko says, "and not the gold, that they rebuilt the temple." He passes his own Old Testament over to Locke, and inside it is the missing piece of the orientation video. Locke watches this splice, becomes obsessed with the button, and all of his actions from that point on lead to what happens in season 5. Is it possible Locke was born with the knowledge of how to alter the Others' Temple, and that is his true destiny?

Highlight: Richard Alpert's shocking line: "Put the gun down, Widmore." *Whoa.*
Did You Notice?:
- In "Because You Left," when Richard is taking the bullet out of John's leg, he says, "I didn't go anywhere. You went." John thought he was referring to when he disappeared in 2005, but maybe Richard was referring to John blooping away in 1954.
- In the season 2 episode, "The Other 48 Days," Ana Lucia finds a pocket knife with "U.S. Army" etched on it. She estimates that it's about 20 years

The 1954 Olde Otherton camp site was also set up in Kualoa Ranch, just a short distance away from the Jughead tower. (ALLISON JIRSA)

old, but it's more likely it belonged to one of the soldiers that the Others killed in 1954.

- At the beginning of the episode, when Desmond is getting a doctor to come onto the yacht to help Penny deliver the baby, you can see the flag of the Philippines and a sign saying, "Mabuhay," which is Tagalog for "Welcome" or "Long live," meaning baby Charlie was born in the Philippines.

- There were a small handful of redshirt survivors on the beach when the flaming arrows took out several of them, and the rest traveled with Miles, Charlotte, and Daniel. After the tripwire sets off the landmines, we officially say goodbye to the last of the background characters on *Lost*. Imagine surviving a plane crash, several smoke monster scares, countless treks across the island, narrowly missing an exploding freighter, living through a flaming arrow attack, and *still* getting taken out by a landmine. That's rough.

- The archivist who cannot find Daniel's name in the Oxford database is played by Mary Ann Taheny, an actress who also played an Oceanic gate attendant in "Exodus, Part 2," who helped everyone board the original Flight 815. She is not meant to be the same character, and the production crew tried to make her look very different so fans wouldn't think the archivist and the flight attendant were the same person.

- Locke fits into the old cliché, "He who hesitates is lost" perfectly. Every time he's holding up a weapon and thinks about it, he doesn't follow through. He doesn't shoot Eddie, the undercover cop in "Further Instructions." He holds a knife to Anthony Cooper in "The Brig," but as despicable as Cooper was, he still can't hurt the man. He holds a gun to Jack in "Through the Looking Glass" but can't pull the trigger. And now he waits a moment too long and realizes he can't shoot Widmore, either. Whenever Locke doesn't hesitate — throwing the knife at "Mattingly" in the previous episode, or knifing Naomi in the back — he has perfect aim.

- The woman who had been incapacitated by Daniel's experiments is named Theresa. In "Deus Ex Machina," Boone tells Locke a story about a nanny he had named Theresa, and how he'd been such a spoiled brat he used to ring a bell making her go up and down the stairs, until she tripped on the way down and broke her neck ("Theresa falls up the stairs, Theresa falls down the stairs"). Ana Lucia's mother was also named Teresa.

- Dan promises Charlotte that he'll be back soon, the same way Desmond promises Penny that he'll return and everything will be over.

- Juliet again seems to have a lot of knowledge about something, but isn't explaining herself to anyone else. She knows the Others speak Latin, and she speaks it fluently. She knew that Richard would be on the island somewhere, and when Locke asks her how old he is, she says, "*Old.*" Instead of just coming out and giving an approximate age — 200 years, 1,000 years, longer — she keeps giving him enigmatic answers, as if this is his problem to figure out and she's not going to offer him any help.

- When Desmond storms into Widmore's office, the scene is presented in complete contrast to the one in "Flashes Before Your Eyes." In that episode, the cameras were mostly behind Desmond, and he sat in a chair before Widmore looking very small, as Widmore stood behind his desk, towering over him and making him feel like a peon. The painting on Widmore's wall of a polar bear with the word "Namaste" on it was to Desmond's right as he faced Widmore in that episode, and now it's on the left. Desmond doesn't kowtow to Widmore this time, and instead crashes

The Keehi Boat Harbor on Sand Island is dressed to look like a seaside village in the Philippines. (RYAN OZAWA)

into the room, refusing to sit down and standing over Widmore the way Widmore once stood over him. He announces flat out that he's not going to answer any of Widmore's questions (and he keeps that promise) and it's clear that he catches Widmore off guard when he asks about Faraday's mother and reveals that he knows about Widmore funding Dan's research. Widmore can't push Desmond around anymore; in "Flashes Before Your Eyes," he was refusing to let Desmond have Penny's hand in marriage. It's over a decade later, and Desmond no longer needs Widmore's permission for anything.

• Penny and Desmond have named their son Charlie. It's interesting they chose the same name as her father, who terrorized them and kept them apart for so many years, and Charlie Pace, the man who opened up the frequency to the island, allowing Penny to follow the signal and find

Desmond again. Only on *Lost* could fans be speculating if Penny did, in fact, give birth to one of them, who will then time travel back to become the man we now know.

- Penny jokes that she and Charlie tried fishing in the Thames, but they were unsuccessful. Little does she know that there's an engagement ring sitting at the bottom of the river that was meant for her.
- Locke says he was born in Tustin, California. When we see his original flashback in season 1's "Walkabout," he's working at the box company in Tustin. Looks like he didn't travel much.

Interesting Facts: In popular culture, the word "Jughead" is more commonly a reference to Archie's best friend Jughead, the goofy character in the *Archie* comics who is always wearing a blue denim beanie. His surname is Jones, which is the name that Widmore wears on his uniform.

Martin "Cunningham" is the name of a minor character in James Joyce's *Ulysses* (see page 79).

Nitpicks: *Lost* is a big, successful show. So why can't they hire actors who are actually British, rather than ones who are faking the accents . . . badly? The actress who plays Ellie does a *terrible* British accent that is so unconvincing it distracts from every scene she's in. She seems to think that a necessary part of pulling off a British accent is to speak through clenched teeth. Also, how does Charlotte's nosebleed go from a tiny river to Niagara Falls in half a second?

Oops: When Desmond is at Oxford, the sign for the Physics Department points him to Claredon Hall. The real name of the lab at Oxford is spelled "Clarendon."

4 8 15 16 23 42: Miles says they've walked over the fresh graves of 4 U.S. soldiers. The Department of Physics at Oxford is Claredon [*sic*] 142-08. The Jughead is a Mark 16 nuclear bomb.

It's Just a Flesh Wound: Several people get blown up real good at the creek. Widmore snaps Cunningham's neck. Charlotte suffers a severe nosebleed and loses consciousness.

Any Questions?:
- At the beginning of the episode, Desmond is running through the streets yelling, "Efren Salonga," which is the doctor's name. How did he have the man's name? Who gave it to him?
- Where did Bernard and Rose go? They're too significant to have been taken out by flaming arrows without us seeing it happen, so why aren't they with the others?

- Penny asks Desmond to promise her that he'll never go back to the island. He replies, "Why in God's name would I go back there?" The line is too specific not to feel like foreshadowing: Will Desmond end up back on the island? Why? How?
- Does Dan know about Miles's special skill? When Miles mentions offhandedly that they just passed over fresh graves, Dan doesn't look at him strangely, but instead says, "Did they mention what year it was?" Why hasn't he discussed Miles's skills with him before?
- Why does Desmond tell the librarian at Oxford that he doesn't remember what year he visited Daniel? It wouldn't have been difficult to figure out. He wasn't in the army for very long, and he says to Penny at the end of "The Constant" that he won't phone her again for eight years, so considering he called her in 2004, why couldn't he remember that he visited Daniel in 1996 if that would have helped track him down faster?
- What happened to Faraday's lab? Did Daniel destroy it out of anger over what happened to Theresa, or was it dismantled by someone at Oxford? Why is everything still there? Did someone get wind that his experiments actually had some merit and they didn't want to destroy the lab? Or did Theresa's accident cause Oxford to shut things down immediately so they're not faced with a massive lawsuit?
- When Locke acts at the beginning like he's the only one who's been time traveling, why doesn't Sawyer set him straight? Why does Juliet change the subject before anyone can say anything differently?
- The caretaker at Oxford says Des isn't the first one to come poking around looking for Daniel. Who are the others? Widmore? Ben? Locke?
- Why does Juliet speak Latin to young Widmore? She tells him that they are not his enemy, but she's speaking in a language that the people she is with don't understand. In doing so, she makes it look like she's acting separately from her companions, which would immediately make the two Others suspicious.
- Why is Theresa still alive? Minkowski succumbed pretty quickly to the consciousness-jumping, and Desmond would have if he hadn't found his constant. Charlotte's nose is bleeding already and by the end of this episode she doesn't appear to be long for this world. So why hasn't Theresa suffered the same nosebleeds and brain hemorrhaging? Is Theresa insane? Or is she perpetually consciousness time traveling?

Operation Castle

The detonation of Castle Bravo.
(U.S. ARMY PHOTO ARCHIVES)

As Dan says in "Jughead," the United States military detonated several nuclear bombs in the South Pacific in the 1950s. On January 31, 1950, President Harry S. Truman declared the U.S.'s intention to develop a hydrogen bomb. At the time, the Cold War was causing grave concern among American citizens who were worried that the Russians would get ahead of them in the nuclear arms race and wipe out the United States before they could catch up. On November 1, 1951, as part of Operation Ivy, the world's first hydrogen bomb, "Ivy Mike," was detonated in the Marshall Islands in the South Pacific. It was the eighth series of nuclear bomb tests in the United States (the previous seven tests involved atomic bombs), and it was a huge success.

The next U.S. bomb test in the South Pacific was Operation Castle, carried out between March 1 and May 14, 1954, on Bikini Atoll. Now that the U.S. had a workable hydrogen bomb that was housed in a casing that allowed them to transport it (called the "Sausage") the next step was to develop a bomb that could be delivered via airplane. Operation Castle was going to test the possibilities of a "deliverable weaponized design," called the "Shrimp." The first test, Castle Bravo, was such a spectacular detonation that it exceeded all expectations, with a yield that was twice what anyone had predicted. Unfortunately, while the detonation was deemed a success, it came with a price: because of the large diameter of the bomb fallout, several crewmen suffered radiation exposure, eventually rushing to underground shelters to await rescue. The cloud rose almost 40 kilometers in the air, with a diameter of 100 kilometers.

The plan was to detonate several of the new Shrimp bombs to see if any of them would work, and in case they didn't, another Sausage bomb had been brought along as backup. Its name? Jughead. Because of the success of Castle Bravo, Jughead was never detonated, because it was already considered obsolete. So, apparently the U.S. Army deployed some soldiers to dispose of Jughead on a nearby island that had special electromagnetic properties, where they met this guy named Richard Alpert. . . .

- Why is Widmore funding Dan's research? Does he think Daniel is his best chance at getting back to the island?
- How did Jughead get on the island? Where will they bury it? Will the radiation leak have anything to do with women not being able to have children?
- Richard tells Daniel that he was forced to kill 18 people, and that he answers to a higher power. Who is he talking about? Jacob? If so, why did Jacob order them killed?
- Daniel tells Ellie that she looks so much like someone he used to know. Who? Theresa?
- Dan tells Ellie that the island will still be there 50 years from now. How did he know it was 1954? Was it a guess based on the age of the bomb?
- Richard tells Locke that they have a very specific process for choosing their leader, referring to the test he gave Young Locke in "Cabin Fever." Was Ben given the same test as a child? What were the objects placed in front of *him*?
- When did Widmore first come to the island? How did he get there?
- In "Exposé," Locke tells Paulo that "things don't stay buried on this island." Even if Richard's people bury the bomb, will it resurface?

Ashes to Ashes: "Cunningham" (probably not his real name) was an Other who worked alongside Widmore. He ended up with his neck snapped when Widmore needed him to shut up. The last of the background socks end up dead when they set off landmines near a stream. We all breathe a sigh of relief, thankful there will be no more Nikkis or Paulos. The original 71 survivors of Oceanic Flight 815 (48 in the front half of the plane, 23 in the tail section) have come down to Sawyer and Locke (and, I hope, Bernard and Rose). Everyone else is dead or off the island.

5.4   The Little Prince

Original air date: February 4, 2009
Written by: Brian K. Vaughan, Melinda Hsu Taylor
Directed by: Stephen Williams
Guest cast: Guillaume Dabinpons (Robert), Susan Duerden (Carole Littleton), Melissa Farman (Danielle Rousseau), Tom Irwin (Dan Norton), Marc Menard (Montand), Stephanie Niznik (Dr. Evelyn Ariza), Emerson Brooks (Tony), Bruno Bruni (Brennan), Ane Tranetzki (Bellman)

Focus: Kate, Aaron

When Locke's crew flashes back to one of their early days post-crash, they must come to terms with what they've been through since the Oceanic 815 crash. Meanwhile, off the island, Kate tries to find out who is demanding a blood test from her, Sun receives a mysterious package, and Ben gets everyone to meet him at a marina.

This episode, like the book it was named after, is about trust — opening up to others, trusting those closest to us with deep secrets, and distrusting others who are lying and conniving. Interestingly, Locke's crew begins to trust one another, opening up and telling the truth, whereas off the island, trust is breaking down in a big way. Sawyer admits to Juliet how he feels with Kate gone and Locke tells Sawyer what really happened the night the light shone out of the hatch. Only Daniel is still hiding what he knows about Charlotte's nosebleeds. Off the island, Hurley trusts no one, Kate's trust in Jack disappears when she realizes he's with Ben, Jack discovers Ben has been harassing Kate behind his back, Sayid clearly hates and distrusts Ben (Ben isn't exactly Mr. Popular in this episode), Sun has been lying to Kate and is out for revenge against someone, and an evil lawyer threatens to take all of them down.

Sawyer is the one who truly wears his heart on his sleeve in this episode. In the previous one, he admitted that everyone he cared about blew up on the freighter — meaning, of course, Kate. Locke knows that Kate is Sawyer's vulnerability, and in this episode he explains that he needs to convince everyone who left to come back, and says specifically to Sawyer, "Don't you want her to come back?" Sawyer mumbles in response, "It doesn't matter what I want." Throughout Sawyer's "relationship" with Kate, Kate has pretty much called the shots, intentionally or not. He steps back when she appears to be going to Jack, and he steps up eagerly when she seems to be interested in him. So it's only natural that he would assume he has no say in this matter, either. He believed they all died on the freighter, and now Locke is suggesting they're alive, they've been rescued, and there's a chance they'll all come back. For Sawyer, not only *Kate* died on that freighter, but his hope as well. Locke brings that hope back, but Sawyer doesn't know what to do with it. If she's alive, great. But what good does that do him if he's stuck on the island? Would she really come back for him?

It's only when Sawyer actually sees Kate — the one he fell for in season 1, the woman of mystery he only dreamed about before they climbed into a polar bear cage together — that the full weight of her absence becomes real to him. He watches her (in the past) as she heroically delivers Claire's baby. And when the island zaps him away from that moment, it finally hits him like a ton of bricks: Kate is gone. Just like the image of her from that early day on the island is gone forever, so is the woman he'd fallen for.

Juliet becomes Sawyer's confidante in this episode, even though he's at first reluctant to let her play that role. When she insists, we see Sawyer pour his heart out in a way we only saw him do once — and even then it was as part of a drinking game with Kate. But unlike the construction worker from "Because You Left," who suggests that if he could go back in time he'd kill Hitler, Sawyer believes "what's done is done." You can't change the past, so why even try? He's resigned himself to having lost Kate, and now he'll have to find a new reason to go on.

In "The Little Prince," Kate tries to find out who is trying to take Aaron away from her.
(MICHAEL ROBLES)

Kate, meanwhile, has already found her reason, and that's Aaron. We flash back to a few days after the rescue, where Kate holds Aaron and has already formed a strong bond with the baby. Even then she admits that she couldn't bear to lose him. So now, three years later, she is the only mother he knows, and she would do anything for him. In this episode, she confronts the lawyer, Mr. Norton, who is demanding a blood sample from her, but she's met with a brick wall of defiance on his part.

It comes as no surprise that Norton is Ben's lawyer, and that Ben is the man behind demanding the blood sample, simply because everything Norton says is a lie. I checked with a California attorney, and the storyline of Kate being asked for a blood sample by an anonymous plaintiff is completely ludicrous. There's no legal way anyone can ask you for blood for no reason at all, without having

Naveen Andrews (left, with his jacket pulled down), Matthew Fox (with his back to us), and Michael Emerson (right) wait between takes as Jack's ugly truck sits nearby. (RYAN OZAWA)

backing evidence that your blood is required to be evidence in a crime. As the attorney explained, "The constitutional right to know the charges being made, to face your accusers and to defend yourself were all thrown out of the window in that scene." Kate would have been caught in the court system for months and years, not asked to submit to the test on the spot.

However, once we consider who Norton's client is, it's clear this isn't a research error on the part of the writers. Like Ben, Norton is a talented manipulator and liar. He doesn't have a court order from a judge, and he knows he has no right to demand anything from Kate. Ben has assured him that Kate is frightened of being found out, she's harboring secrets of her own, and if she countersued the lawyer and his anonymous client for harassment, the media spotlight on her would be immense and the truth of Aaron's parentage would no doubt come out. Norton is banking on Kate's fear, and he's made a good bet. She knows her hands are tied, and Norton does, too.

Kate's not the only woman who is fighting for someone she loves in this episode. Sun has become a completely different person since the death of Jin. Before he died she was at first submissive, then free and independent, and then loving. She is a sensible person, but a caring one. She was always the person Claire left Aaron with when Claire had to go anywhere. She was the person Charlie and Sawyer targeted when they were pulling off "The Long Con" because they knew she would be one of the most sympathetic people in the camp to attack. But now, Sun has changed. She's dark, she's calculating, and she's vengeful. She's hiring surveillance to follow Ben and Jack. She's angry about Jin's death and doesn't mind exploiting Kate's guilt on that count. Her moments of sweetness seem forced to us, and we know she's not to be trusted anymore. Now, we're sadly reminded that regardless of what we thought we knew before, Sun is Mr. Paik's daughter. And she knows how to get things done.

At the end of season 4, many fans were unconvinced that Jin was dead. I argued that we didn't actually see anyone standing on the deck of the freighter, and I held out hope that he was still alive, that maybe the island didn't want him dead yet and he could cheat death the way Michael did. The end of this episode provided me and many other fans who had been ridiculed for our devotion all summer ("Come on . . . Daniel Dae Kim had a DUI, there's *no way* he's still alive!") with a gleeful moment of *"I told you so!!"* (And no, I wasn't above gloating at the time.) From the moment we realize the French people in the raft are Rousseau and her crew (and you must have figured that one out before the big reveal at the end) to rolling him over in the sand and discovering that Jin was still alive, the end of "The Little Prince" provided a squeefest of epic proportions for fans, and made the following week's wait for the next episode an excruciatingly long one.

Highlight: Sawyer in the middle of the time jump. As the group is being shot at while in the middle of the ocean in a boat, the island prepares to flash them away, and Sawyer looks up and screams, "THANK YOU, LORD!!" only to bloop into a full-on downpour in the middle of the night, to which Sawyer adds, "I TAKE THAT BACK!!"

Did You Notice?:
- You could tell Kate was holding a doll in the opening scene while talking to Jack whenever the camera was looking at her and Aaron's face was hidden. Aaron's head is the size of a watermelon, yet this baby had a tiny, tiny head.
- "I have *always* been with you," Kate tells Jack. I added for her, *"Except when I was having sex with Sawyer."*
- As a doctor, Juliet knows how to remain calm in a crisis (something Jack could never do very well).
- Right after Locke's crew sees the shaft of light, watch how first Sawyer, then Locke, and then Charlotte bend a branch to walk past it, but snap it in the face of the person behind them, each actor looking more annoyed than the one before.
- The scene of Kate helping Claire through her labor and delivery reminds us that Kate was actually the first person to hold Aaron after he was born.

Matthew Fox stands by Jack's ugly truck in the scene where Jack runs across the street to talk to Kate in her car. (RYAN OZAWA)

- The footage of Emilie de Ravin was taken from the original episode, "Do No Harm," and was not refilmed for this episode. The scenes shot from Sawyer's perspective were re-shot for this episode with a blonde stand-in.
- Locke tells Sawyer what happened that night at the hatch — something he hasn't told anyone else — probably because of their new bond over killing Cooper.
- The boat with the Ajira water bottle in it has six seats and there are exactly six people. Convenient!
- The canister that Locke turns over says "Bésixdouze" on it. This is a reference to Saint-Exupéry's *The Little Prince*, where the narrator relates a story about a man who had discovered a new asteroid called B612, known in French as Bésixdouze (see page 48). In 1993, a real asteroid was discovered by two Japanese amateur astronomers and was called Bésixdouze.

- When Rousseau and her crew are on the boat, they keep referring to Montand by name. Montand was the man Rousseau mentions in "Exodus, Part 1" when they're heading to the *Black Rock*; she tells them he went into the Dark Territory and lost his arm. The other person she refers to by name is Robert, who is widely considered to be her husband, even though she only refers to him as "my love" when telling Sayid about him.
- On the beach, Montand is listening to Hurley's numbers being repeated on his radio.

Interesting Facts: In one of the time bloops, Locke's crew finds a boat on the beach with a water bottle emblazoned with an Ajira Airways logo. Like Oceanic Airlines, Ajira is a fictional airline. It first appeared in a promotional video for The Fray's song "You Found Me" that played on ABC.com in November 2008, and advertised the first hint of a mini-ARG for the fans, sending them to airline website www.ajiraairways.com. The tagline for the airline is "Destiny Calls" (the same tagline as season 5 of *Lost*) with the motto, "Get lost in the world." The airline's website offered adventure trips, posted to the site by Antonio B. MacCutcheon (the same name as Widmore's whisky) that were relevant to the show: an Australian walkabout, a polar adventure, tropical island adventures, swimming with sharks, and exploring Polynesian ruins in the South Pacific. In one section on the site, readers were instructed to print a boarding pass and fold it using origami, and when the reader followed the instructions properly, the words came together to create GUM, which is the three-letter code for the Guam airport. If one passed the bar code on the boarding pass under a barcode reader, Hurley's numbers came up. The site was a fun little place to play while fans eagerly awaited season 5.

Nitpicks: This is a tiny nitpick, but Kate and Jack are so far away from Mrs. Littleton's hotel room, there's no way they could have made out who opened the door without looking through binoculars. The only way the audience knows it's Claire's mother is because the camera zooms in on her. Secondly, how could Claire's mother not know about a boy named Aaron? Of course, she couldn't know Aaron is her grandson, but she's hardly out of the loop. She attends the memorial service and tells Jack that her daughter and he are actually half-siblings, and she believes her daughter was killed on the flight. With the intense media coverage surrounding Oceanic 6, wouldn't she have noticed one of them was a baby named Aaron?

Oops: There's a major continuity error in the time flash where the characters encounter their earlier days on the island. In "Deus Ex Machina," Boone is hurt when the Beechcraft crashes, and Locke carries him back to the caves and leaves him for Jack. Then Locke leaves and goes back to the hatch and bangs on the door and a dim light turns on. It's not a bolt of light into the heavens, as in this episode. Meanwhile, back at the caves, Jack tends to Boone all through the night and into the next day. We cut to the beach, where it's daytime and Claire is talking to the guys building the raft. Kate is helping Jack with Boone, and she goes to the beach to get supplies. On her way back, she finds Claire in labor. She runs to Jack to tell him, but he's transfusing blood into Boone, so Kate rushes back to Claire and helps her deliver the baby. So Locke seeing the light and Claire giving birth happen about 24 hours apart. Also, in the original scene where Claire was giving birth, Jin and Charlie are standing behind Kate, but they're nowhere to be seen when Sawyer comes upon them.

4 8 15 16 23 42: Sayid was unconscious for **42** hours. Kate's address is **42** Panorama Crest. Ben tells everyone to meet him at the Long Beach Marina, Slip **23**. Norton's car has a **4** and an **8** in the license plate.

It's Just a Flesh Wound: Charlotte recovers from her fainting spell, but she's not doing very well. Miles and Juliet get nosebleeds. Locke's crew are shot at, with no casualties, but when Juliet shoots back it looks like she hits somebody in the boat behind them. Jin has a bad sunburn, chapped lips, and some scratches on his face.

Lost in Translation: "Ajira" is Hindi for island.

Sun's surveillance report is partly legible, but it doesn't actually contain anything relevant. The document is simply a printout of a web page that was used in an unrelated alternate reality game online (one of the clues led players to this surveillance report). The original report is short and it was cut and pasted repeatedly, so as Sun flips through the pages, she's just reading the same few paragraphs over and over.

When Rousseau's crew are in the raft, they are speaking non-subtitled French. One of my French-speaking readers, Benny, provided me with a translation. A dash indicates that it's unclear who is speaking, and square brackets are stage directions.

> **Robert:** We never should have followed those damn numbers.
>
> – It's not my fault, Brennan was at the sonar.
>
> **Brennan:** If you listened to Montand, he already said the instruments malfunctioned.
>
> **Danielle:** Man at sea!

Robert: What? I thought we were all here?

    – We are all here! It's not one of ours.

    – Then who is it?

    – Start paddling!

    – Paddle!

    – Paddle, come on!

    – Hurry up, he's going with the current!

Montand: There's only him — no boat, nothing.

[Brennan complaining]

Danielle: For the love of God, Brennan, shut up.

    – Bring him aboard!

    – There.

    – He's still breathing.

[Next morning, as Jin awakes]

Montand: Robert, look, the signal is coming from the island.

Robert: Can you determine the source?

Montand: Of course, look.

Robert: You think the island is inhabited?

Danielle [to Jin]: Are you okay? How are you feeling?

[In English, Jin tells Rousseau he understands a little English, and he arrived on a boat]

Robert: Who is it?

Montand: Who cares who it is? What's he doing here?

Danielle: He says he came on a boat.

[In English, Jin explains to Robert the boat sank, and he didn't know how long he was underwater, and doesn't answer Montand's increasingly angry questions about how he got there]

Danielle: Montand, leave him, he's in shock! [to Robert] Do we have water to give him?

Robert: Here.

Danielle: Thanks.

Any Questions?:

- Beyond getting in her dig about what happened on the freighter, does Sun blame Kate in any way for Jin's death? The automaton way she says, "It's what any friend would do" sounds completely insincere, like she's not really Kate's friend.

When you watch the scene of Jack crouching by Kate's car (on the right) all you see is the two characters. But here we can see the production crew outside the car making that scene work. (RYAN OZAWA)

- How did Sun find out Ben was off the island, and was working with Jack? Did Widmore tell her after Ben invaded his room in "The Shape of Things to Come"? Is Sun an unwitting agent for Widmore; does he hope that she can get to Ben before Ben can get to Penny?
- So who was the guy who came into Sayid's hospital room and attacked him with a tranquilizer gun? Was he sent by Widmore? Could Ben have sent him, thinking tranquilizing him is the only way he could keep Sayid in one place long enough to get him back to the island?
- Did Jack, Sayid, and Ben take the failed assassin with them? If they left him there, that would cause too many questions . . . and no doubt lead directly back to Jack.
- Ben tells Sayid to save the dirty linen for later. What's the dirty linen?
- Dan asks Miles if he's sure he'd never been to the island before and explains

that the nosebleeds are happening relative to the time spent on the island. If that's true, Charlotte's been there the longest, followed by Miles and then Juliet, who've both gotten nosebleeds after Charlotte. We know Juliet was there for at least three years, but Charlotte and Miles have only been there for a few months. Charlotte talks about the island like she was born there; could she have been a child on the island? Could Miles?

The side of the van that Ben and Sayid are driving says "Canton-Rainier" on it. If you rearrange the letters, they spell "reincarnation."
(RYAN OZAWA)

- The flash from 1954 to 2004 knocks Charlotte unconscious, but the flash from 2004 to 1988 doesn't seem to have any effect on her at all. Could her sensitivity to it have something to do with going forward in time rather than back, or perhaps the number of years they jump? Or is it just an inconsistency that she doesn't get worse with every jump?

- Where was Vincent when they got to the camp? His leash looks like a little noose.

- Whose boat does the group take? Why are they hostile to them (other than the fact they just stole their boat)? The camp looks long abandoned as if we're in a time after 2005. Maybe it was Bernard and Rose . . . what if it was themselves?

- What did Jack say to Claire's mom? Is it possible he let too much slip and now she'll put everything together, or will that be the last we'll see of her? It's definitely possible that she could start piecing things together. When she was in a coma in the "Par Avion" flashback, Claire visited her in the hospital and told her she was pregnant and was giving the baby up for adoption. Could Mrs. Littleton retain a residual memory of that moment, and might she realize that Aaron is her grandson?

- What was Montand's problem? He seemed really angry all the time. I'm happy knowing he's going to lose a limb.
- Why was Ben trying to take Aaron? Was it all a plan to bring them to that point so he could lure Kate back to the island or was he really trying to take him?

✍ The Little Prince by Antoine de Saint-Exupéry (1943)

The Little Prince, or *Le petit prince*, is one of the most beloved books of all time, and has been widely translated into many languages around the world. The timeless story of a little boy from a faraway planet who is seeking knowledge (but only finds stupidity) has been influential in literature, and now television.

The story is set in the Sahara Desert, where a pilot, who narrates the book, has crash landed and is trying to fix his plane. He recalls how imaginative he was as a boy, and would draw pictures of a boa constrictor eating an elephant. But because the picture was basically a lump with the head and tail of the snake sticking out on either side, when he'd show the picture to grown-ups, they thought it was a hat. So he eventually gave up a life of art, and became a pilot instead, but every once in a while he'd show that picture to people . . . and they'd always think it was a hat.

In the desert, as the pilot begins to worry about what will happen if he doesn't find food or water, he hears a small voice behind him asking if he could draw a sheep. He turns and a little boy dressed in flashy garments is standing behind him, and again asks if he could draw him a picture of a sheep. The pilot shows the child his picture, and the child waves it off, saying he doesn't want a picture of an elephant inside a boa constrictor; he wants a picture of a sheep. So the pilot attempts to draw a sheep, and each drawing is criticized by the boy until he finally draws a picture of a box and says the sheep is inside it. The boy is mesmerized by the drawing, and claims that he can see through one of the holes in the drawing, and the sheep has gone to sleep.

The little prince, for that is what he is, begins asking a series of questions about everything he sees around him. When he stops long enough to allow the narrator to get some questions of his own in, he learns that the prince comes from outer space, and lives on a tiny planet the size of a house. As he listens to the description of the planet, the narrator believes that the little prince lives on Asteroid B612. He remembers a Turkish astronomer who discovered the asteroid and tried to present his findings in 1909, but because of his strange clothing, no one would believe him. The astronomer returned in 1920 wearing a European suit, and everyone believed him. The narrator explains at this point that the reason he's referring to the asteroid by its numerical name is because grown-ups are very caught up in numbers, and don't seem to understand the beauty of an object unless they know how much it's worth. They wouldn't be able to see a drawing of a box and find a sheep sleeping inside it like the little prince. But then, he realizes, neither can he, and he begins to worry that he's become as materialistic and shallow as other grown-ups.

The little prince explains that on his planet his biggest problem is the baobab trees. He spends all day trying to cultivate the good seeds and pulling up the bad ones, but every once in a while a bad seed escapes his notice, and if it grows into a baobab tree it will engulf his planet and destroy it. So he must keep on top of it. He tells the pilot how he enjoys watching sunsets, and he has three little volcanoes on his planet that he needs to clean out every day.

The little prince asks the narrator if a sheep will eat flowers with thorns. The narrator, busily trying to fix his plane, gives him increasingly frustrated responses, and finally says that thorns are just a flower's way of being cruel, and that he has important things to attend to. The prince becomes angry and has an outburst during which he says he knows a flower that is unique in all the world, and means everything to him, and yet a sheep can eat that flower in one bite. He asks the narrator if that isn't important, and begins sobbing. The narrator feels terrible. He soon finds out that the prince has a rose, and it's a haughty, pride-filled flower that needs constant care. The prince puts a lid on it to protect it from the sun's rays, he waters it constantly, and no matter how much care he gives it, the rose remains coy with him, telling him how she could die at any instant and that he needs to care for her even more. The prince finally decides to leave the planet, and he puts a cover over her, and she tries to hide the fact that she's crying, and for the first time assures him that she'll be all right.

The prince then recounts the planets that he has visited to find out more about the universe. On the first planet he meets a king, who sits alone waiting for a subject to arrive. When the little prince meets him, the king proclaims him a subject and demands that he follow his commands. The little prince refuses. The king explains that everything is under his command, so the little prince asks him to command the sun to set. But the king says he can only command things that he knows will happen, or he'll look silly. When the little prince gets up to leave, the king commands him to stay, saying first he'll make him his minister of justice, and then an ambassador. The little prince leaves without answering.

On the next planet he met a vain man, who sees the little prince as an admirer. He wears a strange hat so when his admirers clap their hands, he can tip it in acknowledgment. Unfortunately, he lives alone. He never has anyone else around him, which suits him just fine because then he can be sure he's the most attractive person on the planet. When the little prince tries to talk to him, he doesn't hear anything except praise. So the little prince leaves.

On the third planet he meets an alcoholic, who is a sympathetic character in that he's aware that there's something wrong with him, but he's also pathetic. He explains to the little prince that he drinks to forget that he's ashamed of drinking. Baffled by the circular argument, the little prince leaves.

His next stop is on a planet inhabited by a businessman who claims to own all the stars in the sky. He spends all of his time counting them, and doesn't have time for anything else. The little prince asks why one would own stars. The businessman explains (between counting) that when you own things it makes you rich, and then you can buy other things that also make you rich. The prince thinks his reasoning is much like the alcoholic's. The prince tries to explain that the businessman can't hold the stars or do anything with them and that a person doesn't really have a right to own something that he doesn't help in some way, telling him that he tends to his rose and cleans out his volcanoes, yet the businessman does nothing to help his stars. The businessman is speechless, and the little prince goes on his way.

On the fifth planet is a lamplighter, who lights his lamp when the sun goes down, and extinguishes it when it comes up. Unfortunately, he lives on a tiny planet, so he must light and extinguish the lamp once every minute. He's very tired, but continues to do his job, and when the little prince asks why, he says he has orders. He never says who the orders come from, just that he must do his job because it was asked of him. As futile as the man's task is, however, the prince sees him as being the most sincere so far, because he's thinking of someone besides himself. The little prince regretfully leaves the planet (there isn't room for two of them), thinking of all the sunsets he will miss.

On the sixth planet he meets a geographer. Intrigued by someone who actually has a real job, the little prince begins asking him about the geography of his planet. The geographer explains that he's never seen his planet, because he remains in his study all day making the maps. He sends out explorers, who bring back the information to him about the world, and every once in a while he must conduct a study into their moral character to make sure they're giving him accurate information. For example, he says, an alcoholic could cause chaos if he reports back that he saw two mountains when there was only one (to which the little prince replies, "I know someone . . . who would be a bad explorer"). The little prince describes his planet to see if the geographer will document it, and when he says it's inhabited by a flower, the geographer explains that he doesn't document flowers because they are ephemeral. At the little prince's insistence, he explains that by ephemeral, he means that "which is threatened by imminent disappearance." Alarmed that his rose is under threat, and feeling immensely guilty, the little prince next visits Earth.

The first creature the little prince meets upon arriving on Earth is a snake in the desert, who explains that if the little prince wants to return to his home planet, all it would take is one bite from the snake, and his venom would send the little prince to the heavens. Oddly, the snake seems to need the little prince's permission to bite him (like a vampire needs permission to enter a house). When the prince asks him why he speaks in riddles, he replies, "I solve them all."

The little prince continues walking through the desert, where he meets a small flower. Because the flower had only seen a handful of people in its life, it tells the little prince there are only six or seven people in existence. The little prince keeps walking and finds a mountain, where he calls out to someone, and hears his echo in return. He continues talking, thinking the echo is another person, but finds it peculiar that people on Earth need someone else to talk first, and then they only repeat what that person says. He thinks of how his flower always spoke first.

Next he passes a rose garden, and is shocked to see thousands of flowers exactly like his. He realizes his rose is not unique in the world, and he's not a prince over much of anything, and he begins to cry.

A fox suddenly appears, and begins talking to him. The prince, who is immensely lonely, asks if the fox will play with him. The fox explains that he's not tame, but if the prince tames him, then they can be together. Here, in the French version, the word tame doesn't have the same meaning as in English, but is more like earning a person's trust by getting to know them more deeply. In other words, the fox wants to become friends with him. He tells the little prince to come back every day at the same time, and the fox will become excited every day around the time the prince is to arrive. Every day the fox will get a little bit closer to him, and eventually he will be tamed. The prince does as he asks, and when the fox is tamed and the two are good friends (and the little prince is the only boy the fox cares about, and the fox is the only fox the prince cares about), the prince says the time has come for him to leave. The fox is devastated, and the prince asks what good it is to create strong ties with another person if it just makes one upset. The fox tells him to go and look at the roses, and that he'll understand. The prince does so, and realizes that his rose *is* unique, because it's special to him. He doesn't care about a single one of the thousands of other roses, and instead only worries about and loves the one on his planet. Just as he's a very special boy to the fox, and the fox is the only fox he cares about in all the world, so, too, is his rose special to him. He returns to say goodbye to the fox, who gives him the advice that is central to the book: "One sees clearly only with the heart. Anything essential is invisible to the eye." The boy realizes he is responsible for his rose, and that's what makes her unique.

Next the little prince visits a switchman, who tells him that people are constantly in a hurry, moving from one place to the next, but wherever they are, they want to be somewhere else. Then he meets a salesclerk who sells pills that replace drinking water and tells him it could save him up to 53 minutes a week. The boy replies that if he had an extra 53 minutes, he'd spend it walking toward a water fountain.

Here ends the little prince's story, just as the narrator has run out of water. It's been eight days since he's crash-landed, and he's beginning to worry about his survival. The little prince suggests they look for a well, even though the narrator believes that will be futile. They begin walking, and the prince tells him water can be good for the heart. He stops and looks at the sky, telling the narrator that the stars are more beautiful to him because up there is a flower that means the world to him. He then says the desert is beautiful because somewhere inside it is hidden a well. The narrator surprises himself by suddenly remembering a large house he lived in as a child, which he had been told had a treasure buried in it somewhere. That house was more special to him because of the possibility of something he couldn't see being hidden inside it. And suddenly he understands the lesson of the fox.

They come upon a well with a pulley, a bucket, and a rope, which surprises the narrator, who is used to holes in the sand that act as wells in the Sahara. As the little prince drinks, the narrator realizes how right he was — the water tasted better because they'd traveled to get it. They had to work hard to find it and to pull it up with the creaky old pulley and rope, and it tasted sweeter because it had been born of their work.

The little prince asks the pilot to draw a muzzle for his sheep so it won't eat the rose. The narrator feels sad, knowing the prince has made plans to return to his planet. He draws a muzzle and hands it to him, and the prince explains that the next day will be the first anniversary of his arrival on Earth. The narrator asks the little prince if he'd returned to this exact spot because it had been the place where he'd fallen to Earth, but the little prince doesn't answer, and instead tells him to tend to his engine and return to the well the following evening. The narrator feels afraid, knowing that the little prince has tamed him.

The next night, he returns, and he can see the little prince sitting on a wall and talking to someone. He's arguing, saying that it's the right day, but it's not the exact place. Then he hears him say, "Your poison is good? You're sure it won't make me suffer long?" and a feeling of dread washes over the narrator. He looks at the base of the wall and sees the snake. He moves toward the wall, and the snake disappears. He goes to the little prince and sees the boy is frightened, and his heart is pounding wildly. The pilot senses something terrible about to happen, and tells him he has his sheep and muzzle ready for him. The little prince says he'll be more frightened later that night, and the pilot tries to talk him out of it, realizing that he couldn't bear never hearing the little prince laugh again. The boy repeats that important things can't be seen, and that his gift to the pilot will be that every time he looks up at the stars, he'll hear laughter. Just as the rose is special to him, now the stars will be special to the pilot because he knew the little prince, and that because he doesn't know exactly which star is the little prince's planet, all of the stars will be special. Then he tells him not to come that night.

That night the prince slips away when the narrator isn't looking. The narrator catches up to him, and the little prince explains that he needs to get back to his planet to take care of his rose, but that his body is just too heavy to take with him. He tries to explain that his body will be nothing but an old shell, and that the narrator shouldn't be sad about that. He asks the pilot to stop walking, and explains one last time that he's responsible for his rose, and that she needs him. He walks out to the desert, and the narrator sees something flash by the little prince's ankle, and then the prince falls silently to the ground.

At the end of the book the narrator explains that it's been six years since that day, and that at daybreak he hadn't found the little prince's body, so he's convinced that the little prince isn't dead. At night when he looks up at the stars, they're like a million tiny bells laughing. But he's also realized that when he drew a muzzle for the sheep, he hadn't drawn a strap on it, so there was no way the little prince would have been able to secure it on the animal. He worries that the sheep has eaten the rose. When he focuses on that instead, the stars sound like they're crying, but then he convinces himself that the little prince would keep a close eye on the rose and would never let that happen, and the stars laugh again.

The book ends with a plea for the reader to keep an eye out for the little prince, and should they ever see him to please contact the narrator.

At the core of *The Little Prince* is a very simple message: the things that are truly important to us are felt in our hearts, not seen with our eyes. While a crowd of people might all look the same to us, if we see within that crowd one single person that we know, our hearts skip a beat and we instantly recognize them. The reason we look to that person with so much love is because we trust them, and trust is only felt in the heart, not in the eyes. In this season of *Lost*, most of the characters seem to be seeing — and acting — with their hearts, just as the book says we do.

The very first image we saw in the series was a close-up of Jack's eye, and throughout the first season, almost every episode opened with a close-up of the eye of the character who would be the focus of the episode. But much as Locke's argued throughout season 2, the little prince repeats that what truly matters isn't what you can see with your eyes, but what you believe in your heart. Locke believed in pushing the button. There was nothing he could see that told him it was necessary, and common sense told him it was just a useless task. But he believed in what he was doing. Now as Locke heads to the Orchid station, he believes that he can save the people on the island. He doesn't know how or why, he just feels deep down that this is what he has to do.

In the flashback of this episode, we see Kate's relationship with Aaron. Just like the fox teaches the little prince in Saint-Exupéry's book, she has formed a bond with Aaron, and now he means more to her than any other child in the world. He has "tamed" her, as the fox would say. Just like the little prince, Aaron is a little boy with platinum blond hair who was born in a foreign place.

The little prince travels on many adventures, and along the way learns a lot about humankind and its follies, and begins to come to a better understanding of himself, his past, and his feelings. Similarly, the characters on *Lost* have gone through a huge journey of self-awareness, and many of them have come to terms with their deepest concerns and worries. As they fight for survival, all of the materialistic worries they had are stripped away as they worry about more fundamental things, like food, water, shelter, and keeping each other safe and protected. What they once thought was important now seems like child's play, just like the narrator comes away from his experience with the little prince a completely different person.

Most of the action in the book takes place in the Sahara Desert, which becomes a place of enlightenment for the narrator. In season 4 Ben ejected himself off the island and into the Sahara Desert, and it will come up again in season 5. The book is also about perspectives. The prince knows only one rose, so he believes she is unique until he sees the other roses. The flower the little prince encounters in the desert believes there are only a handful of people on Earth because it has only seen a few of them. On the island, perspective is everything. When the survivors see some shabbily dressed people and they call them the Others, their perspective is as the outsider, looking in on these people who are actually native to the island. Because they don't know their whole history, they only know them as people in the jungle wearing tattered rags, and don't understand they are civilized people who live in houses with clean clothes. Similarly, the characters judge each other, assuming certain things of one another without really getting to know each other.

Like the Oceanic 6, the little prince made it off his small planet and joined the real world, only to realize that what he really needed and wanted was back home on his planet all along. Most importantly, we know that John Locke has died in order to return to the island, which is exactly how the little prince returns to his home planet. The narrator is crushed when the little prince leaves him, and if Kate is forced to separate from Aaron, we know she'll be similarly devastated. But just as the narrator doesn't stop the little prince, knowing he can't keep him from his destiny, no one can stop any of the *Lost* characters once they have their minds set on something.

5.5   This Place Is Death

Original air date: February 11, 2009
Written by: Edward Kitsis, Adam Horowitz
Directed by: Paul Edwards
Guest cast: Guillaume Dabinpons (Robert), Melissa Farman (Danielle Rousseau), Fionnula Flanagan (Eloise Hawking), June Kyoko Lu (Mrs. Paik), Marc Menard (Montand), Bruno Bruni (Brennan), Jaymie Kim (Ji Yeon)

Focus: Rousseau, Everyone

Jin accompanies Rousseau and her team on their first day on the island. As Charlotte's health quickly deteriorates, Locke faces huge obstacles trying to get his followers to the Orchid, while off the island, Ben faces huge obstacles trying to get followers.

Since season 1, the writers have been promising the viewers that we would get a Rousseau flashback. First, they said it would be in season 3, then season 4. Then when Rousseau *died* in season 4, it seemed like that flashback would never happen. Oh, thank you, blooping island, for finally giving it to us.

In the first two seasons, the flashback was a simple device where we went back in time in the character's mind and saw what had led them to that point. In season 3, the writers shook things up a little when Desmond seemed to actually time travel back to a time where he could have completely changed his life in "Flashes Before Your Eyes." Then, in the season 3 finale, the writers introduced the flash*forward* to keep things exciting. Now, in season 5, they've come up with yet another way to show a character's story away from the present — by having a present-day character travel to another time for a front-row seat to that person's flashback. Unfortunately for the other characters, the one who goes back is Jin, who has a tenuous grasp of the English language and probably won't be able to relate most of what he saw to them. Lucky for Daniel, that same limitation prevents Jin from warning Rousseau about what's going to happen.

Most of what we know of Danielle's backstory was outlined in the season 1 episode, "Solitary." In that episode she captures Sayid, and, desperate to have another human being to talk to, tells him how she got to the island, and most of her story matches what we see in this episode. She tells him she was part of a science expedition that was three days out of Tahiti when the instruments malfunctioned. There was a storm, and it was nighttime, and they ended up on the island. She shows Sayid a music box and tells him it was an anniversary present from her lover, Robert. She says the team dug out the underground shelter she's living in soon after they arrived. She then says Robert and the others became sick, and she was forced to shoot him. She explains that he had a gun, too, but she'd removed the firing pin so he couldn't hurt her. In "Numbers," she changes her story about how she came to the island, saying that they'd heard a voice saying Hurley's numbers over and over, and they changed course to check it out before they hit the storm and got shipwrecked. She says they spent weeks searching the island for the radio tower, but then the team got sick. After they all died, she went and changed the message. In "Exodus, Part 1," Danielle explains that there were six team members altogether. Everything started in the "Dark Territory," at the *Black Rock*, and that's where her team got infected. She says it was there where Montand lost his arm. She adds that she gave birth by herself in the jungle and had Alex for one week, until one day she saw a pillar of smoke about five kilometers away and then "the Others" (which is where the survivors got the nickname from) came and took her baby. When Smokey attacks in "Exodus, Part 1," she tells Jack and Kate that it's a security system, whose sole purpose is to protect the island.

Almost all of her story is shown in this episode; some of it is consistent, other parts are inconsistent. Jin sees the music box playing on the beach, and there are six team members — Danielle, Robert, Nadine, Lacombe, Brennan, and Montand. We see Montand lose his arm at an ancient wall, not at the *Black Rock*, but maybe the ship is nearby and because Danielle never wanted to go back to the wall, she associated the attack with the *Black Rock* (or, more likely, the writers simply scrapped the earlier story because they wanted to introduce this new island landmark). Interestingly, when Jin flashes away from her at the wall and then returns, he sees a plume of black smoke, but this time it's at Danielle's camp. We see the scene where she's forced to kill Robert and has removed his firing pin. The episode does have inconsistencies, however: it wasn't two months before the team became sick; they were infected the day they arrived. Also, they've clearly set up a makeshift camp on the beach, and haven't dug out the underground shelter.

As you watch Rousseau's first day on the island, it's hard not to compare it to that of the Oceanic Flight 815 passengers. Charlie has a guitar case (well, he found it a few days after they crashed, but he has it nonetheless) and Brennan carries a violin case. There's a woman who is pregnant, in her third trimester. Montand hears a recording from the tower, just as Sayid did, and they all go to investigate (similarly, the 815 passengers' first expedition through the island is to get to a high point where they can hear the signal). Once in the jungle, they lose someone, and Robert takes the leadership role, like Jack, and offers to split up to find the person. When Jin urges them to go forward, Robert refuses to leave anyone behind, as Jack would have done. Nadine falls from the sky, dead and bloody, and the smoke monster pulled the pilot up into the sky in the first episode (they look up and see him in the tree, dead and bloody). Smokey uproots trees and frightens everyone the same way he did the first night the 815 passengers were on the island. People begin turning against each other and immediately doubting what's happening.

When Jin bloops away from Rousseau's group, he is finally reunited with the rest of the survivors, and realizes there's another crisis happening: Charlotte's increasingly rapid deterioration. Almost as if the island is trying to kill her, the flashes start coming fast and furiously, and Charlotte can't take them anymore. Her final discussion with Daniel, when they're separated from the others, is heart-breaking, and we can't help but think of Theresa. Just as Daniel's former girlfriend has been reduced to an incoherent woman lying there talking as if she's a child one minute, and herself the next, so, too, does Charlotte begin babbling various things in different voices, as if she doesn't know whether she's three or thirty-three. In the past Daniel had abandoned Theresa, unable to cope with what he'd done to her, but he refuses to do it now with Charlotte. But where Theresa is still alive, Daniel loses Charlotte. Her final words to him are shocking, however — she says the reason she wanted to find the island so badly is because she'd been told never to come back . . . by Daniel. Does this mean he's going to time travel to a moment where he will find young Charlotte and warn her? In "Because You Left," Dan was adamant about the "rules" of time travel, namely that you're not allowed to interfere and change things if you go back in time. Will his heart get in the way and he'll try to do exactly that? In that same episode, after all, we see Dan in the 1970s. Seeing that such a warning did nothing but strengthen Charlotte's impetuous resolve to return to the island, one wonders if he might reconsider. But if Dan's own adage — "whatever happened, happened" — is true, then it would seem he will always go back in time and give Charlotte this warning, no matter what his brain tells him to do.

Daniel's not the only one acting with his heart in this episode. Off the island, Sun is also following her heart. For three years she's let anger and vengeance eat away at the person she used to be, and has become hell-bent on making Ben pay (officially the other person she blames for Jin's death, which is interesting, since

Widmore is the guy who *sent* the boat that she thinks blew him up). Now, faced with the possibility that Jin is actually alive, Sun makes the impossible choice between going back to find Jin (and possibly never returning) and staying to be a mom to Ji Yeon. She chooses to follow Ben, and the scene of her talking to Ji Yeon shows what a monumental decision this is.

Many of the storylines in this episode show the lengths to which people will go to protect those with whom they are romantically involved. Rousseau is deeply in love with Robert, which makes her act of shooting him even more upsetting. When Charlotte dies, we know Daniel will never be the same again. Jin would rather never see Sun again than risk her or the baby returning to the island. Sun will sacrifice a life with Ji Yeon just to see Jin again.

Knowing Jin is alive hasn't changed her feelings toward Ben, however, and there's a wonderful moment where Sun and Jack are

As Charlotte's condition worsens, Daniel refuses to leave her side.
(© MARIO PEREZ/ABC/RETNA LTD.)

sniping in the car about Ben and Ben just slams on the brakes. The verbal torrents of fury he unleashes on them are the most sincere he's seemed in a long time, as if he truly believes he's been stalking and spying on each one of them to save them. Has Ben really been protecting them? Is it possible he's not the bad guy they've all been making him out to be? Could his mission be as sincere and genuine as Locke believes his is? If so, one can imagine why Ben would be so upset in this scene. If he's really devoted the last three years to protecting all of them, then the angry ingratitude from the two of them would, understandably, set him off just a little. But then again, knowing what we do about Ben's connection with Sayid, it would appear it was *Sayid* who's been going through hell in the past few years keeping them safe, not Ben.

On the island, Locke is the leader, and he seems to be a little more successful than Ben. While one of his number is dying, he's still trying to get everyone to the Orchid, hoping that he can get off the island and stop the time jumping, so no one else succumbs. Locke truly does believe in his mission, and it shows. He hesitates when Jin throws the wrench into his plans, but Locke is an honest person, and he looks Jin in the eye and gives him his word that he won't bring Sun back. Locke is probably telling the truth, and if this ruins his mission, he'll have to find another way to save everyone.

But the biggest moment of this scene is when Juliet steps up and says that if what he's doing is really going to save all of them, then thank you. The look on Locke's face speaks volumes. Ever since he arrived on the island he's been on a mission to save and protect everyone. He believes they were all destined to end up on that island, and despite bad things happening along the way, Locke truly believed all his efforts were for the greater good. But he's been called crazy, he's been yelled at, he's been doubted, and Jack even tried to kill him. Now, finally, someone simply says thank you. This is a huge moment for Locke.

That thank-you is small potatoes for what Locke endures once he lands in the chamber of the Frozen Donkey Wheel. After he snaps his shin bone (in the goriest scene on *Lost* since . . . Montand's arm popped off), he faces Christian, who one minute says he's there to help him the rest of the way, and then refuses to help him the rest of the way. It's a wonderful irony that Locke's "shepherd," so to speak, is the father of his most vocal detractor. But just as Locke agrees to abide by Jin's wishes after a tiny hesitation, when Christian tells Locke that he'll have to die, and "that's why they call it a sacrifice," Locke has one small moment of hesitation before he agrees to go ahead. Maybe Locke is crazy, like Jack says, but he's still the bravest character on the show.

Highlight: There were two laugh-out-loud moments in this episode for me: Miles's response when Sawyer tells him to translate what Jin is saying — "He's Korean. I'm from Encino" — and Charlotte's response when Dan asks her if she knows any other languages: "Just Klingon."

Did You Notice?:

- As Sun approaches Ben and company at the marina, she walks by a boat called the *Illusion*.
- Several fans pointed out that in the pilot episode, when the expedition team finds Rousseau's message, it alters slightly with every iteration. In one of the iterations, she says, "It is outside and Brennan has taken the keys." It's not clear what keys he would have taken — there aren't a multitude of

locks on the island — but the writers were consistent in using the name of someone she mentioned almost 100 episodes ago, which is impressive.

- Brennan is also the surname of Kate's childhood sweetheart, Tom, who we see in season 1's "Born to Run."
- In "Pilot, Part 2" the Losties make their first expedition trying to find a high point where they can hear a message being transmitted. Yet Montand could clearly hear it right on the beach. Perhaps something has changed on the island since 1988.
- Montand mutters, "First a boat. Then a helicopter. Next thing you know he'll be talking about a submarine." I wished Jin spoke French so he could say, "Well, now that you mention it . . ."
- Nadine is walking behind everyone right up to the moment where the baby kicks Danielle and she doubles over. Then Nadine instantly disappears.
- When Smokey first approached Eko in "The 23rd Psalm," Eko stared right into the eye of it, unblinkingly, and Smokey retreated. Smokey similarly approaches Montand in this scene, and grabs his leg only when Montand breaks eye contact and turns to look at the others.
- Darlton have confirmed in a podcast that the structure we see in this episode is the wall of the Temple that Richard and Ben talk about at the end of season 3. The declivity of the wall (the spot where Montand was pulled under it) is covered in hieroglyphics, some of them the same as the red symbols that appeared in the Swan station when the countdown clock reached zero.
- Rousseau told the survivors in "Exodus, Part 1" that Smokey was the island's security system. But considering she was told that by a zombified, half-dead, crazed version of her lover, that information . . . might be a little suspect.
- Rousseau is a helluva shot.
- Jin runs by the music box in his haste to get away from Rousseau, and it's what Rousseau asks Sayid to fix in "Solitary."
- Poor Ben. He had five of the Oceanic 6, and lost Hurley. Then he was back up to five with Sun showing up, and now he's down to two.
- Now that we know Charlotte was born on the island, her knowing triumph at finding the polar bear skeleton in the desert with the Dharma collar suddenly makes sense, as does her happiness when she first lands on the island in the water and begins laughing and splashing around.

- In "The Lie," Juliet explains that when they time-jump, whatever they have with them "comes along for the ride." That explains why the rope is still there when they time-jump away and Sawyer's holding onto it. It wasn't originally in the ground, but it didn't disappear because Sawyer was holding it. It opens up an interesting possibility, however: maybe whoever built the well knew where to build it because Sawyer held the rope in place and gave them their clue.
- There must be some significance to Locke's right leg. In "Walkabout," when we see Locke wake up for the first time on the beach after the Flight 815 crash, he looks down and wiggles the toe of his right foot. In "Deus Ex Machina," Locke gets a piece of shrapnel in his right leg when he and Boone try to open the hatch with the trebuchet. In "Lockdown," Locke's right leg is impaled by one of the bars on the blast door. In "Because You Left," Ethan shoots him in the right leg. And now, only a few days later, Locke shatters his right shinbone.
- Sun tells Ben that Locke never told her about Jin, which means he kept his promise to Jin.
- When Desmond says, "Are you looking for Faraday's mother, too?" the look on Ben's face suggests he had *no idea* she was any relation to Daniel. It's not often we see Ben blindsided like that.
- Desmond recognizes Hawking the moment he sees her.
- Daniel's clearly named his rat, Eloise ("The Constant"), after his mother. Awww . . .

Interesting Facts: Charlotte says that she knows "more about Ancient Carthage than Hannibal himself." Carthage is an ancient city (now an archeological dig site) in Tunisia, which is where Ben landed when he was ejected from the island in "The Shape of Things to Come," and where Charlotte found the polar bear skull in "Confirmed Dead."

Nitpicks: Before this episode, fans knew the white-haired woman as "Ms. Hawking" because the production notes and script referred to her as such in "Flashes Before Your Eyes," even though her name was never uttered on screen. At the time these episodes first aired on ABC, the network would rerun the previous week's installment in the hour before the new episode as an "enhanced" version, meaning it had pop-up subtitles that explained things like, "This is Jin. He is Sun's husband" for people just tuning into the show, in an attempt to lure in new viewers who were intimidated by the density of the show. The week that

"Jughead" aired, the network reran "The Lie" before it, and at the end of the episode, when Ben entered the church, the pop-up information explained that the woman's name was Eloise Hawking. So during "Jughead," when someone first referred to the girl as "Ellie," fans immediately assumed she was the very Eloise from the church, and that Eloise had spent time on the island and Daniel had encountered his mother in the past (which would explain why he tells Ellie that she reminds him of a girl he used to know). Many fans do not like the idea of important information being communicated in podcasts or in pop-ups or in interviews. Even Team Darlton have said they don't have time to regulate the enhanced episodes, and that if anything in those episodes contradicts what is happening in the actual episodes, we should take the episodes as canon and ignore what the pop-ups say. This is probably a situation where the network has more say than the showrunners, but if you want fans to know the information, then tell us in the episode. If we're supposed to start wondering if Ellie could be Eloise back in "Jughead," then have Ben refer to her by name at the end of "The Lie."

While I loved the reunion of Jin with Locke's crew, it seemed a little odd that he hadn't encountered them before that point. Locke and the gang end up on the beach and they find some of the things from Rousseau's team. Rousseau and her crew were likely a little further down the beach and the materials washed up elsewhere. But if Jin was running from Rousseau's shots and tripped just off the beach, and then flashed and everyone was standing right next to him, why didn't they hear Rousseau shooting before the time jump? They would have been in the same time as Jin was, so it just seems strange that they were suddenly all there, when no one was there the moment he tripped.

The Desmond/Penny story is being shown to us as happening simultaneously with the events in L.A. But it would have taken Desmond several weeks to sail from Greece to Oxford to Los Angeles, so either Desmond's story is being told on a completely different timeline or this is a big continuity error.

Oops: When Jin asks Rousseau where she came from, the sky is dark and cloudy, but by the next sentence it's bright and sunny. Also, Jack challenges Ben, insisting that Ben hadn't gone to Locke. Ben says no, Locke came to me, making it sound like he didn't actually lie. But he did: in the hotel room, Jack asked Ben if he'd *seen* Locke since the island, and Ben said no.

4 8 15 16 23 42: Montand hears the numbers being broadcast. Rousseau says they left on November 15.

It's Just a Flesh Wound: The smoke monster kills Nadine and severs Montand's arm at the shoulder. Brennan and Lacombe die (it's not clear if they died from gunshot wounds or of "the sickness"). Rousseau shoots Robert in the head. Charlotte's nosebleeds get worse, and she dies of a brain hemorrhage. Juliet and Sawyer get nosebleeds. Locke breaks his right leg.

Lost in Translation: When Ben hands Sun Jin's wedding ring, she's reading the inscription on the ring when she says, "We will never be apart" in Korean.

Any Questions?:

- Sun tells Kate in "The Lie" that it would be nice for Ji Yeon and Aaron to play together. In this episode she tells Ji Yeon she's found a friend for her. Are the writers foreshadowing that one day the two children *will* be together?

- If Widmore sent Sun to L.A. because that's where Ben is (and in "Jughead" he sends Desmond to the same place) then why isn't Widmore heading there himself? If he's so hell-bent on returning to the island, and Ben and Ms. Hawking are trying to get the Oceanic 6 back to the island, why isn't Widmore there for the ride?

- The recording of a man saying the numbers that Montand is listening to sounds an awful lot like Hurley's voice. Will Hurley go back in time and leave that message? Is the fact that the numbers are on the island not a coincidence, but instead Hurley heard about the numbers first, and then went back in time and *made* them something significant?

- Jin says he knows where the radio tower is, but did he ever actually see it? He was never part of an expedition to it, and when everyone trekked to the tower at the end of season 3, he was one of the renegades who stayed behind on the beach to ambush the Others.

- In season 1, why does Rousseau have no recollection of Jin when she first sees him? Is it because the events happened so long ago, or because of her insanity, or is it an inconsistency?

- What happened to Robert, Lacombe, and Brennan? Are they zombie versions of themselves? Are they themselves but the smoke monster has gotten to them? Are they manifestations of the island? Are they really sick like Danielle thought they were?

- Why did Charlotte hide the fact she spoke Korean? Every time someone finds out she speaks Korean, it's like she just admitted she'd killed someone. I said in my previous book that it doesn't make sense that an anthropologist would speak Korean and not French (she requires a translator in one scene where someone speaks French to her) and there must be a bigger reason for why, but now she's dead and we have no explanation for why she spoke it, or why it was a huge secret that she did. Maybe she was an anthropologist who specialized in Asian cultures?

- Charlotte reveals that she was on the island, and is now dying because she came back. Does that mean if the Oceanic 6 return to the island, they'll all die, too?
- Is the island controlling the flashes, and if so, does it speed them up to kill Charlotte? Why does the island not want Charlotte there? Is the purpose to kill her, or to get Locke moving more quickly to the Orchid?
- Sawyer's nose starts bleeding. Why aren't Jin's or Locke's noses bleeding yet? They've been on the island the same length of time as Sawyer has.
- Charlotte tells Dan that she and her mother left the island and she never saw her father again. Was he in the Dharma Initiative? Was he one of the Others? Could her father be Widmore?
- If Charlotte knew Daniel as a child, and he's with her now, couldn't he be her constant? Or do constants only work if you're consciousness traveling and not physically time traveling?
- Is there a deeper meaning to Locke breaking his leg before leaving the island? Is he simply not meant to walk off the island?
- Is Eloise the Ellie we saw in "Jughead"?
- If Eloise is Dan's mother, and she was on the island as Ellie, it's possible he was born there, too. If so, why isn't he having nosebleeds yet?
- Does Christian refuse to help Locke get up because he's ephemeral and can't actually touch Locke? If that's the case, how was he holding Claire's baby in "Something Nice Back Home"?
- Just two episodes ago, Ms. Hawking suggests that if Ben doesn't get *everyone* to her immediately, "God help us all . . ." [Music swells, terror sets in . . .] And now she's more like, "Oh well, two's better than nothing! Let's all to the bat caves!" Huh?

Ashes to Ashes: Charlotte Staples Lewis was born on the island, and was told by a crazy man who scared her that she needed to leave the island and never come back. Resolved to do the opposite, she devoted her life to finding the island and returning to it. She became an anthropologist and eventually found her way onto Widmore's team of scientists and back to the island of her birth, where she suffered a brain hemorrhage and died.

Bloop!

The following is the full list of all of the time bloops the survivors endure before Locke leaves and makes the record stop skipping. (**Warning:** the last one contains minor spoilers for "LaFleur.") While Locke is told that the time jumps are happening because Ben knocked the wheel off its axis (and it certainly looks like it's broken when Locke goes underground to move it) the island seems like it's completely in control, moving the survivors to key moments that the island needs them to see, or speeding up the time flashes when Locke and his crew seem to be moving too slowly.

1: After Ben turns the wheel, the camp is gone, it is daytime and the sun is shining. The action is divided between Locke and the group of people who are with Sawyer. Sawyer's group realizes they're in a time before the Oceanic 815 crash. Locke sees the Beechcraft go down, which means this is probably in 2001 or 2002. Dan explains the record-spinning concept to Sawyer, and Locke is shot in the leg by Ethan. The next flash happens when Ethan is about to kill Locke.

2: The Swan station has been blown up, and the Beechcraft is covered in moss and flora, so it would suggest it's a few years after the Oceanic 815 crash. The flash happens when Locke is trying to get Richard to tell him how to leave the island. All Richard can say is, "You're going to have to die, John." And then, bloop!

3: We flash from night to day, and the Beechcraft is overhead again. The hatch is intact, and it's not clear if it's pre– or post–Oceanic 815 crash (see page 15). All that really matters is that this was before Locke discovered the hatch. They flash as Daniel is trying to give a message to Desmond.

4: The year is 1954, and the Others are living in tents in a clearing and have killed some soldiers in the army. Sawyer's group are shot at with flaming arrows, and the time in this era lasts overnight and into the next day. Locke is reunited with Sawyer's group. Daniel sees Jughead, and flashes away as Sawyer is aiming a gun at Ellie, and as Locke is once again trying to get Richard to tell him how to leave the island.

5: Charlotte's nose is bleeding profusely and she passes out, and when she comes to they head to the Orchid. When they see the beam of light shoot into the air and Claire giving birth, we realize this is about 40 days after the crash when Aaron was born and Locke hit his nadir of despair. They flash away as Sawyer's watching Kate and Claire.

6: Back in the future again, the camp has been built but has been ransacked, and Vincent's collar is all that's left. They find a boat on the beach and leave, and other people are shooting at them. They flash just as they're under siege.

7: Landing in a monsoon, it's November 1988, the night that Rousseau's group landed on the beach. We discover Jin has been time-jumping with everyone else, but has been unconscious and unaware that anything is happening to him. The focus stays in this time period (though we don't see Sawyer's group through it) overnight and into the next day, and Jin flashes away as Rousseau's crew is heading into the declivity in the Temple wall after Montand.

8: About two months later (Montand's arm is showing a few weeks of decomposition), at the end of 1988 or beginning of 1989, everyone is dead, we see Rousseau kill Robert, and we flash as she's shooting at Jin. We don't see Sawyer's crew at all.

9: Jin is reunited with the others, and it's unclear what time period this is because they aren't near any manmade landmarks. At this point the island seems to begin jumping to urge everyone to hurry up and get to the Orchid. It bloops as Charlotte is saying she doesn't feel well.

10: This flash only lasts about five seconds, and again there's no way to tell what time period they're in.

11: Charlotte collapses at the beginning of this one, Juliet and Sawyer both get bloody noses, Charlotte begins babbling incoherently. Again, it's not clear what the date is. Daniel asks for help in carrying her, and the island flashes again.

12: Locke convinces everyone to keep moving, and Daniel stays behind with Charlotte. They find the Orchid station, and it looks similar to the way it looked just before Jack and everyone left the island, so it is probably, at the earliest, the 1990s, or it could even be in the future. They flash when Juliet marvels about how lucky they are to end up in the same era as the station.

13: There's no station yet, so it's before the Dharma Initiative had arrived. There is a well that is open, as if early inhabitants were using it as a water source. This could be a few decades ago, or even a century or more ago. The time flash happens as Locke is lowering himself into the well.

14: There is no well at all, and the only reason the rope is in the ground is because it came with Sawyer, who was holding it during the flash. The cave with the Frozen Donkey Wheel still exists (when Locke lands, he's inside it), and the gang turns to see a giant Egyptian statue behind them. They've gone way back in time, possibly centuries. Charlotte dies. They flash away when Locke turns the wheel.

15: In the final flash, the top part of the well is there but it's been filled in, like it was no longer needed as a water source (or perhaps someone was hiding the Frozen Donkey Wheel below it). It's 1974, and the Dharma Initiative is on the island. Sadly, Charlotte was only one step away from them possibly saving her life, because everyone's headaches and nosebleeds cease immediately following this final time bloop.

5.6   316

Original air date: February 18, 2009
Written by: Damon Lindelof, Carlton Cuse
Directed by: Stephen Williams
Guest cast: Raymond J. Barry (Ray Shephard), Mary Mara (Jill), Glen Bailey (Magician), Patti Hastie (Barfly), P.D. Mani (Nabil), Kavita Patil (Rupa), Ned Van Zandt (Mr. Dorsey)

Focus: Jack

The Oceanic 5 return to the island.

"We're not going to Guam, are we?"

The opening of "316" is exactly like one we saw almost five years ago: the camera opens on Jack's eye, and pans back to show him flat on his back in the jungle, wearing a suit. The same creepy music and ringing sounds play as he hears people calling for help and begins running to save them. But this time, rather than running to the beach and seeing a burning fuselage, several dead people, and others severely injured, he runs to a lagoon to find Hurley and Kate — people he already knows — in the water. Jack's been given an epic do-over.

In the church, Ben and Jack talk about what's about to happen and Ben explains the painting on the wall. The painting is Caravaggio's *The Incredulity of Saint Thomas* (1601–1602). As Ben talks, Jack listens and sees himself in the saint. Just as Thomas urged everyone to return to Judea with Christ even though he knew they'd probably all die, Jack is returning to the island and helping lead the others there, even if it might mean sacrificing themselves in the process. But, Ben points out, we remember Saint Thomas not for this act, but as "Doubting Thomas," the man who refused to believe Christ had resurrected, even though he was standing before him. It was only when Thomas touched Christ's wounds that he truly believed. While Jack is convinced they need to go back, he doubts the method by which they have to do it. He thinks taking Locke's body back as a proxy for Christian Shephard is ridiculous. After all, if part of his reason for going back is to finally be out from under his father's thumb, why would he want to return with something that reminds him of his father? Ben's little chat makes Jack rethink the situation.

Of course, the real "little chat" of this episode comes from Eloise Hawking, who comes off like an evil Mary Poppins, and who gives us a classroom lecture (complete with chastisement of Jack for not paying attention) that outlines some of what the Dharma Initiative is about, but in true *Lost* fashion, probably creates more questions than answers. We discover that the Dharma Initiative sought out the island, and had used strange global positioning techniques to find it. If Eloise Hawking is the Ellie we saw in "Jughead," then it means she was originally on the island in 1954. In that episode, Richard Alpert says that 18 U.S. Army soldiers came to the island to threaten their peace, and he was forced to kill all of them (it's the uniforms of the dead soldiers that the Others are wearing in that episode). Were those soldiers actually part of Dharma? Was the DI a government organization? How did Eloise Hawking find out about all of this? How are the Others and the DI connected? What she confirms is that there are many pockets of electromagnetic energy around the world, and that each pocket is somehow connected, but the island was the one that interested everyone the most. So if everything really comes down to the electromagnetic energy on the island (which has been pretty clear since the second season) then what was it about that particular pocket that excited everyone? Was it a different kind of electromagnetic energy that they recognized might be conducive to time travel? Is that what all of this was always about?

Eloise gives Jack a private lecture that ties in to Ben's mini-talk about the painting in that both are about the intertwining of science and faith. The reason Jack and Locke were paired up so many times in the second season is because those philosophical arguments they had about science and faith lie at the true heart of this series. Everything comes down to science (or free will) versus faith (and destiny). Do you follow what you believe in, or what has been proven to be correct? Do you make your own luck through a series of choices, or are you destined for certain things to happen to you no matter what you do? Jack was vehemently in the science/pragmatism category, but he's seen too many things off the island that are testing that resolve, and now he's starting to come around to Locke's way of seeing things.

Even though *Lost* is an ensemble show, Jack is still considered the main character. Jack has had a long, difficult journey, and this season will prove to be no exception. While almost every character in the series seems to be grappling with daddy (and mommy) issues, Jack's traveled with his father to the island. Literally. He was haunted by the inferiority he felt bred of being Christian Shephard's son and never living up to his expectations. And the worst part of his ambivalence toward his father is that, as an adult, he'd turned into him. Jack suffers from the same alcoholism as his father, he has failed relationships, he distrusts many people, and he believes that Christian betrayed him in many ways (including coveting his wife, Sarah). No matter how hard he tries, Jack can't seem to get out from under the immense burden Christian always placed on his shoulders. Christian is dead, but he's haunting Jack on and off the island.

And now, Christian has been replaced by Locke, the other older man who caused Jack tremendous aggravation. In life, Locke dogged him with his obsessive missions, and now Jack feels that even in death, Locke is mocking him. Here's Jack, the man of science and practicality, putting shoes on a dead man to recreate the right conditions for a crash that's going to happen again because they're flying over a particular pocket of electromagnetic energy that was discovered by a giant pendulum in the basement of a church. Jack's line to Locke, "This is even crazier than you are," is an understatement. Despite still seeing himself as separate from Locke, Jack is doing exactly what Locke would have, but he doesn't realize it. It was Locke who told him in "There's No Place Like Home" that he was going to have to lie, and then Jack did exactly that. Locke also told him he'd be back, and now he's going back. Jack is starting to believe in destiny, just like Locke did. Jack refuses to read Locke's suicide note, which the old Jack would have thought was ridiculous. How can a note written by a dead guy mean anything? But when he reads the simple words that are written on the paper — "Jack, I wish you had believed me. JL" — they hit Jack like a punch in the gut. The way Matthew Fox reels back in this scene is brilliant. Locke has reached out from beyond the grave, and even though Jack was talking to his corpse that afternoon, Locke *still* managed to get in the last word.

When Jack gets on the plane, he sits next to Kate, and she becomes his philosophical antagonist in the same way he'd been Locke's. He marvels at the fact that they're all on a plane, about to go back to the same place, and that it must "mean something." Kate looks him dead in the eye and says the reason they're on the same plane together is because they bought a ticket. She's looking at the adventure the same way Jack regarded everything: there's an explanation for it, and we made choices to get to where we are now. There's no destiny; I'm doing what I decided to do. She doesn't argue with him harshly as Jack had with Locke, though, partly because Jack doesn't fight vociferously the way Locke always did, and partly because she's just not up to it.

Why Kate is on the plane remains a big mystery. When she left everyone at the marina, there was no way anyone would have gotten her on that plane. And yet only a few hours later, she's lying on Jack's bed, desolate and alone, begging him not to ask her questions about Aaron. We know what that child means to her, and it would take something huge to separate her from him. Maybe Kate thinks she needs to go back to the island to help Aaron, but knowing there was a possibility she'd never get back and would never see him again, she must feel pretty strongly about what is waiting for her on that island. She sleeps with Jack, but there's no love or passion. Is there a chance she's trying to get pregnant by him, so if she can't return, she may not have Aaron but she might have a child of her own? She knows she can't get pregnant

Sayid is the only person who is physically forced onto the plane, but (for now) it's unclear why he's in handcuffs or who the beautiful mystery woman is. (© MARIO PEREZ/ABC/RETNA LTD.)

on the island (Juliet told her that all women who get pregnant on the island will die) so this might be a last-ditch effort to conceive so she can have her own island baby, like Claire did. Or . . . maybe she was just looking for a connection, since she just somehow lost the only true connection she's ever felt with another person.

It's unclear why many of the Oceanic 6 are returning, but they might *all* be heeding Eloise's instructions to Jack, that they must recreate the original flight as accurately as they can. Jack wears a suit, thinks about getting drunk, and brings a coffin, only this time he has the proper documentation for the body and doesn't have to argue with the ticket agent the way he did in "White Rabbit." Kate is wearing a jacket that's similar to the one she had on when the plane crashed the first time. She's alone this time, and not being accompanied by a marshal; Sayid is in handcuffs and in custody, so that could balance out what is missing with Kate. Sun is alone, but she has Jin's wedding ring, which could stand as a proxy for Jin. Hurley has another Spanish comic book (Walt), and is traveling with a guitar case, which might be a proxy for Charlie. (Perhaps the 78 empty seats are reserved for the ghosts of Oceanic 815.) Ben throws off the equation, but he recreates several events from a combination of characters — he's lost the use of his arm, just like Locke had no use of either leg; he's reading on the plane, the way Hurley was in the original flight; he's late to the flight and yells for everyone to hold the doors for him, the same way Hurley did; and he disappears into the bathroom right before the crash, just like Charlie did. Frank Lapidus is flying the plane, and we discovered in the season 4 episode, "Confirmed Dead," that he was supposed to be the pilot of Oceanic 815. Maybe this flight is karmic; if they can right everything that was wrong about the original flight, things might work out better the second time around.

Or not.

Highlight: Jack: "How can you read?" Ben: "My mother taught me." Not only is that one of the best Ben comebacks of all time, but it's also, in true Ben fashion, a total lie — he couldn't have been taught to read by his mother if she died giving birth to him.

Did You Notice?:

- After the opening scene, we zip back 46 hours. Then Eloise says the window closes in 36 hours. Since we know they didn't stand at the opening of the church for 10 hours, they must have been in the air for 10 hours before it happened.
- As the group leaves the church and enters the basement where the Lamp Post station is, there's a sign on the door that says, "CAUTION HIGH VOLTAGE DO NOT ENTER THIS ENCLOSURE." The sign is probably moot, and meant to scare people away from ever exploring what's behind the door.
- The tunnels under the church look exactly like the tunnels through the Dharma stations, right down to the giant iron door with the wheel that opens it.
- When Jack asks Eloise if Ben is telling the truth, she says, "Probably not" in a dismissive way. The look on Ben's face is priceless; he's rarely faced with someone who couldn't care less that he's lying.
- Jack notices a photograph of the island on Eloise's chalkboard dated September 23, 1954, which is exactly 50 years (less one day) before Oceanic 815 crashed on September 22, 2004.
- Eloise mentions that a clever man created a series of equations and invented the pendulum that would get them back to the island, but never mentions

his name. One could probably assume that man is important (and someone we already know), and we'll find out later who it is.

- Eloise says they're standing above a pocket of energy that connects to similar pockets around the world. In season 2's "S.O.S.," during the Rose and Bernard flashback, Rose goes to a faith healer named Isaac, and he tells her, "There are certain places with great energy — spots on the Earth like the one we're above now. Perhaps this energy is geological — magnetic." He says he harnesses that energy to heal people, but when he puts his hands on Rose, he can't heal her, instead saying there are different energies, and this isn't the one for her. Clearly the island was.

- Both Desmond and Eloise show a lot of grace and perfect timing as they walk around the map and never once get clocked by the giant pendulum.

- Eloise hands Jack a binder with the flight number to Guam, and there are coordinates beside it — 34° 03 N, 118° 14 W. These refer to the location of L.A., which is where the plane would be leaving from.

- In Eloise's office, there's a Virgin Mary statue on her desk that looks a lot like one of Charlie's heroin-stash statues.

- Eloise tells Jack that Ben and Sun heard what they needed to hear, but she doesn't say she told them the truth.

- Eloise tells Jack he needs to give Locke something of Christian's whether he believes in it or not, and says, "That's why it's called a leap of faith, Jack." In the season 2 episode, "Orientation," Locke keeps stalking his father by sitting outside his house in a car. Helen follows him and says he needs to drop his obsession, and he must choose between Cooper and her. Locke says he doesn't know how to do that. Helen says we always do things without knowing what will happen next, and adds, "That's why it's called a leap of faith." At the end of that episode, Locke convinces Jack they need to keep pushing the button, and says it's a leap of faith.

- Jack seems pretty thick in the scene in Eloise's office. She tells him he needs to recreate the original circumstances of Flight 815. He doesn't know what she means. She says, you know, with Locke's body? In a coffin? He still doesn't understand what she's getting at. It's only been three years, Jack; you don't remember taking a coffin with you on the plane the first time?

- Ben's Doubting Thomas story brings to mind several Thomases that have been on the show: Thomas was the name of Claire's deadbeat boyfriend, and he's the father of Aaron; Tom was one of the Others; Tom was Kate's childhood sweetheart who owned the toy plane; Tommy was the name of Charlie's drug dealer; Tom Sawyer was one of Anthony Cooper's aliases; when Ana Lucia and Christian are in Australia, he calls her Sarah and she calls him Tom.

- Jack's grandfather Ray is very much like Kate: always on the run and never wanting to stay in one place. He's also a little like Sawyer; when he mentions seeing Kate, he remembers her as "the one with the freckles," which is Sawyer's nickname for her.
- The doctor on the freighter who ended up with his throat slit was also named Ray, as was the Australian farmer who hired Kate in season 1's "Tabula Rasa," who eventually turned her over to the marshal.
- When Kate and Jack are having breakfast, there's an interesting and creepy painting on the wall of an isolated person looking away. It seems to be symbolic of each person about to get on the plane. They're all miserable and alone.
- When Kate is talking to Jack about the shoes on the table, she asks him why he holds onto something that makes him so sad. Her comment not only refers to the shoes, but to Jack holding onto Kate, or her holding onto Aaron. Both remind each other of the island and what was left behind, and it's what they want most but can't have.
- Now we know why Christian Shephard is always seen wearing white tennis shoes.
- Locke's body is being held in the meat locker at Simon's Butcher Shop. Simon was the name of Charlie's father . . . who was a butcher.
- When Sayid is at the security area of the airport, his shirt is a royal blue color, but when he's on the plane, it looks purple.
- When Ben says he didn't know that Locke had committed suicide, you can tell he's lying.
- There's a white flash on the plane as if they all time-blooped off it, which would explain why they don't remember a crash.

Interesting Facts: The title of this episode obviously refers to the flight number of the plane to Guam. It also refers to one of the most oft-quoted verses in the Bible, one that is not only appropriate for this episode, but was carved on the side of Eko's "Jesus stick." John 3:16 states, "For God so loved the world that he gave his only begotten son that whosoever shall believeth in him shall not perish, but have everlasting life." In other words, God loved Jesus so much that when Jesus died and was resurrected, it was a sign from God that everyone shall have everlasting life in Heaven when they die. On *Lost*, however, the passage is more direct, since John died and now he is returning to the island to rise again.

In a podcast leading up to this episode, Darlton teased viewers that Ben would be reading a copy of *Ulysses* on the plane (see page 79) and Damon joked that a significance of the title of the episode was that the following quotation appeared on page 316 of the book (emphasis his): "So off they started about Irish sport and shoneen games the like of lawn tennis and about *hurley* and putting the stone and racy of the soil and building up a nation once again and all of that." Then, after reading the passage, he said, "Coincidence?! Yes."

The Lamp Post station is named such after the significance of the lamp post in C.S. Lewis's *The Chronicles of Narnia*. In *The Magician's Nephew* and *The Lion, the Witch, and the Wardrobe*, a lamp post is the intersection point between two worlds. The doorway from the church is like the doorway of the wardrobe in *The Lion, the Witch, and the Wardrobe*, as if the church is just window dressing. Maybe Eloise is actually a centaur . . .

The comic book that Hurley is reading at the airport is a Spanish version of the third volume of Brian K. Vaughan's amazing series, *Y: The Last Man* (see page 116).

On November 4, 2008, Jorge Garcia posted on his fantastic blog (dispatches fromtheisland.blogspot.com) that the AD had warned him he'd be "starting wet." Dreading it, he joked that he shouldn't even have bothered to shower, but did so out of habit. He did admit, however, that his only solace would be packing a dry pair of underwear to put on at the end of the day. The week after "316" aired, he posted photos of the shoot that day, saying he'd swallowed a lot of water but luckily it had rained, so the water was relatively clean.

Nitpicks: When Jack finds Hurley and Kate in the lagoon, Hurley's flailing around in the water, unable to swim. But we've seen him swim before. In "The Beginning of the End," we see him cannonball into a deep part of the water and then swim back to the shore. In "There's No Place Like Home," when the helicopter crashes into the water, Hurley is the only one not wearing a life-jacket and he manages to swim to the lifeboat with no issues. So why can't he swim here?

Oops: When Eloise and Jack are talking in her office, she hands him Locke's suicide note and Jack is surprised and says he didn't know. Eloise says, "Obituaries don't see fit to mention when someone hangs himself." Except . . . it did. In the section of the obituary that could clearly be seen in "Through the Looking Glass," we saw that the person who died had hanged himself in his loft.

4 8 15 16 23 42: In the opening, we go back in time 46 hours (**23** x 2). Desmond says he wasted **4** years of his life on the island (it had originally been three, but maybe he's adding on the four months and calling it four now). The date on the U.S. Army photo is September **23**, 1954. The flight is number **316**. When Jack gets a call from the nursing home, the administrator tells him this is the **4**th time Ray has tried to leave. In the airport security area, there are two signs, one pointing left for gates 1 to **15**, the other pointing right for gates **16** to **42**. The gang leaves from gate **15**. Hurley buys 78 seats on the plane (7 + 8 = **15**). On the plane, Ben and Jack are sitting in row **8**, and Kate is in row **4**. Frank tells Jack he's been working for Ajira for **8** months.

It's Just a Flesh Wound: Ben has been severely hurt and has blood all over his head and what appears to be a broken arm, but it's unclear what happened to him.

Any Questions?:

- Is there any significance to Ben and Eloise constantly lighting candles?
- When Locke and his crew visit Richard Alpert's camp in "Jughead," Richard says it's 1954. Was the U.S. Army photo taken by the very soldiers that Alpert's crew killed? If so, how did the photograph make its way to the Dharma station? It's not like they had camera phones back then.
- Eloise says the island isn't done with Desmond yet. So what is his purpose? Does this mean he'll be returning to the island?
- Desmond, who none of them have seen in years, reveals that he'd met Eloise Hawking years ago, that she sent him to the island and ruined his life, and that she's Daniel's mother. And no one says *anything* to him? He just dropped more bombshells than Eloise did, and the moment he leaves they all shrug and go back to what they're doing as if he were nothing more than a raving lunatic.
- Not only do Jack, Ben, and Sun say nothing to Desmond, but Eloise's face barely registers an ounce of surprise when Desmond says he was sent here by her son, who needs her help. Does she already know? Or does she not care?
- How did Eloise get Locke's suicide note?
- Is Ben a religious person at all, or is he just playing the part and pretending

to pray while he's in the church?

- Ben says he's keeping a promise he made to an old friend and he just has some loose ends that need tying up. Did he follow through on his threat to Widmore that he would kill Penny? He did just realize that Desmond was in town, after all.

- When the magician in the nursing home pulled the towel off the rabbit, was anyone else checking to see if it had a number on it?

- It's strange that we see Ray all of a sudden when we'd never seen him before. He seems a little creepy himself. If Christian is some sort of mystical prophet, could Ray be someone special, too? After all, the writers could have just had Jack discover his father's shoes in the corner of his closet. There must be a significance to the entire male Shephard line (Ray — Christian — Jack — Aaron).

- What happened to Kate after she left the marina? Where is Aaron?

- Locke's face was smooth when we saw him in the coffin in "There's No Place Like Home, Part 3," but he now has five o'clock shadow. Is this an indication that he's not dead in the way a normal person would be dead?

- What are the chances that Locke would have the same shoe size as Christian?

- I know that Sun is deeply in love with Jin, and who wouldn't want to find out if their previously dead husband was alive, but how can she leave Ji Yeon behind like that? We see Ji Yeon sitting on Sun's mother's lap in the previous episode, so not only is Sun leaving Ji Yeon behind, but she's going to allow the child to be raised by the *Paiks*. How could she?

- Why is Sayid handcuffed to an agent?

- Hurley won't say how he knew about the flight, and he's carrying a guitar case. Was it Charlie who convinced him to come on the flight? Is he carrying the guitar as a proxy for Charlie? Is there something other than a guitar in that case?

- What exactly happens to the plane? Was it only Hurley, Kate, and Jack that actually blooped off the plane into another time period (Jin showing up in a brand-new 1970s Dharma van would indicate they're no longer in the present), or did all the passengers bloop? Did the rest of the plane crash? What happened to Sun and Ben?

- Ben gets up to go to the bathroom as Jack reads Locke's note, and as soon as he disappears the plane experiences turbulence. Did Ben have something to do with the plane going down? We saw him putting something into a hotel vent in "Because You Left." Did he do something with that object to bring the plane down?

- Does Jin know who they are?

Music/Bands: When Jin pulls up in the Dharma van, he's listening to "Dharma Lady" by Geronimo Jackson (see page 140).

✍ Ulysses by James Joyce (1922)

When the writers put Stephen Hawking's *A Brief History of Time* into the hands of a guard and I knew I had to read it (see *Finding Lost — Season 3*, pages 67–72), I groaned. Surprisingly, I enjoyed it (and I must reiterate that it has given me a completely different perspective on the time travel on the show). But then, when they showed Ben holding a copy of *Ulysses* on the Ajira flight, my heart stopped. Do I pretend I didn't see it? Of course not . . . for Darlton had devoted part of a podcast preceding that episode to telling fans that *Ulysses* would appear in an episode and that they *must read it*. I thought I'd never forgive them. And 500 pages into the book, I *still* couldn't forgive them. But then, I finished it, and I realized what a wondrous book this is. Did I understand all of it? No. It's been said that one gets a cursory understanding of *Ulysses* on the first reading, but that it should be read for the first time with no annotations. On the second reading, the reader should look through the annotations (best to find those from a later edition). On the third reading, they should try to remember some of those annotations and study specific pages in terms of the literary styles Joyce uses. And on the fourth reading, they'll truly understand it.

Maybe.

Sadly, the following summary is brought to you by my first readthrough. This book is so rich and dense and packed with so many cultural references it would make your head spin, so this is by no means a comprehensive analysis. I will provide a quick summary of each of the "episodes," or chapters in the book, and then I'll talk about the book's relation to *Lost*.

Ulysses is a modern-day retelling of Homer's *Odyssey*. It is split into 18 sections, each one corresponding to (and named after) a similar section in Homer's epic, which both brings the book into a modern setting (well, for the Modernist era, anyway), and, by contrasting the daily errands of two men, parodying them by showing how heroic they are *not*. Joyce plays with form throughout the book, as the actual language takes center stage several times, switching voices, styles, and making the plot secondary to the semiotics. Much of the book is composed of interior monologues, where we follow (or try to follow) the thoughts of the characters as they jump from topic to topic, get sidetracked, go off on tangents, and ruminate on the world around them.

Chronologically, the book is set roughly one year after the end of *A Portrait of the Artist as a Young Man*. That book had followed Stephen Dedalus from childhood to adulthood, as he moved through boarding school, family tensions, religious piety, shame, and acceptance of who he is, devoting himself to a life of writing.

In the first chapter of the book, we are re-introduced to Stephen, whose mother has recently died after a long and physically debilitating illness. Stephen is still in mourning. He lives with Buck Mulligan, a loud, large, caustic individual who makes off-color jokes and lives a life of leisure by skiving off the people around him (mostly Dedalus). There is another man, Haines, living in the tower Stephen is renting. At the beginning of the chapter, it is about 8 A.M. in the morning on June 16, 1904, and Stephen complains to Mulligan that Haines had kept him up the night before with a nightmare about a panther. Mulligan mocks him about his mother's death, reminding him that his mother's final wish was that Stephen pray by her bedside, and he'd refused her. Stephen then tells him about a grudge he's been holding for months — that Buck had referred to his mother's passing as a "beastly death," and the comment had greatly offended Stephen. Buck blusters through an apology, clearly caught off guard, before collecting himself and turning it back on Stephen for being too sensitive. Stephen and Buck go downstairs to breakfast with Haines. A milkwoman comes to deliver milk. Stephen marvels at her silently, imagining her as a mythic creature of Ireland, but when Haines speaks Irish to her, she asks if he's speaking French (this is the first of many moments in the book where Stephen imagines greatness where there is none). Haines is fascinated by the things Stephen says and claims one day he's going to write a book full of Stephen's sayings. Stephen asks him if he'll see any money from that, and an insulted Haines walks out of the place. Buck admonishes Stephen for being so uncouth, and they all head out for a walk. Haines and Stephen chat on the way down the hill, and Stephen says he has two masters, one English, one Italian (England and the

Roman Catholic Church), and that Ireland acts as an occasional third master. When they get to the water, Buck is undressing and jumping in, and Haines says he'll stay on the shore. Stephen walks away, and Buck demands he leave the key to the tower and some money behind. As he leaves, Stephen mutters under his breath that Buck is a "usurper."

In the second chapter, Dedalus is teaching a class of bored boys, but the effect is clearly contagious. Throughout this chapter, Stephen is saying one thing, thinking another. Joyce uses long passages of stream-of-consciousness writing, where a character thinks of one thing, which leads to another, which leads to another, and we can trace back the thread to see how they got from one point to the next. As he tries to get the boys to pay attention, he thinks about the wittiness of his own words, wondering if he should try them out later on Haines, who would appreciate them. After the boys head out to play field hockey, one of them stays behind, and Stephen thinks about how ugly the boy is, and imagines how much his mother must still love him, which makes him think of his own childhood and his now-dead mother. Stephen is called to the office of the headmaster, Mr. Deasy, for his wages. Mr. Deasy drones on about Protestantism and his loyalty to the English, imagining that Stephen must be an Irish-Catholic who is anti-England. Deasy asks Stephen if he could help him get a letter published, and is typing it while talking in his office. Stephen is at times distracted by the game going on outside the window. When Deasy finishes the letter he hands it to Stephen, who reads it to discover it's about cattle foot-and-mouth disease. They then begin a discussion about Jews (Deasy is very anti-Semitic and believes Jewish merchants are "already at their work of destruction") and Stephen tries arguing that gentile merchants are just as bad. Deasy begins quoting history, and Stephen utters the now-famous literary line, "History . . . is a nightmare from which I am trying to awake." As Stephen leaves with the letter, Deasy races after him and tells him an anti-Semitic joke.

Next Stephen goes for a walk along the beach, and the entire section is written in a stream-of-consciousness style, with Stephen reflecting on the things he'd seen and talked about earlier that day. He sees two midwives on the beach and wonders if one of them is carrying a dead fetus in her pouch to dispose of on the beach. He thinks of the umbilical cord as stretching back to the first man and woman. He thinks about Christ being "begotten, not made" and that he, in contrast, was "made, not begotten," and has nothing in common with his father. He decides he's heading in the direction of his Aunt Sara's house and that he'll drop by, and remembers how his father hates his Uncle Richie, Sara's husband. But as his mind goes back to his younger days and the shame he used to feel for his father and family, he realizes he's gone past the aunt's house and decides not to visit after all. He remembers being a student in Paris and his father sending him a telegram to come home immediately because of his sick mother. This makes him think of Buck's comment again, and he decides he's not going back to the tower that night because he won't get any sleep again. He sees a dead dog in the sand, and another dog that runs toward it, sniffs it, runs back to its owners, and is kicked for going near the carcass. The dog then wanders off and urinates on a rock without much thought. Stephen watches all of this while thinking of other philosophical quandaries, and as with his other musings, the real thing happening in front of him causes him to think of abstract things, which inevitably come back to his own experiences. He thinks of a poem and writes it down on Deasy's letter. Then he urinates on a rock, like the dog, and picks his nose, and then looks around to make sure no one saw him do it.

Episode 4 introduces us to Leopold Bloom, who in many ways is the exact opposite of Dedalus. While Dedalus seems to spend most of his time exploring his own thoughts, Bloom is busy being part of the physical world: talking to the cat, making breakfast for his wife Molly who is still in bed when he leaves, going out to buy himself a kidney for breakfast, watching the way the woman in front of him sways her hips, reading the newspaper, wondering if his wife is having an affair, reading letters from his 15-year-old daughter Milly, and defecating. This episode returns us to 8 A.M., and so we are reading Bloom's morning as it is happening simultaneously with Stephen's. (Joyce reminds us of this at one point when the sun moves behind a cloud, and Bloom's thoughts become gloomy, just as Stephen's had earlier in the novel when he'd noticed the same occurrence.) Stephen, in comparison to Bloom, seems self-centered and thoughtless of others, brooding and blaming. Bloom, in contrast, makes breakfast for his wife, wills himself back to cheeriness after dark thoughts threaten to overtake him, and tries to shake off suspicions that Molly might be having an affair with her music instructor, "Blazes" Boylan. We learn that he will be attending the funeral of his friend, Paddy Dignam — "Poor Dignam!" — at 11 A.M.

As Bloom heads to the post office, he casually walks around the town looking into shop windows and thinking about exotic scents and tastes. This chapter is once again rooted in the sensuality that typifies Bloom's characterization. At the post office he picks up a letter from a woman he's been corresponding with under the pseudonym "Henry Flower." He finds a scentless flower attached to the letter, and the correspondent, Martha Clifford, writes an erotic letter wherein she constantly refers to him as a naughty boy (particularly for using some disagreeable word in his previous letter) but then suggests they meet up. Bloom is amused and happy to read the letter, but has no intention of meeting her. Martha adds a postscript asking him what kind of perfume Molly wears, and he imagines the scent on Molly. He rips the envelope up and lets the pieces scatter in the wind. Most of this chapter is simply the random sensual thoughts of Bloom as he: imagines the smell of his wife's perfume and her lotion that he goes to the chemist's to order for her; watches an upper-class woman in silk stockings getting into a cab and hopes for a look at her leg; sits in church and marvels at the soporific effect of the rituals and the Latin; imagines picking up a woman in the church by pulling off a piece of fluff from the back of her dress; and looks forward to heading to the public baths where he can sit in the

A young James Joyce in 1904, the year in which *Ulysses* is set. He would begin writing the book in 1914, and finish in 1921. (IMAGE REPRODUCED FROM THE ORIGINAL GLASS NEGATIVE IN UNIVERSITY COLLEGE DUBLIN, BY KIND PERMISSION OF HELEN SOLTERER)

water and use his nice-smelling lemon soap. Along the way he runs into McCoy, who acts the grief-stricken friend for Poor Dignam (before announcing that he actually won't be able to attend the funeral and instead asks Bloom to write his name in the register), and Bantam Lyons, an unkempt man who rushes up to him and asks to borrow the paper to bet on the horses (before misconstruing Bloom's offer to take the paper — "I was just going to throw it away" — as a suggestion on a horse). He thinks of how quickly his daughter has grown up, and remembers a son, Rudy, who died 11 years ago only a few days after he was born.

In the next chapter, called "Hades," Bloom accompanies his acquaintances to the funeral for Dignam. He sits relatively isolated in the carriage with Martin

Cunningham, Simon Dedalus (Stephen's father), and Mr. Power, and on the way to the funeral they mostly talk amongst themselves while Bloom sits quietly with his thoughts. When they see Blazes Boylan walking down the street and ask Bloom about Molly's upcoming concert tour with him, Bloom avoids looking out of the carriage and studies his nails instead. They discuss how quickly Dignam died, and while they all think it's a shame, Bloom says it was the best way to go, quickly and with no pain. They all stare at him, horrified, because they are Catholics, and believe a quick death means the victim had no time to repent. Bloom's Jewishness becomes obvious in this scene, and again when he's at the church, watching the entire service as an outsider who is unfamiliar with the rituals. This chapter changes the character of Bloom for us, making him a more sympathetic one, not only for his outsider status, but because it illuminates his own unhappiness. It also shows that despite Bloom being considered an interloper by everyone else, he's not aware of the fact he's a social pariah. When the men in the carriage begin talking about how awful suicides are, Cunningham nervously clears his throat and changes the subject, knowing that Bloom's father committed suicide. Much of this chapter is once again an interior thought process, and we realize Bloom's immense sadness at the loss of his young son, and now discover he also lost his father under unnatural circumstances. He's a son without a father, and a father without a son. As he stands at the funeral thinking ridiculous thoughts — like how it would make more sense to bury people standing up because you could pack them more closely together, and they would actually make good fertilizers for gardens . . . until their heads accidentally started sticking out — one can't help but sympathize with this outsider, who may be rooted in the sensuality of life, but also lives with his own constant — and isolating — sadness.

Very little of the next chapter is internal monologue — instead, it's a mishmash of several conversations at once, broken up by headlines, as if the narrator interjects himself into the text and tells the reader how to read it. It's one of the most difficult sections of the book to read, mostly because there is so much action happening at once, but at the same time it conveys the chaotic nature of the scenes. Bloom, who works in advertising, goes to the newspaper printing offices to explain how he needs the design of an ad changed for a company named Keyes. He then visits the staffroom, where he's mostly ignored, and several other characters are loudly discussing political speeches. He uses the telephone, intending to call Keyes and see how long he wants the ad to run in the paper just as Myles

Crawford, the newspaper editor, enters the room. When Bloom can't reach Keyes, he leaves the office to go to see Keyes directly, and none of the men seem to notice or care that he's leaving. Stephen Dedalus enters the office, dropping off the column that Deasy asked him to deliver, and while he's there Crawford tries to talk him into writing for the paper. As he's chatting with Stephen, Bloom calls the office from Keyes' to secure the ad space and Crawford refuses to take the call, showing that once again, Stephen is the guy people are attracted to and believe in, and Bloom lives on the sidelines, without really being aware of the fact that others don't want to be near him. Crawford and the men who remain discuss poetry with Stephen, asking if he knows of a poet named A.E., and they talk about how they believe he would be a great writer for the paper. But Stephen, the consummate artist, won't lower himself to newspaper writing, and instead suggests they all head to a pub. As they leave, Bloom comes rushing back into the office, crossing Stephen's path directly for the first time in the book (and mentally noting how dirty Stephen's new boots are) and when he tells Crawford that Keyes will place the ad for two months rather than three, Crawford dismisses Bloom, saying of Keyes, "He can kiss my Irish arse," and heads off with the group to the pub.

Where chapter 5 was filled with descriptions of smells, chapter 8, or "Lestrygonians," is rooted in taste. It begins with Bloom standing outside of a candy store and going for a walk in search of lunch. He buys cakes and feeds birds, he remembers the tastes of various foods, and he passes by the aforementioned poet, A.E., who is a vegetarian. He meets up with an old flame, now married with children, and he thinks about women giving birth. He thinks that the Roman Catholic Church is particularly hard on women, forcing them to have too many babies, which "eat you out of house and home" (he thinks particularly of poor Mrs. Purefoy, who has been in labor for three days and still hasn't delivered her baby, and who has many children already at home). He thinks of the difficulty women have in labor, how they get around while they're pregnant (he remembers when Molly was pregnant), and how difficult it is post-pregnancy, having to nurse the babies day and night. He thinks of the astronomical term "parallax," and how he doesn't really know what it means. (Parallax refers to how an object looks different from different perspectives, and in this case is a commentary on the way *Ulysses* is written, with the characters constantly evolving from one chapter to the next, and on how characters perceive other characters in completely different ways, due to their personal points of view.) Bloom stops at the

Burton restaurant, intending to lunch there, until the sights of the men eating repulse him:

> Perched on high stools by the bar, hats shoved back, at the tables calling for more bread no charge, swilling, wolfing gobfuls of sloppy good, their eyes bulging, wiping wetted moustaches. A pallid suetfaced young man polished his tumbler knife fork and spoon with his napkin. New set of microbes. A man with an infant's saucestained napkin tucked round him shovelled gurgling soup down his gullet. A man spitting back on his plate: halfmasticated gristle: no teeth to chewchewchew it.

Disgusted, Bloom leaves and goes to Davey Byrnes' instead, where he eats a cheese sandwich and listens to Nosey Flynn ask him questions about Molly's upcoming tour and Blazes Boylan. He tunes out Flynn and thinks of the food around the bar, and remembers making love to Molly in a field where she passed cake from her mouth to his, and then is suddenly mindful of how their lives have changed since then. Flynn tells Byrne about Bloom and we see a description of Bloom from another character — he gossips about Bloom's marriage to Molly (which he believes is stable) and says Bloom's a good person, but he'll never sign a contract. Bloom leaves the pub and heads outside, where he helps a blind man cross the street (all the while wondering if a blind person has heightened smell and taste) and, as he heads to the National Library, sees Boylan walking down the street and, in an attempt not to be seen by him, Bloom rushes through the gates of the National Museum instead.

In the following chapter, Stephen Dedalus is at the National Library discussing his *Hamlet* theory with literary critic John Eglinton, poet A.E., and the librarian. His theory is that Shakespeare based the character of the ghost of Hamlet's father on himself, being older and graying at the time. The other men are more conservative, with Eglinton challenging Stephen's right to theorize such a thing, and A.E. saying one should not graft biographical details of an artist onto the merits of their work (in this scene Joyce anticipates Roland Barthes' 1967 essay, "The Death of the Author," where he argued vociferously that one should never consider any details of the author's own life when looking at a text). Stephen elaborates on his theory, saying that Anne Hathaway was unfaithful to Shakespeare (and he to her) and that he held a grudge against her for it and stopped mentioning her in the plays. He argues that this again links Shakespeare to the ghost of Hamlet's father, who knows that his wife was unfaithful to him. He argues that Shakespeare's brothers, Edmund and Richard, both had affairs with Hathaway, which is why the characters with those names in the plays are often depicted as bad brothers who are adulterers. A.E. leaves before Stephen is finished, and the men discuss a party where artists have been invited, and Stephen mentally notes with some disdain that he was not invited to the party. A.E. is compiling a book of works by Irish poets, and Stephen is also hurt that he hasn't been asked to contribute to the volume. Buck Mulligan arrives and jokingly chastises Stephen for standing him and Haines up for lunch, instead sending a telegram to them. He listens mockingly to Stephen's theory, interjecting with his own ludicrous suggestions about Shakespeare. As the men return to Stephen's theory, not taking it very seriously, they argue that Shakespeare identified with Hamlet, rather than Hamlet's father, and that the ghost of Hamlet's father was in fact Shakespeare's father. Stephen angrily denies this theory, and says that fathers are insignificant, and are connected to their children only through conception, nothing more, belying his own animosity toward his father. Bloom enters the library, but remains in a different section, and Buck talks Stephen into leaving to get a drink with him. He tells Stephen he saw Bloom at the National Museum, staring at the buttocks of the statue of Aphrodite, and insinuates that Bloom is gay. As they leave the library, Bloom walks up behind Stephen, who moves aside to let him pass, and Buck leans in to mockingly warn Stephen that Bloom has his eye on him.

The next "episode" acts as an intermission in the book, being the middle chapter of the book, and rather than involving any lengthy internal monologues, it instead traces 19 secondary characters in the book as they go about their day. It's one of the easier sections in the book to read because it consists of mostly external description, as if the narrator is simply illustrating the bustling activity on the streets of Dublin by briefly describing one character, and as that character passes another, moves to the second character to focus on what he or she is doing (much like Robert Altman did in the film *Short Cuts*). Most of the characters we've already focused on are simply continuing on their day. We see the man who'd misunderstood Bloom's comment for a tip on a horse inside the bookie's placing his bet; Patrick Dignam, the young son of the deceased, carries some meat through the streets and wonders if anyone notices he's in mourning; Blazes Boylan orders a fruit basket while leering at the salesgirl; a priest attempts to get Patrick Dignam free tuition at the local school; Katey, Boody, and Maggy

Dedalus, Stephen's sisters, discuss how hungry they are and we discover their father has used the family money for drink since their mother died; Dilly Dedalus (another sister) tries to get money from Mr. Dedalus, but he gives her only a shilling and lectures her about wanting anything more from him. We do check in with our two main characters: Leopold Bloom is at a bookshop searching for a book for Molly, and settles on an erotic book called *Sweets of Sin*, while the characters who'd been in the newspaper offices earlier gossip about Bloom and one of them tells a story of once having his way with Molly. Meanwhile, Stephen is at a different bookshop looking through cheap bargain copies when Dilly approaches him with a book she'd bought with the money her father had given her, and Stephen is wracked with guilt at the fact his sisters don't have any money and Dilly is showing the same artistic sense that he once did. But he doesn't give her any of the money that's in his pocket. Meanwhile Mulligan and Haines gossip about Stephen and how they don't think he'll ever be a proper poet. At the end of the section, a cavalcade containing ambassadors of the queen travels through the streets and we see all the characters again as they watch, salute, and discuss the cavalcade. Bloom and Dedalus are connected in that neither notices it passing by.

Episode 11, "Sirens," is more closely linked to Homer's *Odyssey* than some of the other chapters in the book. In Homer's epic, Odysseus ties himself to the mast of his ship so he can hear the Sirens' song but cannot steer his ship toward them. Joyce's chapter once again focuses on Bloom, who is having something to drink at the Ormond Hotel, where he's followed Blazes Boylan, knowing that he has a rendezvous scheduled with Molly at the hotel at that time (4 o'clock). Inside the hotel he listens to the singing, and where other chapters have focused on taste or smell, this one focuses on the sense of sound. Certain sounds interject themselves into Bloom's interior monologue, whether it be the singing of those on the stage or the jangle of Boylan's car as it approaches the hotel, or the *tap, tap* of the blind man's cane as he returns to the hotel to pick up his tuning fork, which he's left on the piano. As Bloom thinks about his day so far, attempts to write a return letter to Martha, and gazes at the alluring barmaid Miss Douce, Stephen's father is in the bar next door, and gets up on stage to sing. Bloom thinks about how his voice was nice at one time, but he'd let it go because of the drink. Other characters talk about Bloom and Molly and her singing career and wonder aloud why she married Bloom. Eventually Bloom has to meet Cunningham about Dignam's insurance. Just as Odysseus manages to avoid crashing on the rocks due to the Sirens,

Bloom pulls himself away from the image of Miss Douce and the music and leaves the hotel, noticing the cider has made him gassy. He sees a prostitute he was once with. He faces away so she doesn't recognize him and as a tram goes by, he passes wind. This chapter is again mostly an interior monologue, with the outside world constantly cutting in, and as with the chapter that's broken up into headlines, this one makes the narrator's presence known when it opens with a series of phrases, all of which will appear later in the chapter, but form their own cacophony at the outset of the section.

The next section is told by an unnamed narrator who sits alone and comments on those around him, and who speaks in various archaic styles — Renaissance, mock heroic, Shakespearean — and includes pages of long lists. The action takes place at a pub (surprise!) where Bloom is going to meet Cunningham. The narrator meets Alf Bergan, and as they go in to the pub they discuss Dignam's death. Alf is insistent that he spoke to Dignam not five minutes earlier, and the other men mock him, saying he must have been talking to a ghost. The narrator offers long passages describing the market outside, the interior of the pub, and his own drink, all in his heroic language:

> Terence O'Ryan heard him and straightway brought him a crystal cup full of the foaming ebon ale which the noble twin brothers Bungiveagh and Bungardilaun brew ever in their divine alevats, cunning as the songs of deathless Leda. For they garner the succulent berries of the hop and mass and sift and bruise and brew them and they mix therewith sour juices and bring the must to the sacred fire and cease not night or day from their toil, those cunning brothers, lords of the vat.

An unnamed "citizen" enters the pub, and he's an Irish nationalist with a xenophobic and racist streak, and when Bloom enters after him, the citizen begins hurling anti-Semitic insults in his direction. Bloom ignores them for the most part, and eventually stands up to him, explaining that despite the citizen going on about how hard-done-by the Irish have been, the Jews have had it worse. As soon as Cunningham arrives, Bloom leaves with him, and the citizen follows them outside, continuing to insult Bloom, who finally turns and shouts back at the citizen that many important men in history have been Jews, and when he names them, he includes Christ. The citizen grabs a nearby tin and throws it at Bloom's departing car.

In the thirteenth episode, "Nausicaa," three girls are sitting on a beach near a church. One of them is tending to her four-year-old twin brothers, the other her infant brother. Sitting with them is Gerty MacDowell, a girl pondering a boy who recently left her, thinking her period is coming on, and noticing a man across the beach who is watching her. This is the first chapter written from a female point of view, and the narrator uses a sort of "Dear Diary" type of tone to convey her sentimentalized perspective. Realizing that maybe she can manipulate a man's passion rather than allowing him to manipulate her, she begins toying with him, and while the twins wreak havoc in the background and Gerty continues to think of her life, she lets part of her leg show and watches the man. One of the girls runs over to the man to ask him the time, but he notices his watch has stopped at 4:30, and estimates that it's past 8 because the sun is setting. When fireworks begin going off, the two girls run off to watch with their charges, while Gerty stays behind. Holding her knee in her hands, she pulls up one leg, letting the man watch her, and he begins masturbating. As the Roman candle firework goes up, up, up into the sky and suddenly explodes, the man has an orgasm. Gerty is satisfied with herself, and her friends call her to come home with them. As she gets up to leave, the perspective switches to the man watching her, who is none other than Leopold Bloom, and he notices that she is lame in one leg, and is thankful he didn't notice that before she'd aroused him. He begins thinking about women and the hold they have over men, and that the girl was dirty (but acknowledges how much he enjoyed her), and wonders briefly if she might have been the mysterious Martha of the letters. He thinks about his watch stopping at 4:30, and with some alarm, realizes that if Blazes Boylan and Molly were planning a tryst at 4, then it might have happened exactly when his watch stopped ("Was that just when he, she? . . . O, he did. Into her. She did. Done"). He realizes he's forgotten to go and pick up Molly's lotion, and therefore hasn't paid for the bar of lemon soap in his pocket that he's been smelling all day. He attempts to write Gerty a note in the sand, thinking she might return the next day. But after etching "I. AM. A." he can't think of anything else to say, and scratches it out. He thinks of how spent and damp he is now, and decides to take a nap. As a nearby cuckoo clock strikes 9, he goes to sleep.

The next episode is one of the most difficult to comprehend. Just as the narrator speaks in a mock heroic language in the pub, and in a girly tone in the previous chapter, voice takes over in this chapter as Joyce tries on various styles to recreate the plot through language. In this section Stephen Dedalus, the men who were in the newspaper offices earlier, and Leopold Bloom are all sitting in a waiting room of a hospital as Mina Purefoy is about to (finally) give birth. The narrator writes in various forms of the English language in chronological order, beginning with Latin biblical writing, to medieval language, to Renaissance and Restoration writers, through to various 19th-century styles. The intent is to show the gestation of the English language through to its birth in the 20th century. In the scene, the men sit around talking loudly about inappropriate topics, all relating to birth, such as fratricide, a mother dying in childbirth, babies who die shortly after birth (which creates a particular pang for Bloom), contraception, Caesarean sections, women who become pregnant after a rape, birth defects. This is the first scene that Bloom and Stephen share where each is aware of the other's presence. Throughout the scene Bloom constantly urges the men to show a little more respect for the situation, all the while thinking that Stephen is too intelligent to be hobnobbing with such people. Meanwhile Stephen talks about God and mothers as if neither is worthy of his attention, and Bloom feels fatherly and protective toward him. Buck Mulligan shows up with his friend Alec Bannon (who is in a relationship with Milly Bloom, Leopold's daughter) and Stephen, disgruntled that Buck has appeared and taken away his spotlight once again, suggests they all proceed to Burke's Pub just as Mrs. Purefoy gives birth to a boy. At the pub, they discuss other non-birth-related topics, and when Bannon realizes that Bloom is Milly's father, he leaves. Eventually the gang is ejected from the pub, and Stephen convinces one of the men to visit the brothel district with him.

Plotwise, not much actually happens in the fifteenth episode, called "Circe," yet this chapter is almost three times as long as any of the ones that have preceded it, mostly because both Bloom and Stephen have grandiose hallucinations throughout the scene that are described over several pages. This episode is written like a play, with stage directions and the name of the speaker preceding each line of dialogue. The narrator is therefore unable to show the interior monologues of the characters if everything must be conveyed through speech, so instead we read their hallucinations. Most of Bloom's delusions involve several people ganging up on him and accusing him of horrible offenses as he cowers before them. In the first one, Molly, Gerty, and Bloom's parents rise up against him. In another, as he feeds a dog some raw meat in an alleyway he imagines he is confronted by policemen, who are accusing him of doing something terrible with the dog. Bloom is approached in reality by Zoe, a prostitute, who walks him to the brothel and takes his lucky potato from him. Bloom imagines becoming a dictator, Leopold I, of the city of Bloomusalem, and imagines making his speech from on high, surrounded by supporters . . . before being called a fraud and brought back down to earth. Zoe takes him into the brothel, where he sees Stephen, and now Stephen has a vision of an apocalypse, with rows of avenging angels rising up against them and Elijah making pronouncements against them (a large section of *A Portrait of the Artist as a Young Man* focused on Stephen's piety as a young man). Bella Cohen, the owner of the brothel, enters the room and Bloom imagines that she turns into a man and dominates him, with him becoming the woman and pleading for mercy. When the hallucination ends Bella demands her money and Bloom settles up with her. He gets his lucky potato back from Zoe and takes Stephen's money for him. Zoe refers to Bloom as a cuckold, and he has another hallucination of Blazes Boylan arriving and allowing the lot of them to watch him having sex with Molly as Bloom masturbates. As that vision ends, Zoe plays some music and Stephen begins spinning in circles around the room, and is suddenly confronted with the ghost of his mother. He refuses to pray while she speaks loudly of God's wrath, and Stephen swings a cane and, in reality, smashes the chandelier. As Stephen runs outside and Bella calls for the police, Bloom tells her the lamp is fine and runs out to help Stephen. Stephen confronts some British soldiers standing outside the brothel and begins yelling at them that they're not wanted in Ireland. Several imaginary characters appear to egg on the fight, and one of the soldiers punches Stephen in the face. Bloom rushes in to help him up, and as he tries to coax him back into consciousness, he sees a vision of a "changeling," a boy in a private school uniform, watching him from the alleyway. Astonished, he recognizes him as his dead son Rudy, and tries calling out to him, but he's lost his voice. Throughout this chapter, Bloom's apparitions come and go and seem to have little effect on him, while Stephen's affect him greatly and leave him very upset and shaken. We read repetitions of several phrases that had been used earlier in the book, but many of the phrases that were part of Stephen's earlier interior monologues are in Bloom's hallucination, and vice versa. The two characters become more conflated in this scene.

After the spectacular climax of the novel in the hallucinatory chapter, the novel moves into its third and final section, which is a 300-page denouement. In "Eumaeus," Bloom helps Stephen up and takes him to a cab shelter. On the way they run into Corley, a friend of Stephen's who is down on his luck, and Stephen offers him his teaching position (which he assumes he'll soon lose) and gives him a half-crown. Bloom frowns at this over-generosity, and as they walk away from Corley he reminds Stephen that just like his friend, Stephen has nowhere to sleep that night. He suggests Stephen go home to his father, telling him that Simon is very proud of him, but Stephen scowls and refuses to. Bloom has never been to the cab shelter where they stop by, because the owner is rumored to be Skin-the-Goat Fitzharris, a man mentioned in passing throughout the book in relation to a set of murders, where Skin-the-Goat was the driver of the getaway car. In the cab shelter they meet a man who claims to know Simon Dedalus, but he begins telling such crazy stories about him — "I seen him shoot two eggs off two bottles at fifty yards over his shoulder" — that Bloom and Stephen both assume the man is talking about someone else. The man continues to tell tall tales about his travels, and Bloom doubts most of them. Bloom begins to drone on about various topics, from his wife to prostitutes to politics, and Stephen is gruff and rude with him. Bloom is annoyed by Stephen's rudeness, but continues to protect him and play the father to him, telling himself that Stephen is acting the way he is because of his upbringing and because he's presently drunk. Despite his worries that Molly might not approve (remembering her reaction over a dog he once brought home) he invites Stephen back to his house to sleep off his drunkenness. The two men head arm-in-arm into the night. This section is written in a purposely amateur style, with the narrator describing events in a dull and tedious voice, and using large words incorrectly where short words would do.

The penultimate chapter feels like the end of the book, with Stephen and Bloom heading back to Bloom's house and having a long discussion about various topics. Bloom has forgotten his key and has to climb in through a window to get it, and when inside the kitchen, drinking cocoa, the narrator offers certain hints that Boylan had been there earlier that day. Bloom remembers having met Stephen twice before, both times when Stephen was a child. Stephen writes some alphabetical letters on a piece of paper in Irish, Bloom writes the same ones in Hebrew, both showing the other language that define them, yet which they are not fluent in. Stephen recites a poem where a Jewish girl beheads a Jewish boy, and Bloom smiles at the poem, thinking of his daughter. We are reminded that Bloom is only half-Jewish, that his mother was Irish and he had been baptized (three times) as a Protestant. Bloom gives Stephen his money back, and suggests ways they could get together, but you can tell by the way Stephen responds to him that they'll probably never hook up again. They both go outside to urinate and look up at the stars, and Stephen leaves. Bloom goes back into his house, immediately bumping into furniture that has been moved around. He thinks about his day and puts Martha's letter into a drawer. He thinks about his father's suicide note, sitting in a nearby drawer, and is glad that his father left him money to keep him in his current lifestyle. He thinks about how he wants to own a bungalow, and he imagines a life of poverty where he travels as a vagrant. He goes upstairs to the bedroom, and once again is reminded that Boylan was there. He realizes that Molly has had 25 suitors, and that he hasn't had sex with her in over a decade. He lies down on his bed, with his head near the footboard, and kisses her bottom. She wakes up and he tells her about his day, leaving out the salacious bits and only including the boring parts. He tells her about Stephen, and then presumably falls asleep. This chapter is written as a series of questions and answers that guide us to what is happening in the scene:

> What, reduced to their simplest reciprocal form, were Bloom's thoughts about Stephen's thoughts about Bloom and Bloom's thoughts about Stephen's thoughts about Bloom's thoughts about Stephen?
> He thought that he thought that he was a jew whereas he knew that he knew that he knew that he was not.

Called "Ithaca," this scene parallels the one in *The Odyssey* where Odysseus returns home after a long journey, and it acts as a parody of it. After ten years, when Odysseus returns home, he is disguised as a beggar, and he kills all of his wife's suitors and claims her for his own. But in this section, Bloom recognizes his wife's suitors, and has resigned himself to their presence. His epic journey has lasted one day, and has involved buying meat and soap, going to a funeral, attending a birth, and visiting about 50 different pubs. Rather than return home victorious to his domain, he simply kisses his wife's rump and goes to sleep.

The final chapter is a long interior monologue by Molly, lacking in any punctuation, and it's written as a series of breathless thoughts (and for me, made reading the rest of the book worth it). The section is broken up into eight giant sentences, where Molly thinks about her day and we get a completely new and different perspective on her, as compared to the one we've had so far from Bloom. She starts by reacting with surprise that he's just told her he wants breakfast in bed the next morning, and senses that he's had an orgasm at some point that day. She recalls the sex she'd had with Boylan and how well endowed he was. Her entire monologue is very sexual and, as she goes back through her own sexual history, we realize her suitors were far fewer than Bloom had guessed. She remembers how in love she'd been with Bloom at one time, and how attractive he used to be. She thinks of her career as a concert singer, and considers with disgust the inferior younger singers she's seen on tour. She thinks about how she should lose weight, and thinks about upcoming trysts with Boylan. She then thinks about female breasts and about how Bloom says some very strange things, and wonders if they should be compiled in a book (interestingly, it's what Haines says to Stephen about his strange sayings at the very beginning of *Ulysses*). She hears a train whistle and thinks back to a childhood friend and how difficult it was when her friend moved away from her. She thinks of how Milly had sent her a card that morning, but had sent Bloom a full letter. She remembers a love letter she got once from Lt. Mulvey, and how they had kissed (in fact, throughout her remembrances of past dalliances, we discover that the only person she's ever had sex with aside from Bloom was Boylan). She thinks of Milly again and how much she misses her, and she realizes her period has come on and gets up to deal with it. In passing, she realizes Boylan hasn't impregnated her. After putting on a feminine napkin, she gets back into bed and wonders about Bloom's day and what was true in what he told her. She worries that he might have paid a prostitute, and then begins thinking of Stephen. She knows he's young, but decides if he'll be coming over to their house, like Bloom said, that she should begin reading more books so he'll think her intelligent and might be attracted to her. She thinks of Stephen's mother, and how she died, and then remembers her own son, and how she'd knitted him a sweater when she was pregnant with him, and then buried him in it 11 days after he was born, but realizes she can't keep thinking about the boy or she'll get depressed. She thinks of telling Bloom the next day that she'd had an affair with Boylan, but then remembers the day when they'd made love in a field and she'd passed cake from her mouth to his (the same incident Bloom had recalled earlier in the day). She remembers when he proposed to her, and ends the book in a wildly beautiful and positive affirmation:

> . . . and then he asked me would I yes to say yes my mountain flower and first I put my arms around him yes and drew him down to me so he could feel my breasts all perfume yes and his heart was going like mad and yes I said yes I will Yes.

Despite the ups and downs the characters experience throughout the book, Molly's positive exclamation at the end (which echoed my own, having finished the book) ends things on a hopeful note. No one's life has really changed because of the events of June 16, 1904 (even Mrs. Purefoy has so many children that Bloom suggests this birth probably won't change anything), but some characters have come to some small realization about themselves, and we see the possibility for things evolving and changing.

Like Leopold Bloom and Stephen Dedalus, the characters on *Lost* have evolved throughout the seasons. As we are introduced to both men in the book, we start to form notions of them in our heads, until another person's perspective casts a new light on that notion. Bloom can't even describe himself — when he tries to write an introduction in the sand, all he comes up with is, "I. AM. A." and can go no further. As on *Lost*, while one character sees himself or herself a certain way, another character can completely change the way we see them.

Throughout the book, Bloom becomes more fatherly, and Stephen takes on the role of son, whether he likes it or not. Things that Stephen said or thought earlier in the book make their way into Bloom's speech or thoughts, and vice versa, as the two characters begin to blend and trade places. On *Lost* we've seen how Jack's convictions at the beginning of season 1 have evolved until they almost resemble Locke's. In season 1, Locke was like Bloom and Charlie was like Stephen Dedalus, an artistic type who was falling apart and resented his father; like Bloom, Locke took Charlie under his wing and tried to be a surrogate father to him.

Just as *Lost* gives us new information on each character through flashbacks, many of the characters in *Ulysses* think back to their childhoods or adolescent years, remembering how different or better (or, in some cases, worse) things used to be. The characters in *Ulysses* have minds that are alive and always wandering. And yet, if you staged the book as a play, only showing actions and spoken dialogue from the book, it might be disastrous; the characters don't say much, and don't seem to know how to communicate with one another. Similarly, the characters on *Lost* rarely tell each other their innermost secrets or anything about their past, and the failure of communication between people is at times astounding.

Throughout Joyce's book, characters cross each other's paths, or talk about another character who has just been mentioned or shown in a previous scene, showing how everyone is connected in some way. One of the themes through the early seasons of *Lost* was how interconnected everyone was; their paths had crossed before they got onto the plane, and they seemed fated to get onto that particular flight.

Much of the tension of the book is derived from parent-child relationships, most commonly those between fathers and sons. Bloom constantly thinks of his dead son Rudy and how it has hurt his marriage and turned him into a shell of who he once was. He looks to Stephen as a son, but throughout the day Stephen is mourning his mother and is disgusted by any mention of his father. Simon Dedalus is a disgrace to his son, a man who can't take care of his family and who certainly couldn't take care of Stephen. As a result, Stephen is sullen and withdrawn, and when Bloom, who takes some joy from life, tries to talk to Stephen, he doesn't get much out of him. Bloom also remembers his father, who killed himself and similarly left Bloom to deal with the shame that comes from a family tragedy like that. One of the ongoing themes on *Lost* is the ever-present parent-child tension that each character seems to carry with them. Every person seems to resent their father, and a few of them throw in their mother to boot. In season 5 the tide is turning on that, as some characters are becoming parents and seeing things through a new lens. But the children are also causing new tensions, and one can only imagine how the next generation of Losties will resent their parents who had once lived on an island.

Ulysses is set up as a heroic journey, parodying and paralleling Homer's *Odyssey*, and the characters on *Lost* have endured their own epic journeys. Like Dedalus and Bloom, they have undergone journeys of self-discovery, internalizing their emotions and coming to an understanding of who they are. But they have also had physical journeys, crashing to the island twice, traveling around the island, and even traveling through time. (Take *that*, Joyce and your one day!)

Death and birth are central to *Ulysses* — at the beginning of the book Bloom attends Dignam's funeral and ruminates on death and how it has affected his life so deeply, and later Bloom attends the birth of Mrs. Purefoy's baby, and all of the men discuss birth and its ramifications for 70 pages. Similarly, death and birth are central to *Lost*. Many main characters have died on the show, while pregnancy is a death sentence on the island.

Many of the themes of *Ulysses* are universal ones that are touched on in *Lost* and so many other books and films. But I think the main link that the book has to *Lost* is in their very nature as a cultural text. I will admit that, when I was reading this book, I thought to myself, "*Who* says this is the greatest book of the

20th century?! No doubt some pretentious git who just loves that he understands a few of the sentences, and declares it the greatest book ever written because it puts him above all those who can't possibly understand it." So many people are daunted by the size and complexity of *Ulysses*. It's written in English (mostly) but the combination of words makes it very difficult to understand, and James Joyce packs every page with cultural, historical, and philosophical references. He drops in many ongoing motifs, like the hilarious advertisement that keeps popping up for Plumtree's Potted Meat ("What is a home without Plumtree's Potted Meat? Incomplete. With it an abode of bliss.") Phrases and comments in conversations and interior monologues that seem insignificant at the time appear several times throughout the book, increasing in importance with each repetition. Ireland as a vast island that both protects and traps its people is mentioned several times.

Many people have tried reading *Ulysses*, but few make it to the end. They give up when they find they can't follow it anymore, while those who stick with it, study it, bone up on the references, and understand it on a deeper and richer level than the majority of its readers love it all the more because of how much work they have put into it.

This sounds a lot like a certain show on television.

Lost demands so much more of its viewers than just sitting back and taking in the show. The diehard fans study every cultural, historical, scientific, religious, and philosophical reference on the show, and come away with a deeper experience having done so. Like Plumtree's Potted Meat, there are lots of repeated motifs thrown in there to keep fans on their toes, like Geronimo Jackson appearances, or references to rabbits. Yet many people made it to season 3 and realized this show is far too complex and simply asks too much of them. They gave up, changing the channel the same way so many people stick *Ulysses* back on the shelf. Those of us who did the extra work are rewarded for it, and call this the greatest show on television. Perhaps that makes us the pretentious gits of the television world.

But just as Joyce scholars are legion, so are the fan-scholars of *Lost*. The show is controversial, it's difficult, it deals with deep and painful emotions in a sometimes sterile way, but in the end it's a character study that has taken us through the depths of hell and (we hope) will end with a positive affirmation.

Lost is, simply, the *Ulysses* of television, and its fans will follow it right to the end and continue to follow it every step of the way our hearts going like mad and yes we said yes we will Yes.

5.7   The Life and Death of Jeremy Bentham

Original air date: February 25, 2009
Written by: Carlton Cuse, Damon Lindelof
Directed by: Jack Bender
Guest cast: Malcolm David Kelley (Walt), Lance Reddick (Matthew Abaddon), J.J. Bradley (Kid), Anmar Daraiseh (Hajer), Concepcion Saucedo (Sister Consuela), Stephen Scibetta (Construction Foreman), Grisel Toledo (Susie)

Focus: Locke

We finally see what happened to Locke after he got off the island . . . and before he ended up in a coffin.

This is the episode many fans had been waiting for. Back in the season 3 finale, Jack was shaken to see an obituary in the newspaper, and when he went to the funeral home, no one had come to see the deceased. From what fans could make out of the obituary, the person who died was named Jo__ Lantham, and he had been found hanging by a rope in his loft apartment. He was from New York City, and had a teenage son. It's since been proven that most of the obit was a huge production gaffe, and several things in it were wrong and weren't supposed to be seen by viewers (the worst being the date — April 5, 2007 — which should have been the beginning of 2008). Fans speculated that it was Michael — he was from New York and had a teenage son, and if he made it off the island again, Jack could have been shaken by the fact that Michael had been driven to suicide after going through what they'd all endured. Some thought it was Sawyer, who wouldn't have had any ties and therefore might have had an attendance-free funeral. Others thought it was Locke — he would elicit the disgust that Kate showed when she saw the obit, and it would make sense that she would be shocked that Jack would be so upset. But the details of the obituary led people away from that conclusion.

Season 4 concluded with the big cliffhanger that Locke was the one in the coffin after all, and we were just supposed to ignore that obituary (score one for the casual fans who do *not* obsess over the minutiae on the show). Leading up to the big reveal, we discovered that whoever was in the coffin was going by the name "Jeremy Bentham" and he'd visited each of the Oceanic 6, plus Walt, in an attempt to get them to come back to the island. Since season 4, fans had been wondering why Locke had changed his name, why everyone was so secretive

"Dammit, Jack, why won't you listen to me?!" In my new favorite *Lost* photo, Terry O'Quinn goofs around in Locke's coffin between takes. (© MARIO PEREZ/ABC/RETNA LTD.)

about it, what those meetings had been like, and why Locke ended up in the coffin. This episode finally gives us the answers. Well . . . some of them.

It's been a long road for John Locke. From the beginning of the series, the writers have set him up as the foundation of the show, and many fans (me included) pegged him as the key to everything after watching the first true masterpiece of the series, season 1's "Walkabout." Locke is always seen apart from the others, and when he appears in scenes with people like Jack, they're usually to show the contrast between Locke and everyone else. In previous *Finding Lost* books I've detailed the development of many of the themes that revolve around the character of John Locke, including the rise and fall and rise of his faith, how his second-guessing of himself has led to the wrong decisions, how the treatment he received from his parents has made him who he is, and how his character has changed through each season. Another ongoing theme that's repeated in Locke's story is how many times he's disappointed other people — and, in turn, himself.

One of the most haunting scenes in the series is when Locke's birth mother, Emily Locke, looks at his tiny body in the incubator and says she can't do it, and abandons him ("Cabin Fever"). The camera pans to the little baby, staring after his mother, who he'll never see again — until she deceives him when he's an adult. The nurse comments that for a baby as premature as he was, he shouldn't have made it, but he fought harder than any baby she'd seen. From the beginning, then, Locke has tried hard to prove his specialness to those around him, but when Emily leaves him, and gives the guy his first real taste of disappointment (even though he doesn't actually know it yet), she sets him up for a lifetime of following the same pattern. When he's five years old, Richard Alpert comes to his house in the guise of someone from a school for the gifted, and Locke's foster mother tells him he needs to impress the man. Locke tries to, but he makes the wrong decision, and Richard leaves in disgust at Locke's "failure." Locke's foster mother berates him for screwing up.

As a teenager, Locke's teacher pulls him into a room and explains how much potential John has as a scientist, and urges him to enter a science fair. John refuses, wanting to go his own way, and he disappoints his superior once again. As an adult, he is tricked by his own conniving parents and loses a kidney, and he's so disappointed in himself that he seeks revenge, until he's talked down by Helen. Helen is the first and only person in his life who really believes in John, who doesn't think his potential has been wasted, and who trusts that he can be a better person. But when John refuses to let go of his anger toward his father, he lets down Helen, too, making the biggest blunder of his life.

Desperate to start over and find another connection, now that he's lost Helen, John joins a commune of hippies that has a grow-op on the side. He befriends an outsider named Eddie, not realizing he's an undercover cop, and brings him into the fold. When his new family realizes they are under investigation and John has just led the fox directly into the henhouse, John is abandoned once again, and he tries to take revenge by killing Eddie, but can't bring himself to pull the trigger.

Alone and depressed, John is approached by a man who says his mother is being conned by Anthony Cooper. Locke tries to ignore it, remembering all the times he's screwed up in the past while trying to make things right. But he can't let it go, and he confronts Cooper . . . and ends up being thrown out of an eighth-storey window, which leaves him paralyzed from the waist down. Now unable to move, he has nothing to do but lie in a hospital bed and reflect on what a sad and pathetic life he's had, and how despite all the hardships thrown at him, his

Imagine looking out your window one day to see the production crew of *Lost* setting up a car accident with John Locke (on the corner of South and Pohukaina Streets in Kakaako). That's what happened to this photographer, who immediately began snapping photos. (BILL SPENCER)

current situation is due largely to his own bad decisions. He finds out about the walkabout and begins training, thinking that maybe this will be the thing that can change his life forever. He learns about knives and surviving in the wild. With Helen gone, he begins an artificial relationship with some sort of phone-sex operator whom he calls Helen, and he asks her to come to Sydney with him. She turns him down and ends the "relationship." With his renewed confidence somewhat shaken, Locke gets on a plane to Sydney to go on his walkabout . . . only to be told that he's not allowed to come along if he's in a wheelchair. He dejectedly boards Oceanic Flight 815 and crash-lands.

After the crash he can miraculously walk again, and people are following him because he has survival skills. He suddenly has more self-esteem than he's had in his life. His faith in the island grows despite Jack berating him and trying to keep him down, but he begins to make mistakes, the biggest being the one that led to Boone's death. People start to divide, some with him, some against, but it's not because they think he's stupid or an ineffectual loser, it's because they think he might be crazy. While that label might bother Hurley, it doesn't worry Locke, and he continues on his spiritual journey.

Until Ben leaves the island, Locke has been a blind follower — he doesn't know why he's doing the things he's doing, he only knows that there must be a reason, and he'll follow his destiny until it decides to tell him why. But once the time flashes begin, Locke's destiny becomes clear: he must leave the island and die to convince the others to come back. The thought that his entire journey was simply meant to lead to his own death is upsetting, but he faces it head on and agrees to do it.

Once off the island, he visits each of the people who left the island: he faces Sayid's scorn, and when he finds out what happened to Sayid, he smartly hides the fact he's working with Widmore. Walt seems to be the only person who's happy to see him, but Locke can't bring himself to involve this child in what's happening, and lets him go. Hurley is frightened of him, and believes him to be evil. Locke hits a new low point with Kate, who shows she never got to know Locke at all, and reminds him that he hasn't changed from the person he was when Helen left him. He discovers that Helen is dead, proving that even if he were to make something of his life, he has no one to share it with. He loses his shepherd/driver, who showed him nothing but disdain on the entire trip. And then he comes face to face with Jack, his biggest opponent, the man who will debate with him any chance he can get. And once again, Jack gets to the heart of

Locke's biggest fears, and suggests there's nothing special about him at all, and that he's just chasing his tail.

There's a reason I'm recounting all of the low points of Locke's life and showing what a big disappointment he's always been: in this episode, when he's standing on the table with a cord wrapped around his neck, John Locke's face conveys the multitude of those moments, and John's disappointment in himself and the world is one of the most heartbreaking scenes in the entire series. In season 2, Locke delivered a quietly devastating sentence in only three words: standing amidst the chaos of a hatch that's about to explode, he simply says, "I was wrong." And in those three words, he sums up every important decision he'd made in his life until that point. Now, in a quiet room, the chaos is all happening inside Locke, and he looks at Ben, with the red cord around his neck, and says, "I'm a failure." Both of these brief sentences are delivered with a conviction and absoluteness that Locke doesn't show at any other time. These are the only two times that he believes what he's saying one hundred percent. It's a poignant and tragic moment, once again showing what a brilliant actor Terry O'Quinn is.

Of course, one of the reasons Locke has never had any confidence is because no one *else* ever seems to have confidence in him. Throughout his time on the island, Jack ate away at Locke's faith by questioning everything he did. Ben tricked him countless times, and people Locke had helped turned their backs on him. Now Locke is caught between two evil geniuses, and he doesn't know which one (if either) to trust.

Charles Widmore and Benjamin Linus: two characters who didn't even exist in the first season of *Lost* and are now at the center of what the island could be about. In season 4's "The Shape of Things to Come," we saw a showdown between the two men in Widmore's bedroom, where Widmore vowed to find the island again, and Ben said he'd kill Penny. Ben believes Widmore is responsible for the death of Alex, and Widmore says Ben is responsible for ejecting Widmore from the island in the first place. Their war has been happening for decades, and now Locke is caught in the middle of it. So which one is evil, and which is good? Are either of them good? Are either of them evil?

In this classic scene, the director uses lighting to convey the two sides. Ben is lurking in the shadows, Widmore is bathed in white light. Ben comes off as the evil little rat, threatening Widmore's daughter and vowing revenge, while Widmore is the tired good guy, wishing the "*boy*" would go away and just leave him alone. If you ignore the lighting, and watch the scene the opposite way, you can just as easily see Ben as the devastated father whose daughter was just killed, facing the man who's made his life a living hell, and Widmore is the eerily calm bad guy who has no time for Ben and waves him off with a dismissive flick of his hand.

One of the themes of the series, established in the very first episodes, is the idea of black versus white. But the irony of that theme is that none of the characters on the show are black or white — they're all gray. Ben and Widmore are no different: like so many other powerful people in history, they have an agenda, and they don't care who gets in their way; they're going to get the job done. They don't see themselves as evil, and they have ardent followers.

In "316," Jack looks at Ben on the plane and asks him what's going to happen to everyone else on board when the plane crashes. Ben looks up from his book, and, surprised by the question, says, "Who cares?" Ben stopped caring about innocent casualties long ago. He knows what he wants and he's going to get it. We've seen him kill and we've seen him order the deaths of others. Every word that comes out of his mouth is a lie, even if he's asked a casual question. But Ben ardently believes that he's one of "the good guys." To him, the innocent people don't mean anything because what he's doing will lead to a much greater good. He's serving a higher power, and if some people have to die along the way, oh well.

Widmore is no different. In season 4, he had his eye on one person — Ben Linus — and in an effort to make him pay, he sent a freighter of people to the island with the instructions to kill anyone on it if they saw fit. He sent his daughter's lover to the island as a guinea pig to see if he'd make his way there, knowing the man would be trapped there and away from his daughter, which is where he wanted him. He enabled the execution of Alex, which happened right in front of Ben's eyes. But we've all seen the bad things that Ben has done, and Widmore claims to be doing everything to stop him.

Unlike everyone in Locke's life who has either abandoned him, let him down, or told him how much he's disappointed them, Ben and Widmore both insist that Locke is special, and that everything they've done was for one reason: to instate Locke in his rightful place as leader of the island. Both of them seem to be working on the same agenda: they both want him back on the island (Widmore wants him alive, Ben wants him dead), and they both say they believe in his specialness. They tell him what he needs to hear to continue on his journey, and Locke is wary of both of them, but he's also impelled by the power of their words.

The final scene between John and Ben is a baffling one: Ben manages to talk Locke off the table, preventing his suicide, only to strangle him with the same cord moments later. Fans were confused, and theories sprung up everywhere. Is Ben such a sociopath that he wanted to do it himself? Was he just looking for the information about Jin and Eloise Hawking, and he killed Locke the moment he got the information he needed? Or was there actually something good in what he was doing? In many religions, suicide is an unforgivable sin, and many followers believe that if one commits suicide, the path is straight to Hell. Maybe Ben believes the same thing, and if Locke is going to be resurrected, he had to kill him and not let Locke do it himself. Is it possible that Ben really thought he was doing right by Locke in strangling him?

Or did Locke just become another casualty in Ben and Widmore's war?

Highlight: Widmore's comment about John Locke's name, which is the first time in the series that anyone has made that explicit connection: "Your parents had a sense of humor when they named you, so why can't I?"

Did You Notice?:
- The Ajira flight has crashed on the Hydra island. Caesar is in Ben's office, and at one point Locke is standing on the shore looking over at the main island.
- When Caesar is in the Hydra office, there's a skull on the desk that looks like a miniature version of the polar bear skull that Charlotte found in Tunisia. He flips through a *Life* magazine (see page 109) and when he begins going through the cabinets, he pulls out a series of maps. One of them was the map that Charlotte and Faraday used to find the Tempest station. He also looks at some diagrams that look a lot like the diagrams from the second chapter of Stephen Hawking's *A Brief History of Time*, where he talks about space-time and how objects can move between events by passing through time (see *Finding Lost — Season 3*, pages 67–72). They were probably drawn by Daniel.
- John stands on the beach staring out at the water. For the first few episodes of season 1, he just sat on the beach staring out at the water, even when it started raining.
- Ilana gives John a mango and he eats it on the beach. In *Lost*'s first episode, he's eating an orange.
- When John teleports to Tunisia, his body has the same physical reaction as Ben's did in "The Shape of Things to Come." He lies face up, and then rolls over and vomits.

- Just as many fans predicted in season 4, it seems that there's a wormhole from the island to a spot in the desert in Tunisia (Widmore refers to it as the "exit"). This explains not only how Widmore would have known Locke was going to land there, but also confirms that one of the polar bears from the island must have been sent as a test case through this mechanism, which is why Charlotte found the polar bear in the desert in Tunisia in "Confirmed Dead."
- The newspaper that Widmore hands to Locke is dated January 14, 2005, and it's the *London Daily Tribune* (a fictional newspaper), with the headline "Oceanic Six Survivors Receive Heroes [*sic*] Welcome." Other headlines on the paper include, "Sutton car crash causes major traffic headaches" and "Dollar creeps higher against Euro."
- Widmore gives John a Canadian passport. This plays into the ongoing inside joke that any Canadian reference points to evil (see *Finding Lost — Season 3*, page 105) but there's a practical side to it: Canadians can travel around the world more easily than Americans can. Some Americans have begun wearing a maple leaf on their jackets when they travel to make other people think they might be Canadian, due to longstanding prejudices against Americans.
- John's passport has him born on February 15, 1948. That's 8 years earlier than his actual birthday, which is in 1956.
- The passport says he was born in New York, which would explain why the obituary said he was born there.
- When Locke first sees Abaddon in "Cabin Fever," Abaddon tells him about the walkabout, and then says the next time John sees him, "You'll owe me one." But we don't see Locke pay him any debt in this episode, or act like he owes him anything. (See *Finding Lost — Season 4*, page 153, for the significance of Abaddon's name.)
- There's no reason Locke couldn't have hobbled around on crutches, since he still has one good leg. The fact that Abaddon pulls out a wheelchair instead is deliberate: he had to have known the impact seeing that would have had on John (he saw how much it had upset him when Locke was in the hospital), and that it would remind him of his vulnerability. It's like he was setting him up to fail.
- When Abaddon is driving John in the car, they come upon some goatherds. Near them is a sign that says "Noire," which is reminiscent of the term

"bête noire," meaning "dark beast." Perhaps this is an off-island reference to Smokey.

- On the building that Sayid is fixing up, the nine times table is written on the side, up to four. Interestingly, Sayid spent nine months with Nadia.
- When Locke mentions Helen Norwood, it's the first time we hear her last name.
- Walt, that *other* special person, senses Locke's presence before he sees him.
- Locke talks to Walt in front of Southfield's auction house. In "The Constant," Widmore was in Southfield's in England, where he was buying the journal of the first mate of the *Black Rock*.
- Hurley is painting a picture of the Sphinx. Perhaps the dead people have been conveying to him that the island's allusions are turning to Egyptian mythology.
- Kate is incredibly harsh to Locke. The last time she had any major dealings with him, he banished her from New Otherton and sent her back through the jungle alone. She asked him for a favor at the time and he turned her down, so she doesn't feel like she owes him anything now. But her words are still very hurtful.
- Kate tells Locke that he's probably obsessed with the island because he doesn't love anybody (unlike her), making fans wonder whether she was referring to Jack or Sawyer in that scene (and, if Sawyer, why wouldn't she want to return to the island?). But it's likely she's referring to neither, and she means Aaron.
- Abaddon says that Helen is right where she's supposed to be. That's what Christian said about Aaron.
- Abaddon refers to death as a choice and Locke says to him, "How could you think that's a choice?" This conversation foreshadows Locke's own choice to kill himself.
- Matthew Fox is amazing in the scene where he talks to Locke. He's slurring his words at the beginning, so we know he's been drinking or is stoned, and he's enraged for most of the scene, yet mostly holds it in as if he's going to explode with it. Throughout the scene he acts like it's taking every ounce of strength not to reach over and snap Locke's neck.
- Locke says to Jack that of all the hospitals he could have ended up in, he landed in Jack's, and Jack retorts that he's only there because his accident was nearby. This is reminiscent of the conversation we saw in "316," where

Jack says to Kate that it's destiny they ended up on the same plane, and she says no, they're together because they bought a ticket.

- We saw in "Something Nice Back Home" that Jack began having visions of his father when he was still with Kate and clean-shaven, so Locke's mention of Christian leaves Jack even more shaken than Locke intended. He's probably been trying to convince himself that Christian is dead, despite the visions of him, and Locke's statement sends him over the edge.
- Westerfield Hotel can be anagrammed to "Die Where Felt Lost" or "Oh Free Will Tested."
- Locke bought his suicide cord from Angel's Hardware.
- If you look at the combined reactions of the Oceanics when Locke visits them, one can see how he might have been driven to suicide: Sayid posits that Locke must have nowhere else to go, which is why he needs to return to the island; Kate tells him he must have never been in love before; Hurley, thinking John is dead, says "no biggie" as if he couldn't care less; and Jack says he's just an unimportant old man.
- In season 4, Locke broke the Losties up to help keep them away from Widmore. Jack took the other half of the castaways to follow the freighter folk, because he wanted to get away from Ben. Now Locke has joined forces with Widmore, and Jack with Ben.
- Locke is sincere to Caesar and Ilana, first telling her that he was going to be buried in the suit, and then explaining to Caesar what the Dharma symbol represents, how long he was on the island, and that he'd been killed. If there was ever a time to lie, it's now, and yet Locke is more honest than ever.

Interesting Facts: If you look closely at the *Life* magazine that Caesar flips open on Ben's desk, which is from April 16, 1954, the cover features two headlines: "Color Pictures of the Hydrogen Test," and "Dave Beck, Former Boss of Goons, Emerges as Labor's New Strong Man." The latter story refers to the man who helped found the Teamsters union and was their president from 1952 to 1957. He was succeeded by Jimmy Hoffa when he was suspected of embezzling money, and was later convicted of the crime in 1959. The other story is the more relevant one, since it refers to the first Operation Castle detonation in March 1954 (see page 36). Also, when Caesar flips through the magazine, you can see a still from the movie *The Creature from the Black Lagoon.*

Eagle-eyed fans noticed that when Locke meets Walt, he's sitting at the corner of W. 67th Street and 8th Avenue in New York City, but those two streets don't actually intersect in real life. Rather than being a blooper, however, script coordinator Gregg Nations explained on the Fuselage forum that the mistakes in locations are intentional. He said if they name a place and that place actually exists, they could be sued if that name had a negative connotation in the episode, so they make things up. This goes for names of buildings, publications, or places. He added, "Addresses are checked, too, because there could be a 1234 Main Street in Your Town. If there is, it identifies a specific business and location. If a bad thing happens there, like say a murder, then that's not going to be good for the business and they could sue. So we have to create fictitious addresses in order to not identify a specific location. Same thing with intersections. We have to be aware of real intersections so nothing is specifically identified."

Nitpicks: In season 4, all of the characters referred to John Locke as "Jeremy Bentham," and while the reason for doing so was a fear of being watched, it seemed more like a setup so we get the big DA-DUM! at the end of the season when we see Locke in the coffin. First, knowing him as Locke for years would make it very hard to suddenly refer to him as Bentham, yet Kate and Jack do it easily enough at the airport when they're talking about him. Hurley and Sayid do it just as easily at Santa Rosa. But now that we know who's in the coffin, now that there's no more suspense, Sayid refers to Locke as Bentham, and Hurley says, "You mean Locke?" In the hotel room, Ben and Jack refer to him as Locke as well. Their sudden shift from Bentham to Locke after the big reveal cheapens the earlier use of the alias, and makes it seem like nothing more than a way to create suspense and delay the mystery in the earlier episodes.

In this episode, Locke tells Sayid casually that he's staying under the name "Jeremy Bentham" at a hotel. He never insists that he refer to him by that name. We don't see him use that name with Walt at all, so there's no reason later on that Walt should have used that name when he came to visit Hurley. He's wearing a nametag with "Jeremy Bentham" on it when he comes to see Hurley, but once again he never actually says Hurley needs to refer to him as Jeremy. We don't see him use the pseudonym with Kate, but then again, we only see one part of that conversation. He doesn't give Jack his pseudonym, either, though presumably it would have been written on his medical charts. But that's the sort of thing that would have made Jack scoff; he would have refused to refer to him that way. Fans wondered if there might be another episode to clarify this discrepancy, but at this point it just seemed to be a hoax to keep us speculating about who is in the coffin.

Not only does Locke not insist on being called Bentham, but everything we've learned that Bentham said to them seems to have been made up. In "There's No Place Like Home, Part 3" Jack says that Locke told him Ben was off the island (he didn't) and that after they left, bad things started happening and it was Jack's fault for leaving (Locke also didn't say that, but Jack's guilt could have added these parts). Jack tells Kate at the airport that Locke had told him that he had to go back to keep Kate and Aaron safe. Locke doesn't say that, either. In "Because You Left," Jack says Locke had told him that if they don't go back, "Sawyer, Juliet, everyone from the boat" would die if they didn't return. If he said that, we didn't get to see it. Where did Jack come up with all of these other stories that "Bentham" supposedly told him? Does Dead Locke continue to visit him the way dead people are visiting Hurley?

The other nitpick is about the timing of this episode. From what we know in the past, Jack begins falling apart and leaves Kate, and soon after that, he begins growing the beard. He starts seeing his father walking around the hospital, and he begins taking flights every Friday night. By the time he talks to Kate at the airport, wild-eyed and fully bearded, he says he's been doing it every Friday night for a long time, and that he's been to Sydney, Tokyo, Singapore, and other places. In this episode, the final straw that forces the cord around John's neck is his discussion with Jack. Jack's beard has only started to grow, and probably needs another two months of growth before it'll look like the mangy Jeard of the season 3 finale. When Locke climbs up on that table, his cast is still new, and the cuts all over his head are still fresh and consistent with the cuts that he had at the hospital. Two months haven't passed; this is either the day after he was in the hospital or at the very most, the same week that Locke speaks to Jack. Ben tells Locke that Jack just bought his first ticket, meaning there are weeks left of Jack flying over the Pacific before he speaks to Kate. So Ben must kill Locke about two months before Jack reads his obituary.

I don't believe the writers could have made a mistake with this one. This is just too big an inconsistency for it to actually be an inconsistency, and it's too obvious for them to have overlooked it. Is it possible that John isn't dead the way a normal person would be dead, as I pointed out on page 78? Could he have been hanging in his hotel room for a couple of months, with Ben paying the bills and putting a Do Not Disturb sign on the door, and the body never deteriorating in any way? Maybe something bigger happened, and we'll find out what in a later episode.

Oops: When Widmore is sitting beside John's bed, and John is sleeping, his arms are at his sides. When the camera pulls back to give us a long shot, John's left arm is above his head. Also, Locke's Canadian passport has an expiry date 10 years after issue. But Canadian passports are only good for 5 years. The prop department got the large red maple leaf right, but there are two other leaves in the upper righthand corner and another one on its side in the lefthand corner. Finally, until this episode, Hurley's institution wasn't *in* Santa Rosa; it was just *called* Santa Rosa. The title card in this episode says the institution is in Santa Rosa, California. But that's almost seven hours away from Los Angeles, and the hospital's always referred to as being just outside L.A., so the title card is probably wrong. (Hurley's mother would not have put her son in a hospital that far away.)

4 8 15 16 23 42: On the car the Bedouin men are driving in the desert, the license plate has a **42** in it. It's been **4** days since Locke saw Widmore as a young man. Locke's birth date on the passport is **8** years before his real one. Widmore gives Locke a phone, and if Locke needs to reach him, he just needs to dial **23**. There's a **42** in Abaddon's license plate in Santo Domingo, too. Helen died on **4/8**.

It's Just a Flesh Wound: Locke has his leg reset in a *horrific* hospital scene. Abaddon is shot three times and killed. Locke is seriously injured in a car accident and suffers cuts and scrapes all over his head. Ben strangles Locke to death with a cord.

Lost in Translation: When the Bedouin men find Locke in the desert, they speak to each other in Arabic. The first man says, "This is him," and another says, "Don't let him walk." The rest of the lines are just the men telling each other to help out or how to move him into the car. When they get to the hospital, the man says to the doctor, "This is the man I've been telling you about." The rest of the lines are the doctor calling for help and telling everyone he's in a hurry. When Locke first comes to see Sayid, Sayid is speaking in Spanish, and calls to one of the workers, "I need to finish this ceiling. Pass me another beam." The other man calls up to him that he has a visitor.

Any Questions?:
- In Ancient Rome, the title of "Caesar" denoted royalty. Is there a reason Caesar was named thusly?
- Why did Jack, Kate, and Hurley go back in time, but the rest of the passengers remained in the present? Where is Sayid?
- How long ago did the plane crash? Has it been there for a couple of days,

or did it crash just a few hours before we see Caesar flipping through records in the beginning?

- What does Caesar know about the island? He looks through the records in the Hydra office like someone looking for something specific. Ilana also appeared to know about things. Considering it took the survivors months to even know there were other people on the island, much less find the barracks, it seems strange this guy went straight to the spot. Perhaps Ben's office is really close to the runway.

- Why did Caesar hide the gun from Ilana? How do they know each other? Ilana refers to someone named Roxanne like she's also someone they've known for a long time (the survivors weren't really on a first-name basis for the first couple of days).

- Ilana says "the pilot and some woman" took one of the boats in the middle of the night. Since Kate is with the others, the other woman must have been Sun. Where were they going? And why?

- When did Widmore erect the series of cameras in the desert? Ben lands there in October 2005 and there were no cameras. Locke is there in December 2007. Did Widmore find out Ben was off the island, and he set up the cameras in the spot to wait for the next person who landed there? Were the cameras already there in 2005 (and that's how the Bedouins come upon Ben so quickly in "The Shape of Things to Come") but they were just hidden?

- Widmore was 17 in 1954, which makes him about 70 when he's talking to Locke. If he lived on the island for three decades, as he says, then he wouldn't have left until the 1980s. Was Penny born on the island?

- Did Sayid join this Habitat for Humanity–type project to atone for his sins?

- When Abaddon first sees Walt, he says he's gotten big. How would Abaddon know how big he'd gotten? How did he know how small he was when the plane crashed?

- Is Walt's dream prophetic? He said he saw John on the beach of the island wearing a suit and people around him want to hurt him. What is he referring to? Is it about to happen or will it happen later? Will it happen *because* Walt dreamed about it? In the past, we've seen that whatever Walt thinks about, happens. He doesn't predict events; he controls them.

- John was told to bring everyone back, and many viewers thought that

The Body and Blood of Locke

In "316," Ben tells Jack the story of Thomas the Apostle, a.k.a. Doubting Thomas, who didn't believe that Jesus had been resurrected until he put his finger in Christ's wounds. From the first season, Locke has been set up as the Christ-like character, often shown flat on his back, but always rising again. It would take some time for Ben to go through and check all of Locke's wounds if he needed confirmation that Locke had returned:

- When Locke first sees his mother in a toy store parking lot, he runs after her and is bumped by a car (this isn't a significant wound, but at the time it was filmed in such a way that fans wondered if this was going to be the accident that caused Locke to be paralyzed).
- Locke gives his kidney to his father, Anthony Cooper, which leaves a scar in his side.
- Years later, Locke confronts Cooper, who throws him out of an eighth-storey window, leaving Locke a paraplegic.
- Locke survives a plane crash, which cures his paralysis but leaves a nasty scar under his right eye.
- In "Walkabout," Locke is knocked over by a boar and, for a moment, thinks he's lost use of his legs again.
- When Locke and Boone try to open the hatch with a trebuchet, Locke ends up with a piece of shrapnel in his right leg.
- After Boone's death, Shannon shoots at Locke and the bullet grazes the side of his head.
- Locke is dragged through the jungle by the smoke monster, which almost yanks him into a hole, until Jack saves his life.
- When Locke lowers Kate into the hatch, his hands bleed from the rope burns.
- In the hatch, Locke's legs become trapped under one of the blast doors during a lockdown sequence, and one of the iron rods impales Locke's right leg.
- When Locke refuses to listen to Eko's reason about pushing the button, Eko headbutts him; when Locke *still* doesn't listen, Eko punches him.
- Locke is inside the hatch when it explodes, and when he regains consciousness, he can't speak and has blood on one side of his face.
- When Locke is trying to detail Mikhail in the Flame station, Mikhail headbutts him.
- Locke is beaten and handcuffed to a pipe in the basement of Ben's house.
- Ben shoots Locke in the gut and leaves him to die in a pit of skeletonised casualties of the Purge. Locke almost shoots himself until he's persuaded by Walt to get up.
- Jack beats Locke up at the beginning of season 4 after a failed attempt to shoot him.
- In "Because You Left," Locke is shot in the right leg by Ethan and then falls from the side of the cliff he'd been climbing, landing flat on his back. Locke then suffers the pain of Richard Alpert removing the bullet.
- Locke shatters his shin bone when he drops into the Frozen Donkey Wheel well, which pierces his skin (and is on the same leg he'd been shot in only four days earlier). A few hours later, a doctor re-sets the leg without giving Locke any anaesthetic.
- Ben ties a cord around Locke's neck and strangles him to death.

only referred to the Oceanic 6, but John remembers that Walt left the island, too. Was Walt one of the ones he was supposed to bring back? Or did Locke just want to see him? Was he approaching Walt as some sort of proxy for Sun, since he clearly didn't go to see her? Why didn't he go to see Sun? Was it out of respect for Jin's wishes? If he had Jin's wedding ring to give to her, why didn't he decide to just visit her the same way he'd visited Walt?

- Abaddon tells Locke that he helps people "get to where they need to get to," making him a shepherd or guardian angel of sorts. But what does this role have to do with the mission he orchestrated for Widmore? He was the one who put together the team of Faraday, Miles, Charlotte, Lapidus, and Naomi. If he and Widmore really *do* care about Locke, then why did they send to the island a team of people, led by Keamy, who could have killed him?

- Why does Ben leave the body behind? He cleans the room and leaves the body hanging there, which risks it being found by someone in the hotel, who would have called the authorities. If the body is important, why doesn't Ben take it with him? Something significant must happen between Ben killing Locke and the body ending up in the coffin.

- Who wrote the obituary? Was it Ben? Did he include just enough clues to tip off the Oceanic 6, without anyone else being alerted?

- Was Ben seriously hurt in the crash? Those bruises on his face look worse than the ones he boarded the plane with.

Ashes to Ashes: Matthew Abaddon was a man of mystery who worked for Charles Widmore. He first approached John Locke soon after Locke's attempted murder by his father, which had him paralyzed, and told him about taking a walkabout in Australia — the same walkabout that would put Locke on Flight 815. He was in charge of recruiting the people for Widmore's freighter mission, and ordered Naomi to go on the mission and protect the other people he was sending with her. After John Locke got off the island, Abaddon was his shepherd, the one who got him where he needed to go. However, Abaddon seemed to take pleasure in humiliating Locke. He sent him on a walkabout that turned him away once they realized he was in a wheelchair. He showed up to escort him around by bringing a wheelchair for Locke instead of crutches. And he mocked him along the way, reminding him of what a failure he was. It was as if his mission was to drive Locke to the very suicide he attempted. Abaddon was killed by Ben Linus.

Y: The Last Man by Brian K. Vaughan and Pia Guerra (September 2002–January 2008)

It lasted for a little under six years, with some diehard fans following it right from the beginning, others coming in partway through the series and catching up quickly. It was the story of a group of people in a desperate, seemingly impossible situation, trying to figure out what their lives were all about in the wake of an unforeseen tragedy. It featured several flashbacks, allowing the fans to learn more about the individual characters by seeing what their lives were like before. There were mad scientists, evil organizations, supernatural entities, and several twists and turns along the way. The series was full of mysteries, and after every instalment fans would come up with theories about why all of this was happening and who was behind it, and those theories would be debunked or reinforced with every new storyline. And when it ended, some fans heralded it as the greatest series of all time, while others were unhappy with how it all concluded.

"But wait," you may be saying, "*Lost* hasn't ended yet." I'm not talking about *Lost*. I'm talking about Brian K. Vaughan's comic-book masterpiece, *Y: The Last Man*. Fans of BKV cheered loudly when Hurley was seen reading the third volume in his series, *One Small Step*, in the airport in "316." Vaughan had cowritten the season 3 episode of *Lost*, "Catch-22," and joined the writing staff in season 4, becoming a writer-producer in season 5. It's not a coincidence: after reading *Y: The Last Man*, you'll see he was a natural fit to join the writers' table on *Lost*.

Y: The Last Man, which is now complete and available in 10 separate volumes that compile 60 issues, ran from September 2002 to January 2008. Illustrated by the brilliant Pia Guerra, the premise is simple: a plague of unknown origin suddenly wipes out every living thing with a Y chromosome, with the exception of a young man named Yorick Brown and his Capuchin monkey, Ampersand. Yorick, an amateur escape artist (which serves him well throughout the series), has no idea why he and Ampersand have been spared, and moments before the Earth's population was halved, he was proposing to his girlfriend Beth, who was on a walkabout in Australia. Now he's alone in the world with a feces-flinging animal that he'd been haphazardly training to be a helper monkey for quadriplegics.

For the next five years, Yorick travels the world trying to find Beth. He and Ampersand are accompanied by Agent 355, a female member of the Culper Ring, which is a secret covert organization under the direction of the president

of the United States. Agent 355 became a favorite with the fans for her toler-
ance of Yorick's lame jokes and because she eventually warms to him. Their
other traveling companion is Allison Mann, a scientist who was in the midst
of giving birth to her (stillborn) cloned child the moment all of the men died,
leading her to believe she caused the plague by rendering man's biological
function unnecessary.

Throughout their travels, the trio is on the run from Alter Tse'elon, a lieu-
tenant in the Israeli army, who seems hell-bent on capturing — or killing —
Yorick. Knowing that his existence would cause mass hysteria, Yorick disguises
himself in various outfits, from a gasmask in the beginning to an androgynous
clown in Japan to a Muslim woman in full burkha. He eventually discovers that
maybe he's not as special as he thought, and being the last man on Earth ain't all
it's cracked up to be.

The term "last man on Earth" has entered our lexicon as a running joke, used
more as the ultimate putdown to a man, with the words, "I wouldn't date you if
you were" preceding it. The Internet is rife with *hilarious* photos of what the
world would look like if women ruled it (they usually involve parking spaces that
are twice as wide, a hammer and screwdriver set that consists of a high-heeled
shoe and butter knife, and a toilet seat held down by chains). But in *Y: The Last
Man*, Vaughan bravely suggests that the world would completely fall apart
without men. It would be easy to accuse him of chauvinism, which many readers
did in the beginning. But his point is more complex and humane than that. If
we, as a society, continue to hold women back from equal rights in half of the
world's countries, refuse them education or access to high-powered jobs, then, if
the men all die, planes are flying with no pilots, companies have no leaders, and
military forces almost vanish.

In the first few volumes, the world becomes a wasteland of no power, no
transportation, and little food. But it's not because of the fact that only women
are left, it's because they're dealing with an apocalypse of epic proportions. "I
think that's an extremely complex, extremely difficult thing to deal with,"
Vaughan told IGN.com. "When three billion people die, I don't care what their
sex was, that's an incredibly difficult thing to come back from." In fact, he said
the world would probably be better off if the men died off, rather than the other
way around. The only really anti-feminist thing in the book can be found not in
the text, but in the pictures. As with most comics, all of the women have 24-inch
waists and 36-inch busts, with toned arms and legs and perfect faces. There's only

one overweight woman in 60 issues, and she's got the IQ of a gnat. But considering women with perfect bodies are a hallmark of comics, I'll let that one go.

In the first few issues, Vaughan details all the little side effects of a male-targeted apocalypse that we wouldn't immediately think of: all of the best rock bands are dead, from U2 to The Eels. Most of the film directors, all male actors, all male writers are gone. Bodies are everywhere. Highways and roads in cities are no longer navigable because many cities were in the middle of rush hour when the men died, and the pile-ups are epic. Radio airwaves are silent. Newspapers stop publishing. Women who were pregnant with male babies miscarry the moment the plague hits. All frozen sperm with a Y chromosome begins rotting.

The women who are left behind react to the holocaust in many ways. Some struggle with survivor guilt, wondering why they were spared while their husbands, sons, brothers, and fathers were taken away from them. Others mourn those whom they have lost, or blame themselves for their deaths. Hardcore feminist organizations sprout up, believing the plague was a sign that men were evil. The Daughters of the Amazon is one such group that Yorick runs into early in the series (and like the original Amazons, who removed a breast to better allow them to aim a bow and arrow, these women cut off one breast in a show of solidarity). His sister, Hero, is a member. When they discover a man is alive, they vow to find and destroy him. Religious types either believe the plague was the Day of Judgment, with the men being punished and the women saved, or the opposite — that that plague was the Rapture and they were left behind, with the men being taken away to salvation.

I will try to avoid spoiling the series as much as possible, because it's now one of my all-time favorite books. And I'm not the only one who fell head over heels for it — the series won three Eisner Awards during its run (the highest achievement for an American comic book), and each volume trumpets the best reviews on the cover: "Funny and scary . . . an utterly believable critique of society. A+" (*Washington Post*); "Complete and utter comic gold" (*Publishers Weekly*); "A seriously funny, nuanced fable. . . A" (*Entertainment Weekly*); "The best graphic novel I've ever read" (Stephen King).

But the one I love appears on the cover of volume 9: "Rivals TV's *Lost* as a smart, consistently entertaining work of popular art" (Time.com). Suffice it to say: if you are a fan of *Lost*, you will love *Y: The Last Man*. It has the same sensibilities, the same cliffhangers, the same mystery. Many of the issues, in classic comic book tradition, end on a cliffhanger, with twists and turns rivaling those on *Lost*. The overriding mysteries — what caused the plague, what is Agent 355's real name, where is Beth, why is Alter trying to kill Yorick? — are explored throughout the series, with many possibilities arising along the way. There are several direct comparisons to *Lost*, the most obvious one being in *Volume 4: Safeword*, when another member of the Culper Ring says, "I help get people where they need to be." Matthew Abaddon utters almost the exact line in "The Life and Death of Jeremy Bentham."

Just like on *Lost*, people are thrust into new relationships, and form families with people who had hitherto been strangers to them. In many of the issues we get a glimpse of a given character's childhood, which provides us with a better understanding of that character and why they are the way they are today. And daddy issues? The *Lost* characters have *nothing* on some of Vaughan's characters.

Vaughan's comics are filled with pop culture references, and there are dozens of moments where the reader will laugh out loud at some of the things Yorick says. (When Agent 355 initially meets him and she refuses to give him her name, instead saying, "If you have to call me something, you can call me 355." To which Yorick responds, "And if you'll be my bodyguard, you can call me Al?" quoting the Paul Simon song from 1986's *Graceland*. Agent 355 has no idea what he's talking about.) The comedy of the books help balance out the hopelessness that pervades their situation. How many more years will the human race live if there's no men? Could one man seriously help repopulate the Earth . . . especially when he's holding out for his fiancée on the other side of the world? There are moments so devastating, graphic, and horrible you want to look away, and many a fan has admitted to crying through several scenes. But the book is also filled with hope, in much the same way *Lost* is. No matter how desolate things may seem, there are so many things to live for.

Also, as on *Lost*, characters do things they never thought they'd do. When one character is pushed to kill another, the results of the action linger for the rest of the series. And in many cases, the thing the characters believe they need the most isn't what they need at all, and often they realize that maybe they needed to be looking a little closer to home. As the series inches toward its conclusion, the reader can't help but start to worry. What will happen to the characters? Will Vaughan answer the questions he's raised? After such a commitment to a story, will I be satisfied at the end?

While I was reading the series, I was chatting with a longtime fan who had already finished it, and was eager to hear my thoughts as I read through it. When I finished the last issue, I emailed him to say that I felt empty, devastated, thrilled, and happy. I felt like I'd lost people I'd become close to. As soon as I'd turned the last page of the comic (which I stared at for about five minutes without moving), I immediately rushed back to the first volume to start over again, something I haven't done with a book in a long time. In short, it's the reaction I believe many *Lost* fans will have when we hit the ending. Not all of the mysteries will be solved, and some of the characters won't make it. We'll have to mourn some of them (there's one death at the end of *Y: The Last Man* that will make you bawl like a baby), and we'll rejoice in those who are left. Vaughan manages to bring the series to an exciting climax, but adds a quieter coda on the end that gives it a satisfying close.

Sadly, Vaughan left the *Lost* writer's table at the end of season 5, but his contributions to the series — and, we hope, his suggestions for the series finale — give fans hope that *Lost* will go out with the same emotional bang as Vaughan's comic-book masterpiece.

5.8   LaFleur

Original air date: March 4, 2009
Written by: Elizabeth Sarnoff, Kyle Pennington
Directed by: Mark Goldman
Guest cast: Kevin Rankin (Jerry), Carla Buscaglia (Heather), Christopher Jaymes (Doctor), Molly McGiven (Rosie), John Skinner (Other #1)

Focus: Sawyer
When the island stops time skipping, Sawyer and his crew are stuck in a different era, and we see how they spend the next three years, until the Oceanic 3 return.

"The record is spinning again. We're just not on the song we want to be on." In the last three seasons, we've seen a lot of references to the scientific nature of time travel. In season 3 there were allusions to Stephen Hawking, and Desmond traveled back in time and learned about the universe's preference for "course correction." In season 4 Desmond time traveled again and actually affected something that happened in the past, and through Daniel we learned about the island's unique properties that make it conducive to time travel. In season 5, we've seen the survivors helplessly skipping through time and becoming voyeurs of events of the past.

But what about the emotional impact of the passage of time? On other series, entering into the fifth season usually means the characters are five years older than they were when the show started. But on *Lost*, we've spent four full seasons with the characters, and watched a total of four months pass. Time has moved more slowly, and we feel like we know these people because we've seen what's happened to them every day of their time on that island. But now three years have passed off screen, and we land in the present (well, present to them), and must piece together what has happened and who they are now.

Sawyer has become the heart of the show. After murdering Locke's father in season 3, Sawyer grew as a person and learned he had more to offer. In season 4 he became a leader to a small group of people, and a hero to many of them. His most heroic gesture was leaping off the helicopter in the season finale, effectively saving the Oceanic 6 and marooning himself again. While the group was grappling with the physical and psychological turmoil of leaping though time, Sawyer was also struggling to come to terms with the fact that Kate was gone, and he quickly accepted that she was never coming back.

Or did he? Sawyer always says one thing and thinks another, and while he's become a master at hiding his true feelings from the other characters, the viewers can see right through him. In this episode, when Locke turns the wheel and the flashes stop, Sawyer says their new mission is simple: "Now we wait for him to come back." Sawyer has never stopped waiting. He originally wanted off the island more than just about anyone — he's one of the men who gets onto the raft in "Exodus, Part 1," in an attempt to get away. By season 4, though, he joins Locke's party, opting to stay on the island and avoid the crazy freighter people rather than risk his life and possibly get saved. He chooses to leap from a helicopter taking them to freedom rather than go with them. And now, when a sub is waiting at the dock to take them all away, he refuses to get on it and even talks Juliet into staying. Is he really waiting for Locke to return? After all, Juliet says to him, "The flashes have stopped. We're already saved." What more can Locke really do? No, it's not Locke he's waiting for. He has Jin out there checking the island grid by grid for another reason entirely.

Sawyer has spent the last three years staring at the ocean and awaiting the return of his friends. Many viewers would probably be happy spending three years just staring at Sawyer.

(© MARIO PEREZ/ABC/RETNA LTD.)

Sawyer was obsessed with Kate for four months, and we watched that relationship develop slowly, following its ups and downs. Kate jumped back and forth between Sawyer and Jack, because both of them represented things she wanted: Jack was the calm, stable leader who promised to save them all. Sawyer was the bad boy, the guy who did his own thing and who was passionate about her. But in some ways, she was interested in both of them and neither of them. Off the island, she's discovered that motherhood offers her a satisfaction that the romance with the men never did.

Kate was unattainable; Juliet is not. Juliet is open and passionate. She's not jumping back and forth between people, but stays loyal to one at a time, even if they don't stay loyal to her. When we first see "LaFleur" carrying a flower into Juliet's house and kissing her, it's disconcerting to us because we didn't see their relationship develop, we only see the end result of it. After so many years of wondering about Kate and Jack, or Kate and Sawyer, seeing Sawyer with someone else is a bit of a surprise. But if we think about it from their perspective, Sawyer's been with Juliet for three years: about 10 times as long as he was with Kate. We accept Horace and Amy as a couple, even though we didn't see their relationship develop, but that's because we never saw Amy with Paul, so we have nothing to contrast the new situation with. Juliet's had Sawyer's back from the beginning (when the Other turns to shoot him, Juliet takes the man out with a single bullet before Sawyer can even react) and Sawyer knows that. Sawyer never knew where he stood with Kate, but he knows where he stands with Juliet.

Through Horace we see what happens to someone who is haunted by the ghost of a man who is dead, worrying that his wife may be loyal to that man instead. As far as Juliet's concerned, Kate might as well be dead, because she doesn't think there's any chance Kate would return to the island; and if she did, she probably wouldn't end up in 1977. Sawyer talks to Horace at the end of the episode about how time heals all wounds and how three years is long enough to get over someone. By saying he's gotten over Kate, he's lying to Horace. When he receives a call from Jin telling him that Kate, Hurley, and Jack have returned, he lies to Juliet. And when he watches, stunned, as Kate steps out of the vw van, he realizes he's been lying to himself, too.

Three years was definitely not long enough.

Highlight: The flash of the full-length statue! I just wish we'd gotten a better look.

Did You Notice?:

- There was a season 3 episode called "Enter 77." And now some of the Losties have "entered" 1977.
- After this episode aired, fans noticed that if you listen closely to the 2008 Comic-Con orientation video (see page xvi), just as Daniel is turning off the camera Chang yells, "LaFleur! What are you doing?"
- Jack, Kate, and Hurley are now in the same time period as Sawyer. Interestingly, these are the same four people who were on Jacob's list that was given to Michael in "Three Minutes."
- Sawyer tells Amy that the gang were in a shipwreck when their boat was three days off Tahiti. This is Rousseau's story.
- As the gang heads to Dharmaville, Sawyer tells Miles and Juliet to keep their mouths shut and let him do the talking, and that they have to come up with a lie. He's become the Jack of this gang. The difference is, Sawyer has maintained his fiction for over three years, and has convinced the others to do so as well. He's also risen to the top and doesn't have people questioning his leadership every step of the way. Jack hasn't been so lucky.
- The Dharma symbol on Sawyer's jumpsuit has a star on it, like a sheriff's badge. In season 1, Sawyer carried around the marshal's badge, which also had a star on it. In the season 2 episode, "The Long Con," he declared himself the "new sheriff in town" and told everyone on the beach that

they'd have to come through him to get anything. Now, as head of security, he really is the sheriff.

- When Sawyer runs to the motor pool to get Juliet, he asks another mechanic where she is. The mechanic's name is Tom, which is also the name of one of the most well-known Others. Could some of the future Others be biding their time in the Dharma camp for now?
- Jin tells Sawyer that he finished searching grid 133. When Sayid had been shot with the tranquilizer darts in "Because You Left," Jack put him in Room 133 of the hospital.
- Sawyer tells Horace the *Black Rock* originated from Portsmouth, England, a detail we know to be true when the auctioneer states as much in "The Constant." How did Sawyer know this piece of information? It's written on the hull of the ship.
- The fact that Horace offers Jim and his friends a one-way trip off the island on the sub shows that the Dharma Initiative didn't have the same interest in keeping the island a secret that the Others have. Horace clearly didn't see how special the island was.
- When Sawyer opts to stay behind and wait for the others to return, his "every man for himself" mantra seems to have been replaced by a genuine bond with his friends. He easily fits in with the communal nature of the Dharma camp, a contrast from the Sawyer who hoarded all the supplies when the plane crashed.
- Jeremy Davies is phenomenal in this episode. From the babbling shell of a man when the group first comes upon him and Charlotte is gone, to the desolate person who accompanies them through the jungle, monotonously answering their questions without any interest in what they're talking about, to his stunned surprise at seeing a little Charlotte running through Dharmaville, he delivers a magnificent performance.
- Jumping ahead three years is one way to make Jin an English speaker. Since Daniel Dae Kim's first language is English, he must be immensely relieved.
- The necklace that Paul was wearing is the Egyptian ankh symbol. The ankh is the symbol for eternal life.
- As Sawyer is walking through the barracks, right before he picks the flower, you see two people playing chess, which is a common motif on the show (see *Finding Lost — Season 4*, page 187).

- Sawyer carrying the flower is a reference to his pseudonym, LaFleur, which means "flower" in French.
- When Sawyer wakes up on the couch after being zonked by the sonic fence, Horace says, "How's your head?" and Sawyer just says, "It hurts." Three years later, the same exchange happens after Horace wakes the morning after his bender, only the speakers are switched.
- Horace's reaction to finding Paul's necklace is *completely* out of proportion to the situation. He finds a token that Amy has kept from her dead husband, and he goes nuts, has a fight with Amy, gets really drunk, and begins tossing lit sticks of dynamite around. Wow. There's a stable father for Amy's new baby.

Interesting Facts: The actor playing Jerry in the Dharma station is Kevin Rankin, recognizable to many TV viewers as a character actor on several shows, from playing Tara Maclay's sexist brother Donny on *Buffy the Vampire Slayer* to Doc on *Undeclared* to Johnny on *Six Feet Under* to the wheelchair-bound Herc on *Friday Night Lights*. Playing Phil is Patrick Fischler, also a character actor staple on television and in movies, from a conspiracy-theorist bookstore owner in *Angel* to appearances on *Veronica Mars, Southland,* and most significantly, as smarmy comedian Jimmy Barrett on *Mad Men*. Reiko Aylesworth, who plays Amy, had prominent roles on *ER* and *CSI*, but she is best known as Michelle from *24*, which she starred in for four seasons.

Miles refers to Sawyer as "Boss," and Sawyer calls him "Enos." This is a reference to *The Dukes of Hazzard*, where Boss Hogg's long-suffering deputy was named Enos.

Juliet asks the doctor if he attempted an external cephalic version on Amy's baby. When a baby is in a breech position (i.e., head up) it's too dangerous to be born vaginally, and many pregnant women don't want to have a Caesarean. Doctors will sometimes attempt an external cephalic version, which is where they figure out where the baby's head and bottom are by feel, and then, by manipulating the mother's belly, try to turn the baby from the outside by pushing the baby around. The procedure does carry with it some risks, like the cord getting wrapped around the baby's neck (the doctor monitors the baby's heartbeat on a monitor and if it changes, they stop the procedure immediately) and many mothers experience extreme discomfort afterwards, as one can imagine. It has also been known to induce premature labor. But it's generally a safe procedure if done correctly on a low-risk pregnancy.

In "Confirmed Dead," Ben gives Charlotte's brief biography while they're holding a gun to his head, and says she was born in 1979. And yet here she is running around as a three-year-old in 1974. What happened? Some fans speculated that maybe that little girl wasn't Charlotte, but instead Daniel was so wracked with grief he just wanted it to be. Or maybe Ben's intel was wrong. Or maybe Charlotte and her mother will leave the island via Frozen Donkey Wheel Express, zipping ahead by a decade and forcing her mother to lie about her birth date. But no, it really was her, and no, Ben wasn't wrong. It was a production error, and one that blew up in the media a little more than it should have. When asked about the mistake, Darlton said in their podcast that when they were filming the scene in "Confirmed Dead," Rebecca Mader stepped up and said that if Charlotte was born in 1971 that would make her 37, and there's no way she was going to play a 37-year-old. So, to save the actress's ego, they changed her age to 28. Fans were surprised to hear the news, and a lot of chatter began lighting up comment boards. But when Mader got wind of what they'd said, she disagreed on her Facebook page, posting, "The timeline error was *their* mistake, and they're making it out to be *my* fault. *Not cool.*" Darlton hadn't intended for their comment to be taken so seriously, and they issued an email to Michael Ausiello at *Entertainment Weekly* to set the record straight. They explained that when the discrepancy was raised by fans, they asked around to see how they could have made such a big mistake. They got a note saying that it was changed to match Rebecca Mader's real birth date, and they misremembered that as having come from Mader herself. They clarified that instead "it came several days earlier when our continuity expert Gregg Nations pointed it out and suggested using Rebecca's actual birthday for Charlotte. And so, the mistake was OURS. Rebecca's production draft DID have the date as being 1979." They apologized to Rebecca, and said she never should have been wrapped up in any of it, and it was "not her fault on any level."

Fans everywhere cheered and hooted with laughter when Sawyer referred to Richard Alpert as "your friend with the eyeliner." The online community regularly referred to Alpert as "Captain Eyeliner" or commented on his "guyliner" each week, and so the writers finally addressed it with Sawyer's line. In an interview with *Sci-Fi Wire*, Nestor Carbonell explained that his eyes are naturally that dark: "I could see why some people would think I have eyeliner on because [my eyelashes] are dark. Especially the bottom row, they're pretty dark. I've been dealing with it since I was a little kid, and so to me it's very funny when it comes up. . . . My brother told me to look online and sort of Google something about that, and my name came up as a couple things. One of them was Maybelline Man. I've been dubbed by some people as Guyliner. It's very amusing." Fans aren't the only ones who suspected Nestor was into the Maybelline. Damon Lindelof admitted, "When we first saw dailies of Nestor, we said, 'We gotta talk to him about the eyeliner situation.' But he is completely sans makeup."

Oops: Watch Sawyer's magic beard throughout the episode. Clearly they were filming the *three years later* portions of the episode, where LaFleur is clean-shaven, simultaneously with the *three years earlier* ones, and were putting fake stubble on his face. When he jumps into the filled-in well, his beard is very dark and black. Then they head to Daniel, and it's light-colored and normal again. They head to the beach and it's black again. They hear shots, and run toward them, and it's normal again. By the time they get to where the shots went off, it's dark again. It continues to switch back and forth in the camp.

4 8 15 16 23 42: Before the "record" stopped spinning, we saw **15** time jumps.

It's Just a Flesh Wound: Paul is killed by the Hostiles. Juliet shoots and kills one of the Hostiles, and Sawyer kills the other one. Sawyer, Juliet, Daniel, and Jin are all zapped by the sonic fence. Amy has a C-section. Horace suffers a major hangover.

Any Questions?:

- When Miles and Juliet notice that their headaches are gone and their noses have stopped bleeding, Jin checks his own nose by touching it. Had his nose been bleeding, but he wasn't telling anyone?
- Phil seems genuinely worried that LaFleur is going to punish him and Jerry severely; is there a cruel side to Sawyer that we haven't seen?
- Where did Horace get the dynamite? It's probably not from the *Black Rock*; that stuff was so volatile that when Arzt touched it the wrong way he flew into bits, so it's doubtful Horace could stumble about, clenching it in his teeth and falling all over the place without ending up as sushi.
- In "The Man Behind the Curtain," we see Ben arrive on the island about 10 years after he was born, which would be the early '70s. In this episode, Horace has a son by Amy in 1977, so earlier calculations should be correct. Does that mean Ben's in the camp somewhere? Does Sawyer know this? Also, in that episode, we saw that Horace was with a blonde woman named Olivia, and there's no mention of a child, or Amy for that matter. Why is

Dharma Wants You . . . Sort Of

Lost has been a groundbreaking series in terms of how it has interacted with its audience. Between seasons 2 and 3, there was the epic *The Lost Experience*. Preceding season 4, there was the shorter *Find815* game. And so, fans were eager to play whatever alternate reality game Darlton were going to throw at them between seasons 4 and 5, and when the Dharma Initiative Recruiting Project began at Comic-Con, fans happily jumped on board. Unfortunately, this ARG would be a huge disappointment.

After people signed up to become a Dharma recruit at DharmaWantsYou.com, they were told they'd have to do a series of aptitude tests. These included tests like a "pressurized spatial judgment evaluation," where you were given a series of shapes and had to organize them inside a square so they all fit; the "broad spectrum knowledge analysis," a multiple choice test with a few tough questions, and some trick questions; the "dexterity and attentiveness evaluation," where the mouse cursor became a Dharma symbol inside a large hexagram and you had to avoid balls being thrown at it without hitting the side of the hexagram (I failed this one miserably); and a few others. However, the tests were spread out over a long period of time, with recruits having to wait weeks for the next email. In September, the email contained a video announcement of Hans Van Eeghen (the angry man in the Comic-Con video), saying it had come to his attention that some recruits were using cheat codes they'd gotten from Black Swan. He urged people to avoid Black Swan and if they encounter any cheat codes to ignore them, or it could jeopardize the integrity of the Dharma Initiative. He believed Black Swan was someone inside the Dharma Initiative, and they were doing their best to figure out who he was.

In the sixth test, recruits were given the option of right-clicking their mouse and the cheat codes would appear on the screen. The final test wasn't a test at all, but a message from Van Eeghen telling recruits they'd either been put in the White Swan group, if they'd never used a cheat code, or in the Black Swan group, if they had. And then the White Swan group were given their work assignments within the Dharma Initiative (I was a cinematographer!). And then . . . players were told that due to the current financial climate, the Dharma Initiative had been canceled and everything we'd done was for nothing.

The game didn't have much direction (and — surprise — Van Eeghen turned out to be Black Swan) and given the sudden halt at the end, the build-up was pretty much for nothing. Instead, with the game suddenly over, anyone who had signed up as part of the game received sporadic emails from Darlton featuring podcasts with the two of them talking about the upcoming season, which more than made up for the sudden end of the game.

there a difference between Horace's life then and now? Was Olivia his sister, and we just assumed it was his wife because she has the same last name?

- Why did Charlotte disappear instead of traveling to the new time? Daniel says, "She moved on, and we stayed." He refers to her leaving in Christian terms, as if her body has "moved on" to the afterlife. Is he talking literally or spiritually? Do dead people become part of the island and therefore they don't time-jump like the rest of them? If Charlotte is a child in 1974 when they first arrive at the camp, do the rules of time travel dictate that her dead body can't travel to that spot? Notice in earlier time jumps that Rousseau, Ethan, the Others, Richard, or anyone they visit in a particular era stays behind, and only the survivors jump. Perhaps the island was tossing them from one place to the next because it needed them to experience certain things, and it no longer needed Charlotte.

- What did Paul do? Did the Hostiles actually kill him, and if so, why? Is it possible Amy and Paul had an argument and she accidentally killed him, or he killed himself? We only see one of the Hostiles reaching forward to grab a gun away from Paul's body, but Amy never says they killed Paul. Why was he shot? Why were the Hostiles about to execute Amy? Are they not the peace-loving people that Richard Alpert makes them out to be? Or is it possible that Paul shot first, and the Hostiles were defending themselves the same way Sawyer claimed he was? One theory on my blog was that Paul was an Other, and integrated himself into the DI and fell in love with Amy. He took her on a picnic and told her the truth, and she killed him. Then two Others showed up as retribution.

- When Mikhail stepped into the sonic fence back in season 3's "Par Avion," he began spewing blood from every orifice. But our survivors merely had seizures and passed out. Did Amy set the fence on a lower frequency, one that she could cut out with earplugs?

- If it's possible to pass through the sonic fence wearing earplugs, and the plugs are kept in a compartment that doesn't appear to be locked behind the keypad, wouldn't the Hostiles have figured that out by now?

- When they get back to the camp, why isn't Juliet questioned more about having knowledge of the sonic fence?

- Horace tells Sawyer that he's not Dharma material. Who is? What constitutes Dharma material?

- Why was Amy able to bring the baby to term on the island? What caused the women to stop having babies? The Purge? Could it have anything to do with Jughead?

- How are they going to explain that Car Mechanic Juliet is actually Fertility Specialist/Surgeon Juliet?

- Will there be any significance to Amy's baby? Could it be someone we know?
- Is Richard Alpert's sense of justice as skewed as Ben's? Horace and Sawyer both explained to him that his men shot Paul and tried to kill Amy, and he says his people will still need justice. Does he simply not believe them?
- Why does Richard want Paul's body? He also wanted Cooper's body when Sawyer killed him in "The Brig." Do the Others have a use for dead bodies? Are they bringing them back to life? Is that an explanation for Christian walking around on the island?
- What happened to Daniel? We don't see him at all in 1977. Has he left the island? Is he lurking in the jungle somewhere? Did he time travel away?

Ashes to Ashes: Paul was Amy's husband, and he was presumably killed by one of the Hostiles when he and Amy were having a picnic lunch. He was the head of security for Dharmaville, and LaFleur succeeds him in the position.

Music/Bands: Jerry and Rosie are dancing to "Candida" by Dawn (with Tony Orlando) from the album *Candida*. The song was a hit in 1970.

5.9   Namaste

Original air date: March 18, 2009
Written by: Paul Zbyszewski, Brian K. Vaughan
Directed by: Jack Bender
Guest cast: Dan Gauthier (Co-pilot), Sven Lindstrom (Dharma Photographer)

Focus: Everyone

Sawyer sneaks Kate, Hurley, and Jack into Dharmaville by passing them off as new recruits, while Sayid is caught and considered a Hostile. Meanwhile, after the Ajira crash, Sun gets away from the group and manages to find her way to someone who can tell her where Jin is.

"Namaste" is an episode about leadership, both what it takes to be a leader, and — sometimes the far more difficult role — what it takes to be led. The very title of the episode has many translations, from the simple, "I bow to you" to the more spiritual, "The Light in Me recognizes and honors The Light in

Dharmaville (formerly New Otherton) is actually a YMCA camp, Camp Erdman, in Waialua, Hawaii. The production crew added the porches on some of the houses, and painted them the yellow that we see on the show. (ALLISON JIRSA)

You." (And come on, who among us wouldn't *love* to see Jack say those words to Sawyer!)

As I've said before, Jack was the de facto leader of the group from season 1 onward. He was the doctor, the man who ran in at the beginning of the pilot episode and saved so many lives, and because he remained calm throughout the chaos, people turned to him for stability. He found the caves and led half the group there. He made the decisions for people. He led several expeditions into the jungle. When he meets Ana Lucia — the *other* leader from the plane — he realized how successful he'd been at leading people in comparison to her, who had lost most of her people along the way. Throughout his many arguments with John Locke in the second season he always maintained an unwavering confidence in what he was saying. Unlike John, he never doubted his own words or convictions, even when he was wrong.

When Jack was kidnapped at the beginning of season 3 the rest of the group seemed lost. When he returned to the camp, everyone rejoiced, and he eventually led them in yet another expedition across the island to be saved. Or so they thought. In season 4 the people split off into two groups — those with crazy John Locke and those with rational Jack Shephard. Turns out Jack was completely wrong again, but he continued to lead people in spite of freighter folk, time lapses, and appendicitis. He managed to get eight people off the island, including himself. From there he continued to control things, instructing everyone to lie about what had happened over the previous four months, and he continued to play a role in everyone's lives, directly and indirectly. And then, when he realized for the first time in his life that maybe John Locke was right, it was he who tried to round everyone up to get them back to the island once again. Even Locke said to him, when he saw him in the hospital, that if Jack returns, everyone will.

But it hasn't been an easy road. Jack's said on several occasions that he never wanted to be the leader, people just expected it from him. His leadership has been questioned and challenged right from the beginning, by Sayid, Sawyer, Locke, even Kate. Everyone looks to him to make any important decision, and when he does, half of them disagree with it (it's not a coincidence the writers gave him the last name, "Shephard," which is purposely an imperfect spelling of the word). As the seasons progressed, and as annoying as Jack started to become, one couldn't help but feel his frustration, that longing to just say, "*Fine!* Then *you* do it!" But he was never able to sit back and be led. On the one hand, he complained that people expected him to be the leader, but on the other, he wasn't willing to give up that position.

All those months, sitting on the beach, Sawyer quietly read his books. He never asked Jack to lead him, and he refused to follow. In "The Long Con" he tricked everyone in the camp, and declared himself the new sheriff. But his leadership didn't last long at all, because he soon found himself on another island, in a polar bear cage (that usually puts a crimp in one's leadership status). People wrote Sawyer off as nothing but a stupid redneck. They didn't notice the heady literature he was reading. They never asked his opinion. He might have been forming plans all along, but no one bothered to ask if he had any input, and he wasn't willing to offer it up. He made himself unlikable, and every time anyone tried to warm up to him and draw him in, he would push them away and say something to make them leave. Sawyer had hated the man who had destroyed his life for so long that he not only named himself after the man, but he began believing he *was* Sawyer, and decided to punish himself as a way of punishing the real Sawyer.

After he killed Cooper in "The Brig," he was lost at first, unsure what to do now that he had fulfilled the only goal he ever had in life. But his desolation didn't last long, and soon he stepped up his game to become a superman to the others. He saved Claire from a burning building, he led a group through the jungle. Instead of just being the useless lump on the beach who refused to pitch in and be part of a team, Sawyer was becoming a leader to a small group, one that looked to him for protection and guidance. He jumped off the helicopter to save several lives and returned to the island, where he was led around first by Daniel, then by Locke. But when Daniel was incapacitated and Locke was gone, Sawyer stepped up and found a way to use his con man instincts for good rather than evil.

For the past three years, Jack's been gone, and Sawyer's not only been allowed to step up, he's wanted to. As the group first entered Dharmaville, he told them to keep quiet, and said he'd handle everything. He concocted a lie about where they came from, and they all went along with it, just like the Oceanic 6 agreed to maintain Jack's lie about where they had been. He actually got his sheriff's badge as a star on his Dharma jumpsuit, and has been appointed head of security. He is trusted, no one questions him, and he has sustained his leadership in a way Jack never did.

Meanwhile, 30 years later after an Ajira flight, Sun follows Ben through the jungle. Frank tries to step up as the leader of this ragtag group of new castaways, but he knows more than he's telling them, and he isn't sure that the rescue he mentioned is actually on its way. He tracks Ben (the other leader) and Sun, trying to figure out why Sun would trust and follow Ben. But Sun has something else on her mind, and when she takes that paddle and out-Bens Ben, it's a brilliant moment. Just as Jin turns into a different person when he faces Radzinsky in the Flame station, so, too, does Sun's brutal side come out. Love and loss has turned Sun into someone she never thought she could be, and she will do anything to get Jin back.

If there will be a reunion between Jin and Sun, it probably won't be happening any time soon. Sawyer, on the other hand, has stared at the ocean for three years, waiting for the gang to return. Now that they have, he's not sure what to do, and decides to just lose himself in another book, just like he used to on the beach. But this is a very different Sawyer. As he faces off with Jack — the past and present leaders — he contrasts the way Jack did things (reacted) with the way he does (thinks it through). He harshly recounts to Jack the casualties Jack left behind during his reactionary leadership, and compares that to his virtually clean record. He talks about Churchill, and we see how quickly he forms plans in his head and calmly carries them out. Sawyer has been holding out on us, and the new man he's become is completely different from the one who sat around on the beach hoarding girlie magazines.

But Sawyer's not the only one who's changed. As Jack leaves, Sawyer asks him if it's a relief for someone else to finally be making all the decisions, and Jack smiles and says, "Yeah, it is." It's the first time we've seen Jack look at peace all season.

Highlight: Pierre Chang giving Jack his work assignment: "Based on your aptitude test, you'll be doing janitorial work." One of the best lines on the show *ever*.

Did You Notice?:

- Way back in season 3, when Sawyer and Kate were stuck in the polar bear cages, they were let out during the day to break rocks and move them. Later, in "Through the Looking Glass," Sawyer is walking across the island and asks Juliet what they were breaking all the rocks for. She answers, "We were building a runway." She jokes that they were building it for the aliens before admitting she has no idea what it was for. Clearly someone had an idea and knew the plane was going to land at some point, in that very spot. It's not clear who finished clearing the rocks out of the way.

- The copilot who talks to Lapidus about Hurley being on the plane is similar to the gossiping pilot in "There's No Place Like Home, Part 2," who talks about the bad-luck "cargo" they're carrying on the plane, meaning the Oceanic 6.

- When Ilana first wakes up, she says, "Jarrah?"

- When Sawyer hugs Kate, she's the only one he doesn't give a nickname to. There was no "Freckles," like some of us might have been expecting him to say. It's like he's forcing himself to remain distant, because he's scared of what will happen if he gets too close.

- When Jack tells Jin and Sawyer who else was on the plane, he doesn't mention Ben.

- Radzinsky! Finally! In case you don't remember the earlier reference to him, here's a quick refresher: We saw Desmond arrive on the island in 2001 ("Live Together, Die Alone"). He was pulled into the Swan station by Kelvin Inman, who told him about his previous station-mate, Radzinsky. He says the entire Swan station was Radzinsky's idea. Radzinsky is the orig-

The pontoon boats used by the blooping survivors were first seen in the Philippines village in "Jughead." (RYAN OZAWA)

inator of the blast door map that Locke found in "Lockdown" and that we saw Kelvin working on, and Kelvin also said that pieces of the Dharma orientation films were missing because Radzinsky had edited them. Radzinsky shot himself, says Inman, and he points to a giant bloodstain on the ceiling of the station and says that's all that's left of Radzinsky. He tells Desmond that he took the body outside and buried it, but he had to do it really quickly because he had to be back at the Swan to push the button every 108 minutes. In this episode, Radzinsky's working at the Flame station (where we later see Mikhail).

- On one of the Flame station monitors, you can see an episode of *The Muppet Show*. Glad to see Radzinsky was busy.
- If this flight really was meant as a do-over for Flight 815, Lapidus does a hell of a better job than the Oceanic pilot had done. Then again, it would have been a little hard to land a plane that's in two pieces.

- History repeats itself with the Ajira crash. When 815 crashed, Jack called everyone together and told them help would arrive. He then immediately took off with Kate into the jungle. Frank tells everyone to be calm, then takes off with Sun. Everyone has the same confusion, is going through the suitcases for supplies, and wants to know where the hell they are. Just as Sayid jumped up on a rock a few episodes in and challenged Jack's authority by not wanting to go to the caves, Caesar jumps the gun a little earlier and talks about searching for a radio or food, clearly disagreeing with Frank's instruction to stay put.
- Sawyer tells Juliet the truth, but seems oblivious to her reasons for worrying. He thinks she's just as stunned as he is that they're back.
- When Amy says they've named the baby Ethan, Juliet almost drops the kid.
- Radzinsky finds "the Hostile" in grid 325. In season 4, the only way to get to the freighter was by following Daniel's bearing of 325°.
- Jin might have learned English, but apparently he didn't learn the subtlety of the wink. He pushes Sayid to the ground, tells him if he speaks, he's dead, and as Sayid just stares at him in disbelief, Jin holds a rifle an inch off Sayid's nose. Um . . . *WINK?!*
- Sawyer puts the lei around Kate's neck, but hands the other two to Hurley and Jack to put on themselves.
- Jin tells Sawyer there's a 14-J situation, which means someone has passed through the sonic fence. We first heard that emergency code in "The Shape of Things to Come." The phone rings in Ben's house and Locke picks it up and a woman's voice was repeating "Code 14-J." When they run over to the other house to tell Ben, he freaks out, arms himself, and knows Keamy and his men are close by and that they're inside the perimeter of the fence.
- Pierre Chang appeared to be just an actor playing a scientist at the beginning of the season, but now we see he's actually a scientist (he's pulled out of his lab to help instate the new recruits). That would explain why he's so revered.
- It's not clear whether it was Juliet or Sawyer who specifically assigned the jobs for the new recruits. Juliet's the one who finagles their names onto the manifest, and Sawyer mentions to Jack that he's "taken care of it." It would be funnier if it were Sawyer: even Jack smiles when he realizes that he's been assigned janitorial work, which is the lowest job they've got. But it could just as equally have come from Juliet, who would not only appreciate jab-

bing him for choosing Kate over her, but who might not want another doctor around, now that she's the backup doc. Kate is put into the motor pool with Juliet, as if Juliet wanted to keep an eye on her; or maybe Sawyer put her there so the two women would be together and he could avoid temptation (or maybe the writers just thought the dark blue jumpsuits brought out Kate's eyes better). Neither Sawyer nor Juliet hold any ill will against Hurley, and either one would have put him in the kitchen knowing how much he loved food and loved cooking it.

- Juliet seems to have purposely left Kate's name off the list, as if she wanted to see Ms. Austen sweat a little bit before swooping in to save her.
- Sayid looks shocked when he sees Sawyer for the first time, since the last time he saw Sawyer, he was leaping out of the helicopter, and Sayid probably presumed Sawyer was dead.
- The photographer who takes the photo of the new recruits is the same guy we saw in "Because You Left," who was filming Chang's Arrow orientation video.
- Smokey's in New Otherton when Sun and Frank arrive. If you listen closely, you don't just hear the leaves rustle, but you hear that NYC cab ticket sound that Smokey always makes right before an appearance. This would lend credence to the idea that Christian and Smokey are linked. Watch when Christian hands the 1977 photo to Sun and the door blows open: you can see smoke in the doorway.
- Sun is the only one of the Oceanic 6 who was not at Christian's memorial service, and therefore would not have known that was him. Maybe *that* is the reason she was the only one of the 6 who landed in 2007.
- Sawyer puts Sayid in the holding cell and tells Phil to get Sayid some food, adding, "We're not savages." In "Confidence Man" in season 1, where Sawyer is pretending to have Shannon's asthma medicine, Jack tells Kate he wants to kill Sawyer, but the only thing stopping him is that, "We're not savages, Kate, not yet." In "The Other 48 Days," when Ana Lucia has the man in the pit, Goodwin tells her to let him go, and says, "We're not savages."
- Sawyer says he wants to sit and read his book and think, but it seems strange that he's just sitting there after having waited for so long to see Kate, Jack, and Hurley. One would think he'd want to just sit and chat with them, but maybe he's uncomfortable, and knowing the content life he has

now, he's scared of being drawn in by the three of them and what that would do to the only life he now knows. Not only that, but he needs to keep up the ruse that he doesn't actually know who the new recruits are.

- Sawyer must know that Ben is in the camp, but since he's subscribing to Daniel's "whatever happened, happened" theory, he doesn't think there's anything he can do about it.

Interesting Facts: In a clip show that aired at the end of season 5, *Lost: A Journey in Time*, Darlton confirmed that Ajira Flight 316 landed on the island in 2007. There are no indicators on the actual show that the plane itself traveled through time, other than it being nighttime in the air, and day on the island. There's been no confirmation on the actual show that they are in 2007, but it probably makes it more convenient for the writers to say they are exactly 30 years apart from those in Dharmaville, who are in 1977. So for the sake of consistency, I will refer to the Ajira plane crash as happening in 2007, even if I don't like details being revealed outside the confines of the actual episodes.

Nitpicks: No offense to Hurley, but there is *no way* a baggy sweatshirt of Sawyer's would also be a baggy sweatshirt on Hurley . . . unless it was Hurley's sweatshirt to begin with. Even so, that would have come down to Sawyer's knees. And without any warning, how would there have been a Dharma jumpsuit available in Hurley's size? And while meeting Ethan as a baby was thrilling (and will definitely make fans watch his death scene in "Homecoming" a lot differently now), if he were born in 1977, that means he was 27 when he was shot by Charlie. That's too much of a stretch. William Mapother was 40 when we first saw Ethan in season 1. Unless he time traveled ahead, which is what made him older, and then came back, it's just not believable. Finally, Jack hugs Juliet and tells her that he'd seen her earlier and wanted to say something, and Juliet says, "But we're not supposed to know each other." So why not wait until they're *inside* the house before hugging, especially when creepy Phil is standing just outside?

Oops: When the photographer tells everyone to say "Namaste," Hurley looks at Kate and says, "Nama-what?" and you hear the click of the camera. But in the photo that Christian shows to Sun, he's looking straight on, and not off to the side.

4 8 15 16 23 42: Only 4 people from the plane made it back to 1977.

It's Just a Flesh Wound: Frank's copilot is impaled on a tree branch. Frank suffers a scratch down the side of his head. Sun has scratches on her cheek and chin. Sun clocks Ben with a paddle. Jack's ego is hurt by his new work assignment.

Lost in Translation: When Sun and Frank first get to New Otherton, you can hear whispers. Fans have had a lot of trouble trying to decipher what they're saying (and for the first time, part of the audio sounds like it's reversed) but one thing that's pretty clear is, "Sarah, it's alright." Often in the whispers, a man's voice refers to Sarah, which is not only Jack's wife's name, but the nickname Christian gave to Ana Lucia in "Two for the Road."

Any Questions?:

- Who knew the plane was going to land? Whose idea was it to build the runway?
- Lapidus asks Ben where Jack, Kate, and Hurley went; how could they just be "gone"? Ben looks at him and states flatly, "How would I know?" Does he know?
- Sawyer tells Juliet that he's got to deal with Kate and company before someone else finds them and "they screw up everything we've got here." It's like he waited for them to come for three years, and now that they're here, he doesn't know why he wanted them back. Had he planned on staying in the DI for the rest of his life?
- There was much talk about who Amy's baby could be, and then when it was revealed to be Ethan, the chatter continued. At the beginning of the season 3 premiere, "A Tale of Two Cities," we see Juliet for the first time, and she's in a book club. An older lady comes to the house first, and her name is Amelia. She leans outside and talks to a guy doing the plumbing in a way that's very familiar, almost like a mother scolds a son, and the guy turns out to be Ethan. Could Amelia be Amy?
- If Ethan was born in the DI, how did he become one of the Others? Why is his last name Rom if Horace's is Goodspeed? Was "Rom" just a pseudonym he gave to the Losties? "ROM" is a medical term meaning "risk of mortality"; was the name an indication of the mortality issues Ethan was dealing with among the pregnant women?
- Hurley reminds Sawyer about the Purge, because he'd seen the pit of bodies and knew about it. But how did Sawyer know about it? He acts like he knew, but just didn't do anything. What *was* he planning on doing when the Purge came?
- Sawyer mentions Faraday, saying he has interesting theories on what they can and can't do, but when Jack asks if he's here, Sawyer says, "Not anymore." Where did he go?

"Turn it up! I love Geronimo Jackson"

Ever since Charlie and Hurley found Geronimo Jackson's album, *Magna Carta*, in the Swan station in season 2's "The Hunting Party," and neither of them claimed to have heard of the band before (Sayid similarly said he'd never heard of them), fans have been having a lot of fun with this Easter egg. The writers have inserted Geronimo Jackson references in every subsequent season, and whenever they are asked about the band, they insist they were real. However, either by accident or on purpose, the writers have been inconsistent with their answers, which points to the fact that the band never existed outside the confines of *Lost*.

After Charlie and Hurley look at the album, Locke, flipping through the same stack of records, also finds the band's album and pauses on it for a moment. In season 4's "Cabin Fever," we realize that Locke had known the band for years when we see a poster of them in his high school locker. As an adult, Locke notices the undercover cop Eddie wearing a T-shirt emblazoned with the album cover, and Eddie refers to it as one of his father's old shirts ("Further Instructions"). In "There's No Place Like Home, Part 1," the DJ at Hurley's birthday party has a copy of the *Magna Carta* album sitting next to his turntables.

But most of the references to the band have been in Dharmaville, where they appear to have been the U2 of the music industry at the time. Charlotte, who had lived in the Dharma Initiative compound with her mother (and probably grew up with her mother listening to the music long after they left), says she loves the band. When we first see Dharmaville in 1974, Rosie is dancing with Jerry in the security station, and she's wearing a Geronimo Jackson T-shirt. When Jin finds Kate, Jack, and Hurley in the lagoon in "316," he's listening to "Dharma Lady," a song by Geronimo Jackson, in his van. The song plays again in "Namaste" when the photographer is taking the picture of the new recruits. In "He's Our You," we see a poster for Geronimo Jackson in the Dharmateria, advertising a concert on 08/15/69 at 23:00. The picture is from *Alice in Wonderland*, with the hookah-smoking caterpillar sitting on his toadstool while Alice peers up from below. In the poster, the White Rabbit, Mad Hatter, and Cheshire Cat rush around in the background.

In a podcast during the show's second season, Darlton insisted that Geronimo Jackson was a real band from the 1970s, who disappeared after making one album. In another podcast later that same season, they said the band recorded two albums. On the season 2 DVD, an interview with *Lost* writers Edward Kitsis and Adam Horowitz revealed the band were San Francisco–based, and had put out one album before disappearing to New York in 1971. On the ABC official site, the band biography says they were from the Excelsior District of San Francisco, and that they disappeared in 1972.

"Dharma Lady" is the first chance we get to hear the band, and it pretty much confirms that GJ is fictional (if the inconsistencies in the "facts" didn't provide enough of a clue). "Dharma Lady" is actually a reworking of the song "Excelsior Lady" (which links it to the myth of GJ living in the Excelsior District) by real San Diego band The Donkeys, whose 2006 CD, interestingly, was called *Living on the Other Side*. "Dharma Lady" was made available on iTunes the day before this episode aired. The artwork that accompanied the song was a deranged-looking rabbit wearing a top hat (the Mad Hatter and the White Rabbit meet the Creepy Bunny from *Donnie Darko*), floating in space with a ring of orchids framing the picture.

Tracing the references to Geronimo Jackson has been a lot of fun for fans, but it's probably nothing more than a side puzzle. Unless we find out the band's music was being funded by Widmore.

- Now we know why Ben was very bloody when Locke saw him lying in the barracks. Did he regain consciousness and talk to Ilana and Caesar? Otherwise, how would Ilana have known that Lapidus and "a lady" took the other outrigger if she hadn't heard Ben say it?
- New Otherton looks more like what it would look like a few years after the Purge than the way it did when Ben was running it in the 21st century. It's a huge mess, which is understandable, since the last time we saw New Otherton it was being destroyed by Smokey in "The Shape of Things to Come." But it doesn't look right: you can see the sign for the Processing Center swinging by a chain link, and there are Dharma symbols on the doors. Neither was there in 2004 when the Others were living there, nor were the annual Dharma recruit photos on the walls when we previously saw the rec room. Have they landed in another time? Or did something happen to change the timeline, and the Others never actually ended up living in the houses? This does not appear to be an area that's been inhabited since the Dharma Initiative.

Ashes to Ashes: Lapidus's copilot is the only person who doesn't make it when Ajira Flight 316 lands. He is impaled by a branch. His efforts were essential to Frank's successful landing of the plane.

Music/Bands: The song playing when Sawyer et al pull into the Dharma camp is "Ride Captain Ride" by Blues Image, from 1970. The song's lyrics refer to 73 men sailing into San Francisco and telling everyone to ride along. In the chorus, they sing that the captain is on his way to a world "that others might have missed." When the photographer takes the photo of the new recruits, you can hear "Dharma Lady" by Geronimo Jackson in the background.

5.10   He's Our You

Original air date: March 25, 2009
Written by: Edward Kitsis, Adam Horowitz
Directed by: Greg Yaitanes
Guest cast: Sayed Badreya (Sayid's Father), William Sanderson (Oldham), Dmitri Boudrine (Ivan), Michael Hardy (Floyd), Anthony Keyvan (Young Sayid), Xavier Raabe-Manupule (Iraqi Boy), Joe Toro (Bartender)

Focus: Sayid

Despite the best efforts of Sawyer and Horace, Sayid refuses to cooperate, because he believes he's finally found his purpose for returning to the island.

Sayid has been the focus of five *Lost* episodes before this one — season 1's "Solitary" and "The Greater Good," season 2's "One of Them," season 3's "Enter 77," and season 4's "The Economist." Each episode focuses on Sayid's past as a torturer and how it has both shaped and cursed him. We know he can shut off his emotions to torture a person and do what needs to be done. He can see through lies and knows how to get people to tell the truth by the use of force — in "One of Them" he was convinced more than anyone else that "Henry Gale" was not who he said he was. However, despite being very good at what he does, he hates doing it: in "Solitary" we saw the regret he felt when he had to torture Nadia and how he forced himself away from the camp because of what he'd done to Sawyer. In "Enter 77" we saw how a past torture session catches up to him and the remorse he feels for what he's done, even though he lies to save his own skin.

The other thing we know about Sayid is that he's a lover. He falls hard and completely, and it's the one thing that can cloud his judgment and lessen his powers of perception. His love for Nadia made him escape the life he had in the Republican Guard, and he spent years searching for her. When he was on the island, he fell in love with Shannon, and truly believed that if he could just be with her he could leave his old life. When she died, he began torturing again without repentance. After he left the island, he conned Elsa, but fell in love with her, too, and because of his strong emotions for her, he didn't see she was conning him right back. The moment he realized what she was doing, however, he instantly shut down those emotions and killed her. And now, in "He's Our You," we saw how Ilana was also able to rope him in. He had just spent two years being the very person he never wanted to become, and Ilana stepped in, played on his vulnerability, and tricked him.

Until this episode, we had yet to receive a glimpse into Sayid's childhood the same way we have the others. In "One of Them" another character refers to Sayid's father as "a great hero," and that's the most we hear about him. Now we finally see his father — a brutal, hard, cold man who forces his sons to become men by having them kill another creature. What is so brilliant about this opening scene is that it perfectly and succinctly sums up the character of Sayid that we've seen all along — he is at once caring and brutal. He steps up, puts his arm on his brother's shoulder to comfort him, and snaps a chicken's neck. He feels deeply for his brother, and then shuts off those emotions to kill. When he has his showdown with Ben in Santo Domingo, he says, "I'm not what you think I am. I don't like killing." And he's telling the truth. But when Ben says, "You're capable of things that most other men aren't . . . it's in your nature, it's what you are. You're a killer, Sayid," he's correct, too. Sayid has been this way all his life, with his deep love in a constant battle with his ability to turn off his emotions completely and "do what needs to be done," as he says to Jack in "One of Them."

And now he believes that what needs to be done is to kill a young Benjamin Linus before he can grow up and do terrible things to people, including to Sayid. Young Ben (whom Sayid says is 12, but if Ben arrived on the island at age 10, has to be more like 14 or 15) has had an upbringing similar to Sayid's. He has an abusive father who doesn't care about him outside of what use he is (Roger comments that Ben never made *him* a sandwich) and he clearly beats him in a way we can only assume Sayid's father beat Sayid as a child. Young Ben Linus is, as Sawyer puts it somewhat sarcastically, a "sweet kid," and when Sayid first sees Ben with his father, he realizes Roger is a tyrant like Sayid's own father was, belittling and abusing Ben for his own amusement. Another character might have believed his mission was to free Ben from his father, making him a better person and preventing the monster he would become. But Sayid sees Ben set a van on fire and send it into the camp as a diversion, putting lives at stake by putting his own need to get out of the compound before anything else. He believes that Ben is already beyond saving, just as Sayid was already lost when he killed that chicken. Sayid sees himself in the boy, and the potential of what Ben could turn out to be. Sayid had the chance to become a sweet, tender, loving person (he was able to live that life for nine months with Nadia) but instead became the exact opposite: a torturer. And he always had that killer potential in him, even when he was a child. Ben himself says to Sayid that his killer instinct is in his "nature," meaning there's nothing anyone could do to change it. Sayid has seen what the adult Ben Linus has become, and sees his chance to prevent that person from ever coming into existence.

The adult Ben Linus is a sociopathic liar. Sayid tortures people physically, but Ben tortures them emotionally. He knows exactly what he's doing. He controls Sayid, whether Sayid is killing someone in Russia or trying to get away from everything by hiding in Santo Domingo. Ben knows he can play on Sayid's vulnerabilities any time he wants. Just like with the chicken, Sayid

The burnt-out Dharma van sits in Dharmaville, a reminder of what Ben was already capable of at such a young age. (RIPTON SCOTT)

kills to protect. He wants to protect his friends, so he kills Widmore's people. He wants to protect Hurley, so he puts himself back into the life he was trying to leave.

Sayid describes Ben to Ilana as "a liar, a manipulator, a man who allowed his own daughter to be murdered to save himself, a monster responsible for nothing short of genocide." Which . . . pretty much sums him up perfectly. Ben lies about everything and hurts people for his own purpose. Throughout the season it's been unclear why Sayid shows the scorn he does for Ben, and now we see that Ben has forced him to do terrible things for two years and then just dumped him with no warning. Telling him he is finally "free," he leaves Sayid standing in a cold, snowy street, with nowhere to go and no one to talk to. It's not clear whether Ben really was using Sayid to get rid of people in Widmore's organization, or if he just used Sayid to get rid of his own old enemies. Even Sayid is starting to question if any of the work he did for Ben was legitimate.

So now he realizes why he has returned — to kill Ben Linus. If he can get rid of the child, then maybe 30 years later there will be no lists, people won't be kidnapped or put in cages or tortured, Sayid won't be forced to torture him in the armory, there will be no Purge of the Dharma Initiative, Alex will stay with Rousseau and not be taken, the signals off the island won't be jammed, and the island could continue being a place where the Dharma Initiative did their thing without the brutal interference of Ben Linus.

But while Sayid considers all of this, we can't help but wonder if Daniel was right. If "whatever happened, happened," then maybe Sayid isn't here to change history. What if Sayid completely misunderstood his purpose? It's not clear at the end of the episode if Ben is really dead or not. Just before taking his shot, Sayid hangs his head and says, "You're right; I am a killer," and young Ben doesn't know what he's talking about. But 30 years later, the adult version of Master Linus will look at Sayid and say, "You're a killer, Sayid," as if he never forgot the words Sayid said to him so many years earlier.

In "Because You Left," when Pierre Chang mentions time travel to a construction worker, the worker says, "Are we gonna go back and kill Hitler?" and Chang says no, there are rules. It's possible Sayid mistook his purpose. Perhaps he wasn't sent back to kill Hitler; he was there to create him.

Highlight: Sawyer to Jack: "Three years, no burning buses. Y'all are back for *one* day . . ."

Did You Notice?:

- One of the readers on my blog commented after this episode that if Sayid shot Ben in the heart then Ben would be fine, since he doesn't actually have one.
- Back in "This Place Is Death," Sayid warned that if he saw Ben again, it would be extremely unpleasant for both of them. He wasn't kidding.
- Sayid stepped in and helped his brother do a dirty deed he was being forced to do against his will, just like Eko had done when he was a child for his brother Yemi. The main difference is that Sayid is the younger brother, and Eko was the elder.
- Right after we see Sayid kill a chicken, Ben brings him a chicken salad sandwich.
- Now we have a date for when Ben met Alpert, which is 1973 (he's in 1977 now, and said he met Richard 4 years earlier). It's still not clear why Richard has shaggy hair in that scene when in every other era he's neatly dressed. It might have been a planning error on the part of the writers, who hadn't

quite worked out Richard's immortal look yet (i.e., perfectly coiffed hair, shirt sleeves rolled up, eyeliner just so . . .).

- The scene where the man is frantically running into the house and down corridors, slamming the doors behind him, is one continuous shot, filmed with a cameraman running behind the actor.
- After Ben (looking like Quentin Crisp) tells Sayid that he's free, he passes through a set of gates that are practically closed, symbolizing the prison-like bars that surround Sayid emotionally. The segue to Sayid sitting in the actual cell drives home the fact that Ben has emotionally imprisoned Sayid the same way the Dharminians have put him in the physical cell.
- Juliet refers to her relationship with Sawyer as "playing house," which is what Sawyer suggested to Kate that they do in New Otherton last season. The difference is, Juliet and Sawyer have been together for three years. Perhaps Juliet always feared Kate's return, and for that reason figured she was only temporarily playing a part that would eventually end.
- Sawyer is tender to Juliet when he's with her in the house, but he doesn't act the same way in the company of anyone else, as if he's uncomfortable and doesn't know how to handle the situation.
- Why do some of the Dharma suits have the person's last name embroidered on them, while others have the first? Or, in the case of Hurley, his nickname?
- There were a lot of ham references in this episode. The torturer is Oldham, Juliet is burning bacon, and Hurley brings breakfast over to Jack and Kate and tells them to try the dipping sauces, because they really bring out the ham.
- Oldham steps out of a tent that looks Native American, much like the smoke lodge that Locke creates in "Further Instructions."
- Sayid is drinking MacCutcheon, the whisky that Widmore deemed too good for Desmond.
- Sayid appears to be sitting in the same bar where Jack goes to drink in "316" and where he gets the call about his grandfather.
- When Horace says, "Hello there," to Sayid to bring him out of his stupor, he says it exactly the same way he says it to Locke when Locke is hallucinating and sees him building the cabin in "Cabin Fever."
- When the Dharminians put to a vote what they should do with Sayid, we see democracy at work in a way it never was with the large group of sur-

vivors before. However, this "democracy" seems more like coercion masked as free will.

- Fool Sayid once, shame on you. Fool Sayid twice, shame on him. In "The Economist," Elsa tricked him into thinking she just happened to run into him at a café, got him stuck in a long con, and boom, pulled a gun on him and said she was working for someone else who wanted to know about his employer. Now Ilana meets him in a bar, gets him stuck in a very short con, and boom, pulls a gun on him and says she's working for someone who wants to bring him back for justice.

- When Sayid asks Ilana to delay the flight, she says she'll buy him a rabbit's foot at the gift shop. The rabbit's foot is a repeating motif on the show: Hurley's father had a rabbit's foot on the keychain for his Camaro, and in "There's No Place Like Home, Part 2," when the pilots are discussing their "cargo," one of them is holding a lucky rabbit's foot.

- Young Ben is impressed by Sayid's kung fu skills, but his will be just as impressive some day, if not more so.

Interesting Facts: William Sanderson, who plays Oldham, is a very prolific character actor that probably looked familiar to most viewers. He played J.F. Sebastian, the genetic designer, in *Blade Runner*, followed by dozens of small roles in television and film. It was Larry on *Newhart*, however

The Hawaiian Hall at the Bishop Museum near downtown Honolulu stood in for Red Square in "He's Our You." This same lane was earlier used as the London waterfront scene in "Flashes Before Your Eyes," where Desmond threw Penny's ring into the "Thames." (RYAN OZAWA)

(always seen with his brother Darryl, and his other brother Darryl), that made him a recognizable face. With his distinctive voice and look, Sanderson has continued to have constant work, and recently had a leading role on *Deadwood* as E.B. Farnum, the greedy local hotel owner who would often look into the camera and deliver Shakespearean-like soliloquies.

Nitpicks: Why is everyone so scared of Oldham? He puts some truth serum on a sugar cube and asks a bunch of questions, which isn't exactly frightening. Maybe they've seen what he does when he doesn't administer the serum first. It just seemed like a big overture for such a little tune.

Oops: We flash back to the scene at the marina again and Sayid points to Ben and says, "If I see you again, it'll be extremely unpleasant for *us both*." But in the original scene from "This Place Is Death," Sayid points first to Jack, then to Ben, and says, "If I see you, or *him* again, it'll be extremely unpleasant for *all of us*." The words were deliberately changed to switch the animosity from Sayid versus everyone to just Sayid versus Ben. Several other lines of dialogue in the marina scene are different from the earlier one (both Ben and Kate say different things) and it's unclear why they show a different cut rather than repeating the original one.

4 8 15 16 23 42: Ben says he ran away into the jungle **4** years ago. After Sayid shoots the man in the building, he steps out and you can see the address from the inside, which is **32**. However, because we see it backwards it looks at first like **23**. Juliet asks Kate how she is with a flat **4** engine. The house that is hit by the burning Dharma bus is building **15**.

It's Just a Flesh Wound: Sawyer headbutts Sayid in the face to make it look like he got physical to get a confession from him. Sayid shoots Ben in the torso.

Lost in Translation: When Sayid steps out of the building, you can see Cyrillic writing on the glass of the doors that translates to "Oldham Pharmaceuticals." Behind Ben are the letters В Р И С О, which simply translate to another acronym: VRISO. It's unclear what that acronym refers to.

Any Questions?:

- Did that chicken deflate? Sayid picks up a really fat chicken, breaks its neck, and when he hands it over, it's the size of a drumstick.
- How did Roger "Workman" Linus know about Oldham? You'd think that was intel they wouldn't have handed down to a janitor. Is he someone who used to be in Dharmaville but when his methods differed from everyone else's, he moved out?

- Did Ben hire Ilana and pass himself off as being from the Avellino family? He of all people would know about Avellino's death; he's the one who ordered the hit. How else would Ilana have ended up on that very plane?
- If Ilana's not working for Ben, is it possible she has another motive? Did she know the plane would crash on this island?
- Is Sayid really a killer at heart? Why doesn't he shoot the boy one last time in the head? Is he sure he killed him?

Music/Bands: The song playing in Oldham's tent was "I Can't Give You Anything But Love, Baby," sung by Billie Holiday.

A Separate Reality: Further Conversations with Don Juan by Carlos Castaneda (1971)

The book that Young Benjamin Linus passes through the bars to Sayid is one that changed many lives in the early 1970s, but the story behind the man who wrote it is far more fascinating today.

A Separate Reality was the second book by Peruvian-born anthropologist Carlos Castaneda, now considered the grandfather of the New Age movement. As a graduate student at the University of California, Castaneda had decided to travel to Mexico and find a Native Indian who could teach him about the ways of his people. When he arrived in a bus depot, he met don Juan Matus, a "sorcerer," or shaman, and their meeting is now legendary. Castaneda was shaken by the meeting, and tracked don Juan to his house, where he asked if the Yaqui Indian would take him on as an apprentice. Don Juan convinced Castaneda to try smoking peyote, a highly hallucinogenic cactus plant, and when Castaneda did, he had terrifying hallucinations. He explained them to don Juan the next day, and don Juan told him that no Westerner had ever had such hallucinations, and clearly he was different. Don Juan decided to take Castaneda on as his apprentice. Through various teachings, don Juan taught him that the world is made up of more than one reality, and through height-ened awareness and willpower, one can see the other realities. Castaneda con-tinued doing hallucinogenic drugs with don Juan and his fellow sorcerers, and eventually began seeing the other realities while sober, in his everyday life. He was shaken by what he could suddenly do, and decided to end the apprenticeship after four years.

Castaneda returned to California and turned his field notes into his master's thesis. The thesis was accepted by the University of California Press, which published it as a book called *The Teachings of Don Juan: A Yaqui Way of Knowledge* in 1968, and it instantly became a hit. Michael Korda, the legendary book editor at Simon & Schuster, read a copy on a trip to California. He went out to lunch with Castaneda, who he later described in his memoirs as an extremely likable and friendly man: "I had seldom, if ever, liked anybody so much so quickly — a feeling that remains undiminished after more than twenty-five years." Korda bought the rights to the book and it became a massive bestseller and a must-read within the drug-taking, trippy, hippie culture. Castaneda became a millionaire.

Later that year, Castaneda returned to Mexico and underwent a second apprenticeship with don Juan, and the result of that experience is his second book, *A Separate Reality*. The main focus of the book is don Juan trying to get Castaneda to "see," and his definition of seeing is much like that in *The Little Prince* — it does not involve using one's eyes. Castaneda is reluctant to use any of the drugs that don Juan offers him — peyote, jimson weed (or datura), and mushrooms — and says he wants to try a drug-free alternative. Throughout the book don Juan chastises Castaneda for being a fool, for asking too many questions, for talking too much, for not seeing an answer right in front of him, and Castaneda continues to take furious notes and tries to understand what don Juan is telling him by writing it down, thinking it through, and attempting to make it logical. Don Juan, on the other hand, wishes he'd stop talking, stop taking notes, and just let feelings and occurrences happen to him.

Castaneda attends a *mitote*, a ceremony where several sorcerers get together and smoke the drugs while others watch as they *see*. During this ceremony, they all begin looking at Castaneda, who begins to have a vision of his mother standing behind him. Afterward, don Juan tells him that "Mescalito" (his name for the peyote) had singled out Castaneda, and they could all see Mescalito standing behind him. Castaneda eventually meets another sorcerer, don Genaro, and don Juan tells Castaneda that Genaro can also see something unique in Castaneda, and knows that he has the ability to see, but can't figure out what is standing in Castaneda's way that prevents him from doing so. Don Juan explains several ideas: that of an ally (something from the spiritual world that only the seer can see, who helps them achieve their goals); controlled folly (a difficult concept that is never defined clearly, but seems to involve controlling one's emotional response to a situation by convincing oneself that it doesn't matter . . . don Juan uses the personal example of not becoming anguished by his son's death); and one's will. At the end of the first of two parts of the book, don Juan describes fibers of light, like tentacles that reach out and connect with the world around a person, and that these fibers protrude from one's belly button, and can be willed by the seer.

In part 2, Castaneda gives in and smokes again. Don Juan explains that the smoke will allow him to see the other world. In his first experience, Castaneda falls to his side and sees a gnat in his line of vision. When he sits up again, that gnat is 100 feet tall, drooling in front of him, a terrifying beast. Don Juan explains afterward that the gnat is his guardian, the keeper of the other world, which he must overcome to enter. When Castaneda begins to doubt the teachings, don Juan sits with him and asks him about a promise he once made. Castaneda can't remember the promise at all, until don Juan gives him enough clues that Castaneda suddenly remembers a terrible incident from his youth, when he knocked over a blackboard and crushed a fellow student's hand, and promised that if the child lived he would never try to be victorious again. Castaneda is in awe that don Juan could see this moment from his childhood, and he returns to his path of enlightenment.

Don Juan continues his teaching by telling Castaneda what a warrior is, and how a man becomes one. A warrior, he says, must have a detachment about death, but later, when Castaneda smokes and then abandons himself to death, don Juan chastises him again, showing the difference between detachment and not caring at all. He teaches him about death through various exercises, always starting with Castaneda smoking the drugs, and then following the instructions of don Juan and hallucinating various people, places, and things. Near the end of the book he comes very close to seeing, and don Genaro returns to try to speed things up. After a few tough lessons, don Juan warns Castaneda to go away for a while and ruminate on his teachings so far, all the while worrying that if Castaneda should stick around and continue to follow don Genaro's teachings, the exercises might kill him.

A Separate Reality was a hit like the previous book, so Castaneda returned to what had happened in his initial experience with don Juan, and from his field notes wrote a third book, *Journey to Ixtlan*. The book was released in 1972, and he submitted it as his doctoral thesis, and it was accepted by UCLA. At this point, however, questions began to arise about his work.

The field notes that had been gathered to write these books mysteriously disappeared when his thesis advisors asked to see them (his family maintains he had boxes of notes and they were destroyed in a flood). Other students argued that Castaneda had been lying about everything, and that these books shouldn't earn him a doctorate. No one else had ever met the elusive don Juan, and Castaneda refused to divulge where he was or what his real name was. In 1973, Castaneda suddenly announced that don Juan had died, but he hadn't died a mortal death; instead, he had journeyed to infinity, and that Castaneda was his official successor. In 1976, investigative journalist Richard de Mille (son of film director Cecile B.) published a book called *Castaneda's Journey: The Power and the Allegory*, in which he argued that don Juan and everything that Castaneda wrote in the books was a complete hoax. He didn't believe Castaneda had ever traveled to Mexico (despite Castaneda's wife and young son having lived without him for four or five years at a time while Castaneda was away "learning"). He pointed not only to an inconsistency in don Juan's voice throughout the books (he moves from being serious and teacherly in the first book to joking and almost clownish in the next two, despite the third one covering the same time period and lessons as the first book), but he also said that several of don Juan's teachings were retreads of earlier anthropological works. He located much of don Juan's "lessons" in over 200 books dating back as far as the early 20th century, with concepts like seeing and man being a "luminous egg" quoted almost word for word in them. Also, he pointed out quite dramatically that Yaqui Indians don't take peyote, and the plant doesn't grow anywhere near their territory. In a 2006 BBC documentary, de Mille states outright, "Don Juan did not exist; he was a character in a story invented by Carlos Castaneda." However, at that point Castaneda's followers were legion (to date the books have sold more than 8 million copies) and de Mille's criticism barely made a ripple in the New Age movement that had grown out of a worship of Castaneda's writings.

One of Castaneda's readers, Jay Fikes, decided to follow his hero and do the same fieldwork when he was a young anthropologist in 1976. He traveled to Mexico to the Huichol Indian tribe, who were well known for taking peyote, and he took the drug and experienced some far-out hallucinations of his own. But in doing so, he realized that Castaneda's descriptions of a peyote trip were nothing like the real thing. He began noticing the controversy rising up around him, and traveled back to Mexico and tracked down a man he believed to be don Juan. Now dead, the man had left a widow behind, who said she remembered Carlos Castaneda, but said he'd never asked any questions, never spoke, and certainly wasn't around for very long. And she said the story of his apprenticeship was untrue, because to become an apprentice, a person had to experience five annual excursions into the desert with no women, hygiene, or pleasures, and she said Castaneda refused to do it. No one would simply become an apprentice without having undergone the rituals that preceded it. Dr. Fikes concluded publicly that everything in the don Juan books had been entirely made up, and that the books — and Castaneda's academic credentials that resulted from them — were the biggest anthropological hoax since Piltdown Man. Today the Yaqui Indians claim to be completely misunderstood because of Castaneda's writings, and that their tribes have been overrun in the 1970s by hippies searching for don Juan and peyote. And because of the number of hippies who became seriously ill on peyote, the drug was outlawed, which hurt several other Indian tribes who relied on the plant for religious rituals. Fikes argued that Castaneda had crossed a line in anthropological studies by harming the very civilization he was pretending to observe.

After announcing don Juan's death, Castaneda became a recluse. He refused to allow his photograph to be taken or his likeness to be drawn. He resurfaced in the early 1990s with a mysterious new teaching from don Juan that he'd been keeping secret, called "Magical Passes," which were a series of exercises that don Juan had purportedly taught him, which could bring one to enlightenment. At that point Castaneda's personal life had become complicated. There were three women living with him full time and he had an adopted daughter who was also his lover. He had organized his followers into a cult-like state, ordering them to cut all ties to friends and family and to change their names, because that's what don Juan would have wanted. He told them that like don Juan, when he died he wouldn't die a mortal death but would become a ball of energy and would take his followers with him to infinity. He said they'd leave their bodies behind and would travel the galaxy (which also sounds like *The Little Prince*).

In June 1998, it was discovered that Carlos Castaneda had died two months earlier of liver cancer, and the people closest to him had kept his death a secret. His body had been immediately cremated and the ashes scattered in the desert. In the wake of his death, several followers committed suicide, and the women who were always seen with him disappeared and are presumed dead (the body of his daughter/lover was found in Death Valley).

Carlos Castaneda's teachings and words took people on a path to enlightenment, and certainly blockbusters like 1993's *Celestine Prophecy* (which alone has sold over 20 million copies and repeats many of the things Castaneda says in his books) couldn't have existed without it. His books are still read and praised today — the back cover praise for *A Separate Reality* includes a quotation from the *New York Times* that heralds the book as "extraordinary in every sense of the word." Despite the controversy that surrounded Castaneda, he still had thousands of followers (and many believers today), and many people maintained that even if don Juan wasn't real, the message that Castaneda conveys in his books was beautiful and important, and could still lead readers to enlightenment. His work has influenced countless lives and several generations, and has spawned a movement that has grown and developed into the New Age movement of today. But he leaves behind a deep mystery — were his books a hoax or genuine? — and the reputation of "the most controversial figure in the history of anthropology."

It was inevitable that *A Separate Reality* would turn up on *Lost* sooner or later. There are moments in the book where it almost seems like a character study for the development of Sawyer, Jack, and most of all, Locke. The mysticism and mystery of the book would have made it the perfect primer for the DeGroots as they were originally coming up with the idea of the Dharma Initiative. The most obvious connection specifically to "He's Our You" is probably the fact that don Juan encourages Castaneda to take drugs in order to "see," and similarly, Oldham drops some sort of acid-like substance on a sugar cube and gives it to Sayid, which causes Sayid to see clearly and tell the truth. Sayid assures him he used just the right amount, just as don Juan is concerned with having just the right amount of peyote or "little smoke" for Castaneda to take.

But the book goes far beyond this simple comparison. Often don Juan's long explanations about knowledge versus seeing echo those of Jack's science versus Locke's faith. Don Juan spends many pages in the book urging Castaneda to stop overthinking everything, and instead asks him to just look at the world around him for the proof of what he's saying. At the end of the book Castaneda tells don Juan that a single leaf can only fall once out of a tree in exactly the same way. To challenge him, don Juan has him watch a leaf fall from a branch and to the ground, then he looks up and sees the same leaf fall off the branch and out of the tree, and it happens over and over. Castaneda just saw this wonder with his own eyes, but quickly he begins to try to explain it, positing that he was actually looking at one leaf falling only once, but he was seeing it from a different perspective and it appeared to be falling over and over. Don Juan finally breaks Castaneda out of his thought process by shouting at him, "You're chained! . . . You're chained to your reason." Locke similarly finds himself frustrated by Jack's insistence on common sense and reason on an island that doesn't make any sense in the scientific world. Even when Jack sees the island disappear, he insists it didn't actually happen, and tries to come up with an explanation for what he just saw.

One of the most important links to *Lost* is don Juan's insistence on Castaneda doing drugs, specifically "smoke." He tells him early in the book, "Only the smoke can give you the necessary speed to catch a glimpse of that fleeting world." When explaining what an ally is, he tells Castaneda that the smoke will lead him to the ally and allow him to become one with it. It doesn't require any stretch of the imagination to align Smokey with don Juan's "little smoke"; Smokey has led many of the people to where they need to be. Just as the "smoke" can be lethal, leading a person to his/her ally and getting them killed by it, so too has Smokey proven itself to be very dangerous. Don Juan says the smoke is different for each person, and similarly, the smoke monster manifests differently for different people — Locke thought it was benevolent in "Walkabout," but it killed Eko in "The Cost of Living."

When Castaneda gives in and begins smoking, he sees his guardian in the form of a giant gnat. He stares at it, and then turns away, and the moment he does the guardian comes charging at him. In much the same way, Smokey has staring contests with people (Eko), but when they look away (Keamy's man; Montand) it attacks them. Don Juan explains what death is like at one point, and it seems eerily similar to what Eko experiences at the end of "The Cost of Living" and his encounters with Smokey: "The first stage is a shallow blackout [think of Eko seeing Smokey in "The 23rd Psalm" and seeing his life against a blacked-out backdrop]. The second, however, is the real stage where one meets with death; it is a brief moment, after the first blackout, when we find that we are, somehow, ourselves again. It is then that death smashes against us with quiet fury and power until it dissolves our lives into nothing."

By the end of the book, when Castaneda is using the smoke, he is on the verge of seeing. At one point he is standing by a stream, and when he comes out of his hallucination don Juan says he saw him travel thousands of miles. It's unclear if don Juan means he physically moved — one would assume it's impossible, but later Castaneda sees don Genaro jump from his side to a mountaintop a couple of miles away in an instant. Still the descriptions of Castaneda's hallucinations are similar to those Desmond had when he was consciousness traveling in "The Constant." Don Juan's insistence on separate realities in the first book also plays in to season 5, where one group is in 2007, another in 1977 — two separate realities that seem to be coexisting. Don Juan's idea of one reality superimposed on another is similar to a motif in Philip K. Dick's *VALIS* (see *Finding Lost — Season 4*, pp. 50–55) where the protagonist, Horselover Fat, begins seeing one time period superimposed on another. *VALIS* is another book that Ben has read more than once.

Despite *A Separate Reality* being passed from Ben to Sayid, there is a much stronger link to Locke in what don Juan says. Don Juan tells Castaneda early in the book that "Knowledge is power, and once a man embarks on the road of knowledge he's no longer liable for what may happen to those who come in contact with him." Similarly, Locke's obsession with finding the meaning behind why they were all on the island has caused a lot of pain: he's clubbed Sayid in the head and prevented an early breakthrough in getting a radio signal working; Boone and Naomi are both dead; he thwarted Juliet's chance of leaving the island by blowing up the sub. . . . He's hurt a lot of people, even if he thinks what he's doing is ultimately going to lead to the greater good.

At one point in the book, Castaneda tells don Juan about a man who lived to his eighties and realized he'd wasted a large part of his life. Don Juan replies, "For him, his struggle was not worth his while, because he was defeated; for me there is no victory, or defeat, or emptiness. Everything is filled to the brim and everything is equal and my struggle was worth my while." Similarly, in "The Little Prince," Locke sees the moment where he hit his low point on the island, but chooses not to go over and enlighten his younger self, saying instead, "I needed that pain to get to where I am now."

Don Juan says throughout his teachings that a sorcerer must give up everything — family, friends, possessions — and that he must have a detachment from things. Castaneda constantly questions this idea (though in real life he later insisted on it in his own followers) and finally don Juan asks him, "What else can a man have, except his life and his death?" We have seen John Locke's birth, his life, and his death (and interestingly, don Juan's teachings are echoed in the episode title, "The Life and Death of Jeremy Bentham"). And when Locke goes to see Kate, she tells him that the reason he acts the way he does is because he has no ties. Don Juan would see that as a good thing. Near the end of the book don Juan says that a sorcerer encounters forces around him and doesn't question them, unlike normal men, but instead "he learns to use such forces by redirecting himself and adapting to their direction." Similarly, John Locke follows what the island tells him to do and adapts to each new situation thrown at him, never questioning why.

Locke's focus is on the journey, not necessarily the endgame, just as don Juan says a warrior's spirit "is not geared to indulging and complaining, nor is it geared to winning or losing. The spirit of the warrior is geared only to struggle, and every struggle is a warrior's last battle on earth." Don Juan says that "a warrior selects the items that make his world. He selects deliberately, for every item he chooses is a shield that protects him from the onslaughts of the forces he is striving to use." One can't help but recall Richard Alpert sitting in front of Young Locke as he asked him to choose the things that already belonged to him, as if these items would be the ones to "make his world."

There are echoes of Jack throughout the book, too, and not just in Castaneda's reluctance to open himself to don Juan's teachings. Just as Jack told Kate in "Pilot, Part 1" about forcing fear out, don Juan tells Castaneda, "There is nothing new about being afraid. Don't think about your fear." Later don Juan describes a man of knowledge, and says that he "lives by acting, not by thinking about acting, nor by thinking about what he will think when he has finished acting." In "Namaste," Sawyer accuses Jack of acting first without thinking, yet don Juan would say this man is in control of his life. Similarly, don Juan goes on to describe the Jack of season 5: "A man of knowledge may choose, on the other hand, to remain totally impassive and never act, and behave as if to be impassive really matters to him; he will be rightfully true at that too, because that would also be his controlled folly." One would argue, however, that Jack is not in control of his folly, and it's this that has sent him off the rails time and again. Near the end of the book, don Genaro puts his hand on Castaneda's shoulder, and Castaneda is brought to his knees by the immense weight. This harkens back to season 1's "All the Best Cowboys Have Daddy Issues," where Christian puts his hand on Jack's shoulder to convince him to sign the declaration that gets him off the hook, and that hand leaves such a metaphorical weight on Jack's shoulder that he admits to the board that his father had been drinking on the job.

The flip side of what don Juan is saying also, oddly, applies to Sawyer. As don Juan describes what a warrior does, he instructs Castaneda to "worry and think before you make any decision, but once you make it, be on your way free from worries or thoughts; there will be a million other decisions still awaiting you. That's the warrior's way." This sounds very much like what Sawyer tells Jack at the end of "Namaste," that he's thinking things through before recklessly acting. Don Juan says that a warrior doesn't care about the meaning of life and doesn't overthink things, and again that would be consistent with Sawyer. Jack assumes he isn't thinking things through properly, but Sawyer is only focusing on what he believes is important. He probably would have made a very good shaman.

In *A Separate Reality* there are references to parenting and other problems that point to some of the more general concerns of characters in seasons 1 and 2. During the first *mitote*, where Castaneda sees a vision of his mother, he is overcome by the realization that his mother's love was a "horrendous burden." When Castaneda later opens up to don Juan and tells him that his childhood was difficult, don Juan casually responds, "Everybody feels that way." Any *Lost* fan will probably get a chuckle out of that line, realizing that there isn't a character on the show who doesn't suffer from some sort of regret or sadness about their childhood. By season 5, many of the characters have reconciled themselves with the problems of their childhoods, either by accepting what happened to them or deciding to move beyond the hold their parents have over them (think of Sun finally standing up to Paik when she returns). Similarly, don Juan tells Castaneda about how a group of Mexicans killed his father, and how he'd vowed to destroy them. But after many years of living with this feeling of revenge, he changed, and doesn't want to destroy anyone. "I don't hate anyone," he says. "I have learned that the countless paths one traverses in one's life are all equal. Oppressors and oppressed meet at the end, and the only thing that prevails is that life was altogether too short for both." Despite Sawyer and Locke being the closest matches to don Juan's description of a warrior, however, both of them actually gave in to their revenge fantasies.

Many of don Juan's teachings relate to one of the characters mentioned above, but we have to remember that it's Ben who has read the book twice, and who hands it to Sayid. Ben seems like a charlatan, like someone who read the book to find out how one would *resemble* a sorcerer, without actually being one. That said, don Juan tells Castaneda at one point that a warrior must always take responsibility for his acts, and we will see later in this season that Ben will do exactly that. Don Juan later talks about how detachment is necessary in a warrior, saying, "The idea of imminent death, instead of becoming an obsession, becomes an indifference." While one wouldn't necessarily call Ben or Locke indifferent about their deaths, they both accept it as a necessity — Locke hesitates only for a few seconds when he realizes he will have to die to bring people back to the island. Ben walks headlong into several dangerous scenes as if he doesn't care what happens to him. And the two characters are definitely detached emotionally from others, as is Widmore. But Ben's isn't a complete detachment — his connection to Alex is what drives him to leave the island hoping to destroy Widmore. That rage seems genuine.

Ben could also be a fan of the book for the real-life story of Carlos Castaneda — that of a deceptive, charismatic cult leader who allegedly told lies for profit. If there's one person who would look up to someone for pulling off such a great hoax, it's Ben.

In one of the key moments in don Juan's description of a warrior, he says:

It is up to us as single individuals to oppose the forces of our lives. I have said this to you countless times: Only a warrior can survive. A warrior knows that he is waiting and what he is waiting for; and while he waits he wants nothing and thus whatever little thing he gets is more than he can take. If he needs to eat he finds a way, because he is not hungry; if something hurts his body he finds a way to stop it, because he is not in pain. To be hungry or to be in pain means that the man has abandoned himself and is no longer a warrior; and the forces of his hunger and pain will destroy him.

These words could describe any one of the people who have survived thus far on the show; they have survived because they refused to give up, because they refused to give in to pain or hunger or loss.

Some of don Juan's final words to Castaneda could have been written by the *Lost* writers to the fans: "Your problem is that you want to understand everything, and that is not possible. If you insist on understanding [then] you're not considering your entire lot as a human being. Your stumbling block is intact. Therefore, you have done almost nothing in all these years." In the first five seasons of the show, *Lost* fans have asked countless questions, and with every answer we get, we find five more questions. Perhaps this line is a subtle reminder to us that we need to step back and take in the whole show and be entertained. The answers will come in time, if we just let them.

5.11   Whatever Happened, Happened

Original air date: April 1, 2009
Written by: Carlton Cuse, Damon Lindelof
Directed by: Bobby Roth
Guest cast: Kim Dickens (Cassidy Phillips), Susan Duerden (Carole Littleton), Miko Franconi (Grocery Worker), Susan King (Sweet Young Woman), Scott Moura (Manager), Candace Scholz (Nurse Debra), Sebastian Siegel (Erik), Olivia Vickery (Clementine)

Focus: Kate

Kate, remembering why she left Aaron behind, takes a huge risk trying to save young Ben's life.

Entire books could be written (and no doubt *will* be written) on the parent issues most of the characters on *Lost* carry around with them. Jack, Charlie, Ben, Sayid, and Sun had fathers who were hard, abusive men who put a lot of pressure on them. Locke's father was a scumbag con artist who abandoned him, returning only because he needed a kidney, and his mother gave him up when he was an infant. Hurley's father was absent most of his life, and came back when he realized his son was worth millions. We don't know much about Sawyer's relationship with his parents, but his father went crazy when he found out Sawyer's mother was having an affair with another man, and he killed her and then himself. Jin is actually the one person who seemed to have had a kind, loving father, but Jin was ashamed of what his father did for a living, and told everyone the man was dead. His mother, on the other hand, is an opportunistic witch.

With issues like these, you'd think they'd be spending all their time in 1977 in a Dharma psychotherapy station. If there were such a thing.

But now the children are becoming parents, and it's giving them a new perspective on everything. In "Eggtown," Kate couldn't even pick Aaron up when he started crying, and said she's not good with babies. But once she's forced into a motherhood role, it takes only a couple of days before she's pretending that she's his real mother; she convinces herself of it. Every scene where Kate is alone with Aaron she seems to be a natural mother, playing with him in a relaxed manner, singing to him, joking around with him. Of all the parenting stories, we can't forget how complicated Kate's is, and it probably gives some insight into why she in turn became such a good mother. The man who Kate believed was her biological father, Sam, was in the army, and he loved her very much, but Kate's mother Diane left him and started a relationship with Wayne, a drunken loser who beat Diane and (it's insinuated) sexually molested Kate. In an effort to protect her mother, Kate burns down the house with Wayne inside, only to face an unforgiving mother who is more loyal to Wayne than to her abused daughter. Worse, Kate discovers that her loving father actually isn't her father at all — Wayne was. She killed her biological father, but to her that's not nearly as bad as the fact that a man with whom she shares DNA was capable of the things he did.

Kate of all people must realize what it would do to Aaron should he discover one day that she's not his real mother. But, just like Sam, Kate proves that you don't have to be a biological parent to love a child. The bond she has with Aaron is stronger than most parent-child bonds we've seen on the show, and it's one built on love, not genetics. So, before Aaron is old enough to be seriously traumatized by Kate leaving him, Kate embarks on the most painful break of her life — worse than leaving her family, worse than leaving her husband, worse than losing Sawyer: she leaves Aaron behind with his biological grandmother in an attempt to go back to find Aaron's real mother so everything can be put right.

Similarly, we've seen the terrible side of Roger Linus in "The Man Behind the Curtain," as he verbally and physically abuses Ben. In Ben he just sees the face of the woman he lost, and blames his son for her death. His life has been a shambles ever since he got to the island, his dignity was lost the moment he put on a janitor's outfit, and once again he blames everything on the burden of the son he's been forced to raise. We've seen Roger almost entirely from Ben's point of view, but in a single scene in this episode, we get Roger's side of the story. He never set out to be a bad parent, but his circumstances, his alcoholism, and his weakness to see past any of it has led him to the point where he is at now. He tells Kate that he's tried his best, but maybe a boy just needs his mother (once again making her think of Aaron). There's a small amount of sympathy conjured for Roger in this scene, but it hardly makes up for the fact that he beat the kid so badly the night before that he broke his glasses. What the scene does, however, is give Kate a glimmer of insight into why Ben is the way he is. She was abandoned by her mother; Ben grew up without one. The difference is, Kate is trying to get Aaron's mother back to him.

Before he leapt from a helicopter, Sawyer's final thoughts were of his daughter, Clementine. It wasn't clear in "Every Man for Himself" if Clementine really was his daughter, or if Cassidy was running a long con on Sawyer, but the fact that Kate confirms that she looks just like Sawyer would suggest Cassidy was telling the truth. Kate's meetings with Cassidy (whom she actually knew before the plane crash, as we saw in "Left Behind") give us Cassidy's take on what he did. She's feeling abandoned by him as a lover, but also feels like he left his daughter behind when he could have stepped up and done something. Sawyer, on the other hand, admits to Kate that he wasn't ready to be a father to Clementine, and one wonders if, like Roger, he might have felt burdened by a child who was keeping him in one place.

Sawyer similarly talks about parenting in the same breath as being in love with Kate, and tells her that, just as he was unfit to be a parent, he couldn't have been a boyfriend to Kate. This episode reminds us of the past relationships we've seen, and how different they are now. There's the Kate-and-Sawyer relationship. If you watch the episode one way and take what Cassidy sees as truth, you see that Kate held onto Aaron as some token of Sawyer, and by leaving Aaron behind she leaves the one thing that links her to him. She returns to the island and is devastated by his relationship with Juliet, so she convinces herself that she really came back to find Claire, and not Sawyer. Watch the episode another way and you could take Cassidy as just projecting her own anger onto Kate, who doesn't share these feelings. In this interpretation, Kate loved Sawyer, but she knew as well as he did that it wouldn't have worked out between them, and instead it was with Aaron that she found what love could really be all about. She returns to the island hoping to find Claire and expecting to maybe return to the flirtation with Sawyer that she'd had before, but when she realizes he's with Juliet she understands how awkward her presence must be to both Sawyer and Juliet, and doesn't know how to handle herself around either one of them.

Similarly, you could see Sawyer as telling the truth when he says he's saving young Ben for Juliet's sake, that he was unfit to be Kate's boyfriend, that he's matured a lot and is happy with Juliet. Or you could see those scenes as Sawyer trying to convince himself of those things, while in reality Kate's return has caused a rupture in his life, because he never really did get over her. He still feels loyalty and love for Juliet, which is making these feelings all the more painful. So he begins saying that he's doing everything for Juliet, hoping to convince himself and Kate that this is the truth, even if he's not sure what is true anymore.

Meanwhile, Juliet sees Kate as an obvious threat, but right now her foremost concern is saving Ben's life. There are still a lot of fans who don't like Juliet, and they thought her idea to send Ben over to the Others was just a way to get rid of Kate. But the fact that she also sends Sawyer immediately after Kate, telling him exactly what spot on the fence Kate's at, would suggest otherwise. Juliet is stuck, in love with Sawyer but watching him struggle with his feelings for both her and Kate.

We can't forget about Juliet and Jack, who were also a "thing" before Jack got onto a helicopter and flew away. Kate tells Juliet that they were engaged when they were off the island, and this comes as a bigger pang to Juliet than she'd expected. She's probably still struggling with her own feelings for Jack, which aren't quite what Sawyer's are for Kate, but they're still there. Juliet confronts Jack in the shower on purpose; she wouldn't have confronted anyone else in such an intimate way. Juliet's actions in this scene — confronting Jack while he's naked and vulnerable, yet *never looking down* — speak volumes. It's Juliet's subtle way of telling Jack she's no longer interested, and one can tell that the feeling is probably mutual.

Jack also seems to have muted his emotions for Kate, or so he says. She confronts him about his lack of action, confused that he doesn't want to try to fix a child that's suffering from a bullet wound. This inaction comes from the man who transfused his own blood into Boone; who assisted in torturing another man for asthma medication to save Shannon; who trekked across the island numerous times to get people rescued; who saved an adult Ben's life to help Kate and Sawyer escape; who managed to get a group of unwilling people back on a plane to return them to the place they'd spent 100 days trying to escape.

But as Miles explains the concept of time travel to Hurley (see page 169), Jack listens and decides that maybe in 1977 he just always sat back and made sandwiches; maybe things will turn out exactly the same as they always did. There's no reason to lose his mind trying to fix things if everything will just happen the way it was always meant to happen. It's hard to watch this scene and stop yourself from yelling, "Maybe saving Ben *is* the reason you came back!" But if Miles is correct, then Jack can't change events, and whatever he does is the thing he always did. Jack has completely given in to the idea of destiny over free will in this scene, and has decided to wait for the island to give him a sign. As infuriating as Kate and Jack found Locke on the first go-round, Jack's acting exactly like him. When Kate angrily tells him she liked the old Jack better, the one who tried to fix everything, he looks right at her and says, "You didn't *like* the old me, Kate." Ouch. As useless as he seems to be in this scene, he's sort of got her on that one.

So . . . Kate takes matters into her own hands. As a new mother, she cannot sit by and watch this child just die. Cassidy reminds Kate that she took Aaron from his real mother, and now Kate takes Ben from his real father. Just as she has proven that as an adoptive mother she has taken better care of her child than her parents ever did of her, she now delivers Ben to *his* new adoptive family. Which, if Miles is right, has set in motion the conditions that will make Ben the person he must eventually become.

Highlight: This episode had its funny moments — mostly involving Miles or Hurley — but the highlight of the episode is no doubt when Kate says goodbye to Aaron. That scene would break any parent's heart.

Did You Notice?:

- At the end of "There's No Place Like Home, Part 3," Kate rushes into Aaron's room and hugs him, apologizing to him over and over, right after having had the nightmare of Claire being in his room. Now we see she was probably apologizing to him for having taken him away from his mother.
- There didn't appear to be a noticeable exit wound on Ben's back. Maybe it went through his side and that's why there's no blood.
- Kate's got her Patsy playing again. An interesting choice, since Kate's got Sawyer's picture in her mind, but Juliet's got him. (Not that Kate knows that yet . . .)
- Kate sings "Catch a Falling Star" to Aaron, which is the song that Christian always sang to Claire when she was a baby.
- We've now seen Clementine, Ji Yeon, Aaron, and Charlie, all children roughly the same age. Maybe when *Lost* is over we'll get a sequel called *Losties: The Next Generation.*
- When Kate first mentions Sawyer, Cassidy calls him a "son of a bitch," which is one of his favorite expressions.
- Josh Holloway sounds like he's battling a terrible cold.
- If the fans are right in estimating that Sawyer was put in prison some time in 2001, and that Clementine was born in early 2002, then that would make her between two-and-a-half and three years old when Kate comes to visit her (which seems a little old for her to still be in a crib, but some toddlers stay in them longer than others).

- After Sawyer and Miles take off with the janitor's keys, leaving Horace and Phil behind in the cell room, Phil has a look on his face like something isn't right.
- For all his snark, Miles seems to fall into the role of being Sawyer's underling pretty easily, and takes orders from him without ever talking back.
- Juliet says the doctor is at the Looking Glass station. That's the underwater station where Charlie died in "Through the Looking Glass."
- In "Namaste," Hurley tells Sawyer that he could warn everyone of the Purge and save their lives, and Sawyer says he's not here to play Nostradamus. Clearly he's been talking to Miles (and took Daniel's original explanation to heart) and he's been won over by the "whatever happened, happened" camp.
- Hurley thinks he's won the argument when he reminds Miles that Ben had no recollection of Sayid ever coming to him, but there's a chance Ben *did* remember what happened to him, and knew exactly who Sayid was when he walked into the armory in season 2, or whatever Richard Alpert is about to do to him is going to wipe those memories from his mind. In either case, Miles wins.
- Where Sawyer avoided calling Kate "Freckles" when he first saw her, he uses the nickname here, as if he's more comfortable now that Kate knows about him and Juliet, and he doesn't think it'll be taken the wrong way.
- When Kate goes up to the stockboy to ask where the juice boxes are, he looks directly at her, and never looks down at Aaron. Then when she goes back to him to ask if he saw her son, he looks at her in complete confusion and as she runs away, he looks behind him as if to say to someone that she was nuts. It was almost like Aaron was invisible in that scene and the guy didn't even see him there.
- When the Others come out of the woods, one of them is a young woman in brown with long dreadlocked hair who comes at them as the guy says, "Do not move." She looks a lot like Bea Klugh, the Other who questioned Michael in "Three Minutes" and who was killed at the Flame station by Mikhail.
- When Richard takes Ben, someone steps up and says they need to ask Ellie, and insinuates "Charles" will be angry if he finds out. They're probably referring to Ellie (the young girl we saw in "Jughead" who is possibly Eloise Hawking) and Charles Widmore.

Interesting Facts: Evangeline Lilly said in an interview that before each new season of *Lost*, she goes back and rewatches the previous seasons so she can reacquaint herself with Kate and be sure to play her consistently.

Nitpicks: Just before Sawyer jumped from the helicopter, fans turned up the audio on their televisions and heard him say to Kate, "I have a daughter in Albuquerque. You need to find her. Tell her I'm sorry." In "Every Man for Himself," Cassidy says that she and Clementine live in Albuquerque. First, Cassidy never would have given Clementine Sawyer's last name, so how did Kate find her? Secondly, in "Eggtown," Kate signed an agreement saying she would not leave the state of California for 10 years as part of her probation, which allowed her to stay with Aaron. There's no one patrolling state lines and Kate's probably using cash to buy things, but if she used a credit card in New Mexico, she would have been caught pretty easily. And thirdly, Albuquerque is about 11 hours away from Los Angeles. Clementine seems to know her instantly, like they visit with Cassidy all the time; if so, that's a long hike for playdates. And in the context of the episode, if Kate left everyone at the marina and went to a supermarket with Aaron, she would have had to drive all night to get to Albuquerque, arriving mid-morning. Then if she stayed a few hours with Cassidy and left early afternoon, she would have gotten back to Mrs. Littleton's hotel around midnight. That seems to be a really long trip to take with such a small child. Did Cassidy move after Sawyer last saw her? If so, how would Kate have tracked her down?

And finally, while I realize it's much easier for Kate to leave Aaron when he's asleep, talk about childhood trauma — could you imagine this three-year-old boy waking up the next morning to find his mother gone and a complete stranger with a strange accent sitting over him? This child will no doubt be dealing with abandonment issues when he gets older.

Oops: In the previous episode, Ben was shot on the left side of his chest. But in this episode, the wound is mysteriously on the right side.

4 8 15 16 23 42: Kate loses Aaron while standing at the end of aisle 4.

Any Questions?:

- Where did Sayid go?
- The castaways spent three months combing nearly every square inch of that island when they first crashed. Why did they only ever find one vw van if, as it appears, the DI camp had at least a dozen of them?
- In "Every Man for Himself," Sawyer snitches on a fellow prison inmate

and is given a large monetary settlement. He asks that it be placed in a bank account for Clementine. In this episode, Cassidy is entirely dismissive of Sawyer as if he's had absolutely nothing to do with her child. Does she not know about the money? Was it a trust fund that no one told her about?

- In "LaFleur," when Amy went into labor, there was an intern holding down the fort at the hospital, and in this episode, the doctor has gone to the Looking Glass station. Wouldn't it be more important to stay in Dharmaville and bring the wounded to him? Or is it too difficult to transport people out of the station and into Dharmaville? Considering they only seem to have one doctor (who is *never* available), taking the doc through Hostile territory doesn't seem like the smartest idea these people have ever had. They have three janitors, yet only one doctor?

- In season 4's "The Other Woman," Juliet tells Harper, the Others' therapist, that Ben's been really good to her. Harper says, "Of course he has. You look just like her," but she doesn't expand on that. Fans assumed that Harper was referring to Ben's mother, who he would only know from photographs, and that could be the case. But seeing Juliet stroke Ben's hair tenderly and hovering over him in this episode, is it possible that Ben kept some sort of photo of Juliet, remembering how kind and motherly she was to him, and then tracked down her younger self in 2001 and brought her right back to the island for himself? Is it possible that by "her," Harper was actually referring to Dharmaville Juliet?

- What are Juliet's motivations when she suggests the Others might be able to help Ben? Does she sincerely believe they have the capabilities to help him? Or does she have one of many possible ulterior motives, like trying to get rid of Kate? Is there any chance that Juliet is still on the side of the Others? She's always known much more than she's ever divulged, and now she's turning Ben over to them.

- How fast does Aaron move? Kids move fast — I think every parent knows that from experience — but Kate's in the middle of the store and that Claire lookalike said she found him in the fruit section, which is always on the outer edge of the store. How did he get all the way over to the fruit section without Kate seeing him?

- Why doesn't Kate tell Sawyer that she actually knew Cassidy before the island?

- Claire's mom says to Kate, "Why didn't you come to me in the first place?" and Kate answers that she needed Aaron. But wouldn't the obvious answer be, "Because Claire told us all you were dead"?! When Claire had left her mother, she was in a coma, and Claire assumed she would never wake up from it. In "Par Avion," Claire tells Sun on the beach that her mother was dead, and Sun probably passed that on to Kate. So why would Kate have been looking for Claire's mom if she assumed Claire was an orphan? She meets Mrs. Littleton for the first time at Christian's funeral, and Aaron is nine months old at that point, so she's already very attached to him and it wouldn't have been easy for her to hand him over.
- Why would Kate tell Mrs. Littleton that Claire was alive, when even she's not sure that's true? Why not say she was alive when Kate was there, but Kate doesn't know if she still is?
- When Kate goes to Mrs. Middleton's hotel room, she leaves Aaron alone in another room, unattended. Considering what she's been through in the hours leading up to this moment, why would she leave him alone like that?
- What did Richard mean when he says Ben won't be the same? That he'll lose his innocence? What will he forget? He clearly remembers his father, because we see in "The Man Behind the Curtain" that he'll still be living in Dharmaville when the Purge happens and knows what his father did to him as a child. Will he forget that Sayid shot him? Will he just forget Kate and Sawyer bringing him out there? Will they wipe his memory of everything and then rebuild it for him? Or will he only forget certain things?
- Any chance Rose and Bernard are in the Temple? Where did they go?
- Richard takes Ben to the same spot where Rousseau lost her crew (now we see why we flashed back to that). Does the spot have the same effect on Ben as it did on them, or has it changed? Everyone who followed Montand into the declivity in the wall came back out as crazy zombie versions of themselves. But Richard's not taking him down into the declivity, where it appeared the smoke monster resides later in 1988, he's opening the door of the wall to take him, presumably, to the Temple inside. Will that have a different effect on Ben?
- In "Cabin Fever," Ben says to John, "I used to have dreams." Did they stop when he was taken to the Temple?

- Does Smokey actually exist in 1977? They don't seem to have had any run-ins with him in the time they've been in Dharmaville.
- What did John Locke mean by "Welcome back to the land of the living"?

Music/Bands: Kate is listening to Patsy Cline's "She's Got You," which she was also listening to in "Eggtown" while sitting on the porch in New Otherton.

Miles and Hurley: The Great Time-Travel Debate

The Kate/Sawyer/Juliet/Jack quadrangle made things confusing in this episode, but one coupling made all the fans happy: Miles and Hurley. No, not like *that*. (What would their "ship" be called? Hiles? Murley?) The geek argument that breaks out between the two of them mirrored the one the fans had been having from the beginning of the season.

Hurley has been raised on comic books, movies, television, and sci-fi/fantasy novels that present scenarios where characters go back in time and alter something so the present becomes a completely different place. He references *Back to the Future*, a movie in which Marty McFly, whose parents' marriage is falling apart, goes back in time to when his parents first met, and when things go badly (and Marty's mother begins to have a crush on . . . him) his hand begins disappearing. If he actually screws things up and his parents don't even get together in the first place, then in the future he won't exist.

Hurley has a difficult time getting his head around what Miles is trying to tell him, because in popular culture, mainly in film, when a character goes back in time they *can* alter the future. This idea causes tension in the story, because the viewer can't wait to go "back to the future" to see how life might have changed because of something the character did in the past. His idea of going back in time is the more popular one as a result. The Dharma station construction worker at the beginning of the season talked about going back in time and killing Hitler. In "The Little Prince" Sawyer wonders why Locke doesn't interrupt himself banging on the hatch on day 41 and just tell himself how things will work out. There are several examples of popular movies that have used this trope besides *Back to the Future*. In *Superman*, for example, the man of steel turns back time by literally making the Earth spin backward on its axis, and saves Lois Lane from being killed during an earthquake. In *Peggy Sue Got Married*, Peggy Sue faints at her high school reunion and goes back in time to high school, where she does some things differently, including having an affair with a classmate. When she travels back to the future, that classmate has written a book and dedicated it to her.

But on *Lost*, things are different. This show is taking the road less time traveled. The scene between Hurley and Miles baffled those fans who still saw time travel in a *Back to the Future* way while other fans, who'd been lighting up the forums trying to get the point through to the dolts among us were saying, "A-*ha!* See? *That* is what I've been saying all along!" In case you were still scratching your heads, here's an elaboration of Miles's argument.

According to Miles (who is repeating the words of Daniel), whatever happened, happened. Whatever the Losties do now, they always did. They always traveled to 1977, they just didn't remember it because it hadn't yet happened to them. He's describing the difference between objective and subjective time. Objective time is the linear time in which the world moves in general: 1977 is followed by 1978, and 2004 happens 27 years after 1977. If you're 30 in 2004, then you'll be 31 in 2005, 32 in 2006, etc. But subjective time is what the time travelers of *Lost* are experiencing in their own aging and in their memories. In other words, 2004 is a time that is in their past, and 1977 is in the present, because they are currently experiencing the things happening on the island. So if Miles were 30 in 2004, then he's 31 in 1974, 32 in 1975, 33 in 1976, etc. He doesn't go back in time and become a toddler, he continues to age just like he always would. His aging hasn't been halted until he catches up to his self in 2004 — he's still aging in a normal biological way, even if the broken Frozen Donkey Wheel caused objective time to no longer move in a linear fashion. He could technically die in 1979 as 30-year-old Miles, but 27-year-old Miles will still get on that freighter because we already know that he did that three years ago, when he was 27.

Sawyer is three years older than he was when the helicopter took off, just as Kate is three years older. For her, the last three years have been 2005–2007, but for him they've been 2005 (followed by 15 time jumps), 1974–1977. He's still lived his life for three years, just as she has, he's still three years older, but he's just experienced subjective time in a different order. He could have been killed in 1976, but the younger Sawyer would always get on that plane because he already did, and Sawyer remembers doing it. Ben's life doesn't appear to be

Hurley tries to figure out a way to go back in time and beat Miles at this game the second time around. Miles contemplates shooting Hurley. (© MARIO PEREZ/ABC/RETNA LTD.)

circular yet, because he's still in the past. Therefore, that theory of Sayid always shooting Ben and actually causing the monster to appear is a valid one, because Sayid always shot Ben in 1977, and Kate and Sawyer always took Ben to the Others. As one of my readers explained, if you were walking along a street, dropping bread crumbs, and you passed the addresses 2004, 2006, 2008 and then saw an alley, walked down it, and it somehow popped you back 30 addresses, as you came up the street past 1976, 1978, 1980, you'd start to see your bread crumbs on the street again because you had already dropped those in the past, even though you'd gone back a few addresses. Daniel uses a similar analogy in "Because You Left" when he says, "Time is like a street; we can move forward, or back, but we can't create a new street. Whatever happened, happened."

Just as there are several pop culture references that support Hurley's idea of going back in time to change history, there are time-travel stories that feature Miles's way of thinking. In the cult romance classic *Somewhere in Time*, an elderly woman approaches a young man in 1980, handing him a pocket watch and telling him to come back to her. He goes back in time to 1912, where he falls in love with the young version of the elderly woman and gives her the pocket watch that she will give to him (this is like Richard Alpert giving Locke the compass that he will in turn hand back to Richard Alpert). When he accidentally pulls out a coin from 1979, he is snatched out of the time period and zapped back to 1980, where he dies of depression from being separated from her. When he travels back in time, it is his present, but it's the elderly woman's past, just as Miles describes the difference between Hurley's present and Ben's past. But he didn't change history, he was simply going back to 1912, the way he'd always done, since as an elderly woman she always remembered him being there.

In *The Terminator*, Ah-nold travels from 2029 to kill Sarah Connor before she can give birth to John Connor, the man who will eventually save mankind. The premise of the film is that by going back in time, the cyborg can change history. But instead, the cyborg fails, suggesting that whatever happened, happened, and nothing it can do can change that.

Daniel has found one person who stands as an exception to this rule, however, and that's Desmond. He warns him of something in 2001, and Desmond only has a memory of that having suddenly happened in the past in 2007/8. That memory wasn't with him from that moment onward; it only popped into his head when Daniel said it in 2001, because Desmond and Daniel's subjective times are linked in some way that hasn't been fully explained. Perhaps Desmond's subjective time is not completely subjective, and is somehow outside of him, so that other people can manipulate him in other eras, and it actually does affect him in the present. Desmond went back to Hawking in 1996 in "Flashes Before Your Eyes," but he only remembered having that conversation in 2004. He talks to Daniel at Oxford in 1996, and again only remembers that in 2004. These are not conversations that changed his timeline objectively, because he's altering things and playing with time in a way no one else is allowed to do.

Is Miles correct? Did Sayid always go back in time and shoot Ben, and Ben really did know who Sayid was when he first walked into the armory? Or did Hurley really pwn Miles the way he thinks he did? Can the Oceanic 6 change the future by their actions in 1977?

5.12   Dead Is Dead

....

Original air date: April 8, 2009
Written by: Brian K. Vaughan, Elizabeth Sarnoff
Directed by: Stephen Williams
Guest cast: Melissa Farman (Danielle Rousseau), David S. Lee (Widmore, Age 40), Tania Raymonde (Alex), Marvin DeFreitas (Young Charlie), Devon Gearhart (Young Ethan), Matt Hoffman (Jed), Lehualani Silva (Young Alex)

Focus: Ben

Ben and Locke make their way to the main island so Ben can be judged by Old Smokey for the things he's done.

"There's a war coming, John, and if you're not back on the island when that happens, the wrong side is going to win." With these ominous words in "The Life and Death of Jeremy Bentham," Widmore convinced Locke to work with him so he could help him find everyone who had left the island and try to convince them to go back. It's been fun watching the romantic entanglements of the Juliet/Sawyer/Kate triangle, or watching Miles and Hurley verbally duke it out over the basic concepts of time travel, but when you have any combination of Locke, Widmore, or Ben on the screen, the scenes become positively electric.

When we first saw Widmore, he seemed nothing more than a nasty bully of a potential father-in-law for Desmond, a barrier that stood in the way of Desmond and Penny's love, a man who likely tricked Desmond onto a boat where he ended up shipwrecked on an island. But since then he's become so much more. While we've seen Widmore's life out of chronological order, the writers have brilliantly unveiled this man to us in a way that makes him as enigmatic as Ben. Chronologically, our earliest glimpse of him was on the island as a young man in 1954. He seemed cocky yet unsure of himself, and he already had a brutal side, snapping his colleague's neck the moment he thought the man was saying too much to Locke's crew. According to him he stayed on the island for over 30 years and became the leader of the Others. When Ben entered the camp as someone Alpert claimed the island had chosen, Widmore kept Ben under his thumb and began testing him. Eventually Ben usurped him as leader, and Widmore left the island, vowing to return.

It's unclear how Widmore became the leader of the Others, but he's gone from a jittery 17-year-old when he first meets John Locke, to a menacing 40-year-old

Ben Linus listens to his Very Evil iPod. (Tracks include "Bad to the Bone," "Enter Sandman," and "Sunshine, Lollipops & Rainbows.") (MICHAEL ROBLES)

when he first meets Ben, to a manipulative 50-year-old when he sends Ben on the Rousseau mission, to an angry and vengeful 60-year-old when he's banished from the island, to a confident and sinister 70-year-old trying to find his way back. At each stage, we can tell from his reactions that while others think of the island as a deity, he's just playing along. Richard says to Widmore, "The island chooses who the island chooses, you know that," and Widmore, full of bluster a moment earlier, quickly calms down and acts like he knows exactly what Alpert means, even though it's clear to us that Widmore is hiding something. Perhaps he became the leader of the Others through trickery, telling everyone about an encounter he had with Jacob, when he was completely lying. When Ben is holding the baby and challenges Widmore about what the island really wants, Widmore stands up, speechless and furious, and storms off to a tent. Widmore doesn't seem to understand the spirituality of the island, he just wants the place for himself. Richard, sitting nearby, looks very interested in what just happened. Maybe Ben is the first person to question what Widmore really knows about the island. Widmore comes off as a charlatan, but now that there's someone else there who's picked up on it, he needs to humiliate him and prove that Ben is as much of an interloper as he is.

Ben is instrumental in the Purge, becoming the de facto leader of the Others and usurping Widmore, but Widmore won't disappear. He immediately begins trying to find his way back (presumably the island moved after he was banished). He goes to great lengths, showing how ruthless he can be in his attempts to find the island; he was probably the one who orchestrated Desmond's sailing trip and the Oceanic 815 flight; he then created an elaborate hoax, sinking another plane to make people stop looking for the first one, for fear someone else would find the island; and he sent a freighter full of people to the island once he'd found it, with instructions to kill Ben Linus and everyone else, if needed. When that failed he moved in on John Locke, hoping to find a way back to the island through its new Chosen One. Widmore is capable of just about anything when something stands between him and his precious island.

Ben, on the other hand, stays. Ben believes in the spirituality of the island, but at times he seems as insincere about his commitment to it as Widmore did. As a boy, Ben undergoes a transformation when Richard takes him to the Temple (though it's not yet clear what the exact nature of the transformation is). The island saves him, and in return he vows his allegiance to it. He doesn't want to own the island the way Widmore does; what he wants is acceptance. If he could earn the island's acceptance by giving it his loyalty, he could finally get the acknowledgment he never got from his own father, who wished Ben had never been born. Alpert believes the island has chosen Ben when Sawyer and Kate deliver Ben to him, but Alpert could be wrong. The island heals Ben, but then makes him ill again with spinal cancer. After his operation, Ben doesn't heal as quickly as he should, and Richard begins to question if Ben really is the one Jacob always wanted to lead them.

Just as Richard begins to question Widmore's leadership status when Widmore lectures Ben about not killing Rousseau and the baby, Richard begins wondering about Ben after the cancer scare, looking instead in John Locke's direction. In "The Brig," Richard hands Locke Sawyer's file, helping him kill his father, which Ben says will make him leader. Like Ben and Widmore before him, then, Locke puts one over on the camp by making them all believe he has fulfilled the task before him. However, Ben sees through the ruse, and just as Widmore tested Ben, now Ben tests Locke: he takes him to Jacob's cabin. And then can't believe his ears when Locke admits that he actually heard Jacob talk.

Ben's relationship with Alex shows us something new in him. Widmore's ruthlessness is incredible. He refers to the baby as an "it," and says Ben should have killed both of them. Ben works differently. He cannot kill the baby, and he truly loves Alex as she gets older. He's not perfect, however; he never seems to feel any remorse for the fact he'd taken Alex from her own mother, convincing himself instead that Rousseau was insane and unfit to care for a child. But he does warn Rousseau about the whispers in the jungle, and he doesn't kill her. Alex's death truly shatters him, and while his first thoughts turn to revenge (he immediately sics the smoke monster on Keamy's men), he sits by her body and we see Ben in a genuine light we've never seen before. He attempts to get revenge on Widmore by killing Penny, but his retribution isn't an easy one for him — he introduces himself to her, he apologizes, he explains that this is all part of a war, and it's nothing personal against her. And then when he sees her child emerge, in much the same way he realized Rousseau had a baby, he begins to lower the gun. Perhaps he would have walked away (or maybe he would have taken Charlie the same way he took Alex). If, that is, Desmond hadn't suddenly appeared and beaten the snot out of him.

One could see Ben as a cold-blooded murderer who wanted John dead, and his shock when he sees John sitting next to him seems like proof. He later tells Sun that he had no idea that Locke would come back to life, and if he's telling her the truth, then he really is the bad guy. However, think back to the scene in "316" when Ben talks to Jack about Thomas the Apostle and how he was remembered for doubting the resurrection, and not for his bravery. At the time, the story seemed to apply to Jack, but in retrospect, it just as easily applies to Ben. Locke doesn't remember Ben as the man who was brave enough to do what needed to be done so that Locke could come back to life; he remembers him only as the man who killed him in the first place. But Ben's words in "Dead Is Dead" are more than just bluster. He says, "It's one thing to believe it, John, it's another thing to see it." There are millions of people who believe in a higher power, but if God or Christ appeared to them in their living room, many would probably think they'd gone insane. Faith, as we saw throughout season 2, is the opposite of science. In science, you believe something when you see it. In faith, you believe it without seeing it, and when you see it, you might actually question it. If Ben really believed he was doing the right thing, it's more difficult to categorize him as either good or evil. When he tells Sun that he didn't think Locke would come back to life, he does so in the same tone of voice as when he's talking to Caesar, and we all know he was lying in that scene.

In "The Shape of Things to Come," Widmore refused to accept the blame for "that poor girl's death," and turned things on Ben, saying he was the one responsible. He calls Ben "boy" and says, "I know who you are, boy. What you are." He insinuates that Ben is a thing, not a person (the same way he refers to Alex as "it"). Now Ben agrees that he was the one who killed Alex, because if he'd just come out of the house and left the island, she would still be alive. By calling Ben a "what," perhaps Widmore is referring to Ben's resurrection in the Temple. He knows that Ben isn't the Chosen One, but is an imposter, just like he was.

And now John Locke has come back from the dead. Many of the best scenes of the season are in this episode, where Locke is talking to Ben. Locke has emerged a new and very different man. He's confident, he smiles, he's assured. He used to ask questions; now he has the answers. He seems more knowing about everything around him. Few things surprise him, and when they do, he reacts with a smile, rather than a horrified look of shock. In only one scene does he look a little unnerved: when Ben asks a series of sarcastic questions and Locke stops and tells him how difficult it is never knowing the answers, adding, "Now you know what it was like to be me." Interestingly, he uses the past tense, as if his resurrection changed him fundamentally. He's been reincarnated as a new man. The fact that he tells Sun that he's the same man he's always been only reinforces this notion; you don't have to tell someone you're the same person if you really are.

Locke correctly surmises that Ben isn't looking to be judged for breaking the rules, but for killing his daughter. As Locke and Ben walk into New Otherton (formerly Dharmaville), Locke wonders if it was actually Ben's wish to move into the houses, not the island's wish. Just as Ben had questioned Widmore about Alex, wondering if her death was something the island wanted or if it was simply Widmore's wish, now Locke is seeing through Ben's guise. He guesses correctly the real reason Ben's going to be judged, so perhaps he's correct in his other assumptions. Ben is his usual enigmatic self, assuring Locke earlier that he killed him because he knew he'd come back to life, while telling Sun the exact opposite, that he had no idea he would resurrect.

Facing Smokey, however, is the one time when Ben can't put up a guard and can't lie, because the smoke monster will see to the heart of what he truly believes. The scene of judgment is one of the most awesome of the series. Finally we see how Smokey is summoned (though it's a little bit anticlimactic: Ben unplugs an ancient toilet? Really?), we see where Smokey "lives," we see how he comes out, and we now understand that he's not a security system, but the island's form of judgment. Only those who can feel regret for their actions are spared. In "The 23rd Psalm," Eko faces Smokey, who similarly flashes moments of Eko's life in his face. Eko stares back at those moments unbendingly, but deep down he regretted the death of Yemi. After spending time on the island, however, Eko came to terms with what had happened, and realized it wasn't his fault. In "The Cost of Living," Eko was visited by a vision of Yemi, no doubt created by the smoke monster, and when asked to confess, he refuses, saying, "I did not ask for the life I was given, but it was given nonetheless. And with it, I did my best." His lack of remorse brings forth the smoke monster, which shows him no mercy. Now, Ben is shown all of the moments of his life, and while he, too, could argue that he'd been given a bad life, and with it he did the best he could manage, he doesn't. Instead he looks at moments in Alex's life and admits he was at fault. Widmore might not have been a true Chosen One, but he was right when he said that Ben killed Alex. Ben stops blaming Widmore for Alex's death, and accepts his own culpability in it. And with that, the smoke monster grants him a reprieve.

But is Ben through being judged? Or will the new and improved John Locke, who has arisen, and, according to Ben, "scares the living hell out of me," be the one to truly put Ben to the test?

Highlight: Ben warning Sun that "what's about to come out of that jungle is something I can't control," and then Locke emerges. Ha!

Did You Notice?:

- David S. Lee, the actor playing Widmore at 40, looks remarkably like Alan Dale, who plays him in the present.
- We've had a progression of these men visiting each other, and oddly enough, one of them has always been in bed. Widmore first visited young Ben when Ben was recovering in a bed; Ben visited Widmore in "Shape of Things to Come" when Widmore was in bed; Widmore visited Locke in the Tunisian hospital while Locke was in a bed; now Locke visits Ben in an infirmary when Ben's in the bed.
- Locke looks very amused when Ben says he needs to be judged. You can tell he's jumping for joy on the inside.
- The scene where Ben manipulates Caesar is beautiful — this is the first time we've seen Ben pull off an elaborate con where we *know* he's lying. He convinces Caesar that Locke is evil, which forces Caesar to not only reveal that he's carrying the gun that Ben will steal, but to push Caesar to fight with John Locke, "forcing" Ben to kill him.
- Richard Alpert watches the sparring between Widmore and Ben the way a spectator would watch a tennis match.
- Ben's statement that "friends can be significantly more dangerous than enemies" certainly rings true on this show. Though it's not clear that he and Widmore were ever friends.

- When Ben first enters his house, you can see the Risk game sitting on the table. Sawyer, Hurley, and Locke had been playing the game just before all hell broke loose and Smokey had charged into the camp, which is why everything is thrown about inside the house. However, the fact that a cupboard door has been pulled from its hinges, yet tiny pieces of the game are still on the board seems a little inconsistent.
- When Sun, Lapidus, Ben, and Locke are talking in Ben's front room, you can see on the bookshelf copies of *Flowers for Algernon* by Daniel Keyes, *Roots* by Alex Haley, and *Uncle Tom's Cabin* by Harriet Beecher Stowe.
- When Ben is pushing Alex on the swing, Alpert says if he pushes her any higher she'll fly right off the island. Ben looks unsettled when he says that, as if one of his biggest fears is how to keep Alex on the island when she gets older.
- On the dock, Widmore hisses at Ben, "I'll be seeing you, *boy*," which is how he referred to him in "The Shape of Things to Come." Also, "Be seeing you" was the way people would say goodbye on the 1960s short-lived television show *The Prisoner*, which was a big influence on *Lost* (see *Finding Lost — Season 3*, pages 81–85).
- As Ben is talking to Widmore and approaching Penny's boat, he walks by another boat called *Savage*. After the scene cuts to Widmore and back again, Ben walks by another boat called *Stella Mare*, which means "sea star" in Italian. But it could also be a reference to Stella Maris, which is a term used to refer to the Virgin Mary, or the Star of the Sea. In *Ulysses* (see page 79), the chapter "Nausicaa" takes place outside the Star of the Sea church.
- The name of Penny and Desmond's boat is *Our Mutual Friend*, which is the Dickens book that Desmond was saving to read until he knew he was about to die in "Live Together, Die Alone." When he opens the book, a letter falls out from Penny telling him how much she believes in him and loves him, and it gives him the will to turn the failsafe key.
- Locke says he was always frustrated asking so many questions and blindly following someone, hoping they might lead him to the answers. It's like he was describing the fans of *Lost*. '
- The drawing on the wall above Smokey's abode is of the Egyptian god Anubis and Smokey (see page 258).
- The writers have always related Ben to the movie *The Wizard of Oz* (see

Finding Lost — Season 3, pages 171–175). He says his name is Henry Gale (the name of Dorothy's uncle). The episode of his first flashback is "The Man Behind the Curtain." And in this episode, as the smoke monster swirls around him, it's like Dorothy being caught up in the cyclone and looking out of her window to see the images of people and things flying by.

- Just like Yemi turned on Eko, Alex turns on Ben. Smokey might have let Ben live, but now Ben will live with the pain of knowing he killed Alex.

Interesting Facts: When Ben is being judged, one of the scenes shown to him is Alex telling him that she hates his guts. This is a deleted scene from "I Do," where she asks him where Karl is and he assures her that Karl isn't dead, but is locked up somewhere where he will do what he is told to do. When she says she wishes he was dead, he tells her about his tumor. You can see it on the season 3 DVDs.

Nitpicks: There's a lot of inconsistency when it comes to exactly when Widmore left the island and when the Purge happened. In "Cabin Fever," Locke has a dream where he meets Horace in the jungle, and Horace says he's been dead for 12 years. That would place the Purge in 1992. In this episode we see that Widmore was ejected from the island after the Purge (the Others are living in Dharmaville), and Alex looks like she's about six or seven, so that would put the Purge in the mid-'90s. In "The Life and Death of Jeremy Bentham" Widmore said he'd been searching for the island for the past 20 years, which means he would have left the island in the mid-'80s. *But* when Ben takes Alex from Rousseau, it's 1988 and the Others are clearly still living in the jungle (and Widmore is obviously still there), so the Purge hasn't yet happened. When exactly did the Purge occur? Is there a continuity error in what Horace said, or what Widmore said? Has he actually been looking for the island for 10 years, not 20? Should the Horace scene be discounted because it was part of John Locke's dream and not reality?

I love Michael Emerson, I really do, but I do not buy him as a man in his 20s. The wig doesn't succeed in making him look younger, it just makes him look like Pee-Wee Herman. (The wig he's wearing when Widmore is banished is similarly awful.) But perhaps the casting department simply couldn't find a younger version of Ben who could match Emerson's performance. Also, if Ethan was born in 1977, then he's 11 in the scene where Ben is taking Alex, and that kid playing him is much older than 11. Also, in "Solitary," Rousseau said she'd never seen another person on the island . . . though that could be chalked up to her state of mind.

4 8 15 16 23 42: Ilana's metal crate has the number **823** on it.

It's Just a Flesh Wound: Desmond beats Ben senseless on the docks. Ilana hits Frank in the head with the butt of her gun.

Any Questions?:

- If Ben really did believe that he needed to kill Locke to bring him back to the island and back to life, where did Ben get that idea? Who told him he had to do this? Was it Jacob?

- In the credits, the writers put the word "Young" in front of any character who is a child version of one of the adults, like "Young Ben" or "Young Sayid." Aaron, on the other hand, who appears only as a child, is simply listed as "Aaron." Yet Marvin DeFreitas, who plays Desmond and Penny's son, is credited as "Young Charlie." Could this be a hint that Charlie Pace is Desmond's son?

- Before Ben and Locke get into the boat, Locke carefully removes Christian's shoes and puts them into a bag, and then at the Dharma dock, he sits down, puts his socks back on, and puts the shoes back on. Is there something more to this than just not wanting to get the shoes wet? Does he need to hold onto this link that Jack was forced to establish for the flight? If he loses the shoes or something happens to them, does anything happen to him?

- If it was daylight on the dock, why is it nighttime in New Otherton, especially if the place is only a short walk from the dock?

- Now that Locke is undead, does he know more than he's letting on? He says to Ben, "Hm, that's your house, isn't it?" and when Ben explains it's Alex's room, he says, "Well, I suppose you should get over there and check it out" in a matter-of-fact way, as if he knows Sun will be there.

- Ben acts like he didn't know the survivors were in the DI, even though he met them there. Is he lying or are those the memories that Richard erased?

- Did Ben ever meet Christian? There's a look of familiarity in his eyes when Sun mentions him.

- How did Ben originally find the room in the house from which he could summon Smokey? Did the Others show him? Did he find it on his own?

- Eloise said the island is constantly moving, which is why Widmore can't find it after he's banished. But how does the sub keep finding its way back when it's bringing new recruits or ferrying people back and forth from the island? Do the people on the island know where the island is moving to at all times, and they can keep the submarine captain abreast of its new coordinates?

- After Ben summons Smokey, John emerges from the jungle. Where had he been and what was he doing?
- How does Locke suddenly know everything about the island, including where Smokey is and how to get to it? Did his resurrection bring enlightenment? Could Jin have told him about what happened with Rousseau and he figured Smokey dragged Montand to where it lived?
- In "316," when Ben calls Jack to tell him to go pick up Locke's body, he's covered in blood and dripping wet. Did Ben let himself sink so that Desmond would believe he'd drowned, then crawl out of the water on another dock?
- Ben asks Sun, if she ever makes it off the island, to tell Desmond that he's sorry. What is he referring to? Shooting Desmond? Attempting to shoot Penny? Did we see everything that happened in that scene, or is there a possibility Ben returned and did something worse? Is it possible he took Charlie?
- How badly was Desmond injured by the bullet?
- Was the gun the thing that Ben was hiding in the hotel vent in "Because You Left"?
- What is up with Ilana and her colleagues? What did Ilana mean by "What lies in the shadow of the statue?" Was it a riddle, like "what did one snowman say to the other snowman," a code meant to seek out a particular person? Is she working for Widmore? Is there another group?
- Was Caesar with Ilana and her people or was he just an innocent passenger?
- What did Ilana mean when she said it's time, and they're going now? Going where?
- Who originally carved all those drawings on the wall of Smokey's abode? Was it Richard? How old is that place?

Ashes to Ashes: Caesar had been traveling on Ajira Flight 316 when the plane went down onto a strange island. A paranoid man, Caesar distrusted his fellow passengers, choosing instead to try to find out what the island was about through his own process of deduction. He was known to refer to a person as "friend," even when he didn't consider that person to be one. He was killed by Benjamin Linus.

Smokey: Island Security System or Pillar of Judgment?

It appeared in *Lost*'s pilot episode, and Darlton have said repeatedly that every time we see the smoke monster, we will learn something more about it. So far, that statement rings true. Whether it's finding out more about the nature of the beast, or simply *seeing* more of what it looks like, the appearances of the smoke monster have created an evolutionary process in our understanding of it.

"Pilot, Part 1": The first night on the beach, the monster makes its first appearance . . . though no one actually sees it. It makes its now-familiar howling sound and uproots trees, and as the survivors stand on the beach, terrified and shocked, Rose comments that it sounds familiar, probably referring to both the chain-pulling sound it makes (which sounds like a rollercoaster car being pulled uphill) and that chit-chit-chit sound that is actually a replica of the sound of a receipt machine from a NYC yellow cab. The next day, in the jungle, the monster "appears" again (and again we don't actually see it) and it yanks the pilot out of the plane and throws him in the trees, bloody and mangled. We hear more of its sounds up close, including its growl. Meanwhile, Claire can hear it from the beach and calls the others to come and look.

"Walkabout": Locke comes face to face with the monster, and while we don't see it, he describes it as a white light, and says his now-iconic line, "I've looked into the eye of this island . . . and what I saw was beautiful." From this line we can surmise that the monster might not be all evil.

"Hearts and Minds": The monster chases Shannon and Boone through the jungle and when we see a strange shadow on a tree, we realize it's corporeal. It kills Shannon by lifting her off the ground and mauling her before dumping her lifeless body in a stream. Turns out, it was all Boone's hallucination, albeit a strangely accurate one. We hear all of the Smokey audio trademarks — the fluttering bird-wing sound that warns of its approach, the howl, the growl, and the chain sound.

"Exodus, Part 1": When entering the Dark Territory, the survivors and Rousseau are chased by the monster (which uproots more trees) but they get to safety before it reaches them. Rousseau tells them it had attacked her team, and says it's a security system that has been put in place to protect the island.

"Exodus, Part 2": A few hours later the monster attacks again, and while the others smartly hide, Locke thinks he has a connection with it, and strides out proudly to meet it head-on. However, the eye of the island has lost its beauty, and this time it grabs John Locke by the ankle and drags him through the jungle. We finally get a full-on look at the monster, and realize it's made of smoke. As the sound of the cranking chain reverberates loudly, Jack runs as fast as he can to grab Locke just as the smoke monster is about to pull him down a hole. Locke pleads with him to just let him go, but Jack refuses and talks Kate into dropping a stick of dynamite down the hole. When it goes off, the smoke monster lets go and Locke is free. We see the cloud of smoke get sucked down the hole and it disappears. This appearance suggests that the smoke monster might actually have some sort of mind of its own, and chose Locke specifically. It may reside underground.

"The 23rd Psalm": When Charlie and Eko are at the Beechcraft, they hear the sounds of the approaching monster, and Charlie scrambles up a tree. Eko refuses to back down, and Smokey forms a long cylinder of smoke with a round head facing Eko up close. As Eko stares it down, refusing to blink, the chit-chit-chit noises, which we now see as quick bolts of electricity, show flashes of Eko's past, mostly painful ones. Still, Eko doesn't blink, and the smoke monster retreats. The smoke monster seems to taunt Eko in this scene, testing him to see if he'll back down, and when he doesn't, it leaves him alone.

"The Cost of Living": After Eko has survived the hatch explosion, he begins seeing visions of his dead brother Yemi, and there's a suggestion that the smoke monster might be creating this manifestation. As Eko walks into the jungle, we see the smoke monster quietly following him, silently flitting in and out of the trees around him. Manifestations of people from Eko's past appear before him, telling him to confess, but he refuses. As Eko reaches the stream for a drink, he sees the reflection of Smokey in the water, and when he turns, Smokey makes a quick retreat. Yemi appears to Eko one more time, and Eko refuses to repent for any of his sins. Smokey suddenly appears, rising up to a massive and thick column of smoke, and grabs Eko around the ankle, throwing him up into the air and slamming him into the ground before throwing him side to side against the trees, as if making a giant sign of the cross with his body. Eko dies of his internal injuries moments later. This is the first time we see Smokey as some sort of figure of retribution, and the way it silently follows Eko gives it an animal-like, predatory quality.

"Left Behind": Juliet and Kate, who are handcuffed together, find themselves trapped in a rainy jungle at night when the smoke monster attacks, and they run to hide in the roots of a banyan tree. Smokey finds them, peering inside and taking what appear to be snapshots of the two women (we see bright flashes go off) before suddenly retreating. The next day, the monster appears again, and chases the women one more time as if it didn't like what it saw the night before. Juliet and Kate run through the sonic fence, and Juliet turns it on. Smokey emerges from the jungle looking like Cerberus, the mythical three-headed dog, and slams into the fence, which propels it suddenly backward. This is the first indication that Smokey can actually be stopped by something. Fans wondered why it didn't go up and over the fence, but perhaps this has something to do with the sound waves emerging from the fence. The smoke monster beats a quick retreat.

"The Shape of Things to Come": After denying many times that he has any knowledge of the smoke monster, Ben shows us differently after Keamy shoots Alex in the head. Ben disappears into an ancient room under his house, and returns covered in what appears to be soot. Moments later, Smokey comes charging into New Otherton, attacking the mercenaries while Ben and the others run out of the village. We see trees uprooted once again, and when Mayhew, one of the men, tries to run out of the jungle, the monster grabs him with a smokey tentacle and drags him back into the jungle. Mayhew tries shooting at Smokey with a machine-gun, but it has no effect on the monster. Mayhew dies of his injuries a few days later.

"Cabin Fever": The smoke monster doesn't appear directly in this episode, but when Richard Alpert goes to visit a five-year-old Locke, he notices a picture that Locke has drawn of a man being attacked by a plume of smoke. Alpert is startled and asks Locke if he'd drawn that, as if Richard recognized the smoke monster and knew exactly what it was. This subtle moment is proof that Smokey existed at least as far back as the early 1960s.

"This Place Is Death": During a time jump, we travel to 1988 to see Smokey attack Rousseau and her crew on their first day post-shipwreck, and through this

185

attack we see echoes of earlier attacks by the monster. It silently nabs Nadine in much the same way it sneaks up on Eko in "The Cost of Living," and she drops from the sky like the pilot. It howls and uproots trees, chasing them through the jungle. It approaches Montand close-up and begins staring him down the way it had Eko in "The 23rd Psalm," but Montand breaks eye contact. The moment he does, the monster grabs him by the leg and drags him through the jungle to a declivity in the wall around the Temple, pulling him down. In this episode it stands up like a cobra in front of Montand before attacking him. When it grabs him, it appears to have two arms and a head. It still has that sound of the chain pulling a rollercoaster uphill that we've heard several times, and now it seems connected to one particular ancient site. The research team grabs hold of Montand's arm, and sensing resistance, Smokey reaches up and severs the arm at the shoulder, pulling him down. Then the monster appears to mimic Montand's voice, calling the rest of them to come down and help him (suggesting again that the monster is behind the manifestations of dead people on the island), and it "infects" the team by turning them all into zombie versions of themselves. Robert tells Rousseau that the monster is a security system. Everyone who follows Montand down the hole is dead within weeks. This attack gives us a hint of where the monster might actually reside (and is consistent with it disappearing down a hole in "Exodus, Part 2") and the sound of Montand's voice drawing the rest of them down into the hole is a new and evil trick of the monster's. It's unclear why the monster has attacked these people — does it sense there is something inherently evil or threatening about them?

"Namaste": As Frank and Sun approach the ruins of New Otherton, they hear the chit-chit-chit sound of Smokey and see the rustle of trees. The monster is watching them, but leaves them alone as they enter the village. When they go into a cottage and meet with Christian, who might also be a manifestation of the monster, you can see wisps of black smoke heading out of the doorway as they close the door behind them.

"Dead Is Dead": In the most fantastic appearance of the smoke monster to date, Ben seeks out the monster, rather than unexpectedly being caught by it. We see how Smokey is summoned when Ben goes back into the room under his house and reaches down into a pool of dirty water, turns some sort of plug, and lets the water out. When Ben gets to the ancient room where Smokey "lives," we see a carving of Anubis sitting before the smoke monster, either being judged by it or calling it forth to judge another, so we know Smokey existed in ancient times, and is not a recent addition to the island. It resides under a stone that looks like a kind of grill, and as it emerges it makes a low growl that we've heard before, and quickly grows and surrounds Ben. The monster had faced Eko head-on in "The 23rd Psalm," but in this scene it completely envelops Ben so no matter which direction he looks, he's faced with his worst nightmares. Ben doesn't blink, even though he's overcome with guilt and grief. Sensing that Ben has accepted responsibility for his actions, the monster retreats with one last howl. Alex comes forth, apparently a manifestation of the monster, and threatens Ben. He's been judged, but he has been spared.

5.13   Some Like It Hoth

Original air date: April 15, 2009
Written by: Melinda Hsu Taylor, Greggory Nations
Directed by: Jack Bender
Guest cast: Tim DeZarn (Landlord), Dean Norris (Howard Gray), Marsha Thomason (Naomi), Simon Elbling (Field Supervisor), Cody Gomes (Worker), Linda Rose Herman (Evelyn), Lance Ho (Young Miles), Leslie Ishii (Lara)

Focus: Miles
When Miles enters Horace's "circle of trust," he has to face more than just a cover-up.

Ever since Miles Straume first appeared on the show, fans have been complaining about his unused potential. The island is filled with dead people, and with a skill like Miles's, you'd think he of all characters could be the one to finally answer most, if not all, of our questions. He could find out what really happened to the people in the Dharma Initiative pit (if he's able to isolate one of those bodies from the dozens of others). He could talk to any number of the island dead buried beneath its surface. He could perhaps figure out why some of them appear to be walking and talking. But instead, he's been used mostly for snark. And because he's so damn funny, we've overlooked the fact that his sixth sense has been outrageously underused.

This episode changes all of that. Well, sort of. He manages to talk to one dead guy and realizes there's a huge cover-up going on just outside of

Dharmaville. We see the beginning of the Swan station (and from our position — and Hurley's — we know *that's* gonna end badly), we see construction continuing on the Orchid, and from what Alvarez "tells" Miles, there's an early sign that maybe the Dharminians had an idea of the danger the Swan station posed right from the beginning, but Radzinsky chose to ignore it so his precious dream station could become a reality. Miles's gift provides everyone with clues to the destructiveness of the electromagnetic energy at the Swan, but beyond that, it doesn't do much else.

It seems that once the writers came up with this fantastic idea of including a ghost whisperer as one of the characters, they realized his powers might be *too* strong, and if he suddenly showed up on the beach and said, "Okay, so here's the sitch: turns out there's this guy named Jacob, and he first came to the island in . . ." then the writers wouldn't have much of a show left. So, in this episode, they put limitations on Miles's powers — he needs to have direct contact with the body, meaning bodies buried deeper than Rousseau and Karl were last season wouldn't set off his Spidey senses. And he can't ask them any questions, he can only say what was on their mind in their final moments, which often doesn't tell him much of anything, especially if they were killed suddenly.

"Some Like It Hoth" is a fun episode, acting as a bridge between the drama of the Dharma love quadrangle, the mystery of the Ben/Locke journey, and what's going to come later. What does link it to the themes of this season (and the four seasons before it) are Miles's daddy issues. The parent/child issues have been expressed largely from the point of view of the children, and when we get a rare scene like Roger expressing his remorse for the parent he's become, it gives us a glimpse of the other side of the story. Maybe the parents weren't as terrible as the children believed, and instead, the children were too young to understand their parents' perspective. Miles is alone in actually getting a chance to go back in time to see his father at the time of abandonment. However, Miles, who will unzip a body bag to communicate with a deceased stranger, ironically refuses to communicate with the person whose answers he seeks above all others.

In this episode we see both Hurley and Bram tell Miles that he lives in pain and that he should find out more about his father or get to know him, and Miles exasperatedly tells them they're wrong, and that he doesn't care about his father or want to get to know him. Yet the pain on his face, the obvious rebellion he exhibits as a teenager, and the tears that roll down his cheeks when he finally sees that his father was an active and engaged parent, belie his bravado. He's been able to bury his feelings ever since his mother convinced him that his father cared nothing for him, but just like the targets of Miles's special ability, those feelings don't stay buried for good.

Hurley plays the sidekick in this episode, acting as both Miles's foil and as the voice of reason. While probably every geek fan in the audience figured out that Hurley was writing something relating to *Star Wars* the moment he asked how to spell "bounty hunter," the reveal that he was once again ignoring Miles's claim that you cannot change the future by trying to rewrite *The Empire Strikes Back* and getting Lucas to make his version was hilarious. But this subplot wasn't an empty one: *Star Wars* is, at its heart, the story of a boy who doesn't know his father, and who believes at one point that his father was always an evil man, only to discover by the end that he just didn't have all the facts. In a fictional world of good versus evil, the story reveals a vast middle ground. Hurley argues that if everyone just communicated, they could have avoided a whole lot of pain and could have been happier earlier on. But as any fan of *Star Wars* (and *Lost*) knows, it would also make for a much less exciting story.

Meanwhile, in Miles's flashback, we see more evidence of the splinter group that appeared in "Dead Is Dead." Using their catchphrase, "What lies in the shadow of the statue?" to detect other converts, they appear to also have a connection to the island. The scene where they pull Miles into their van would have happened three years before Miles's present moment, meaning they'd been planning a trip back to the island for years. Who are these people? What does their question mean? And how, not being connected to either Ben or Widmore, did they know that Ajira Flight 316 would land on the island the way it did? Perhaps this episode wasn't as disconnected as it seems: maybe their presence on the island has something to do with what is happening in 1977. Or the fact that Daniel just returned to the island.

Highlight: The look that former punk Miles gives to his father when Chang says he prefers country music.

Did You Notice?:

- Eagle-eyed viewers might have noticed that Lara is the same woman who wakes Chang up at the beginning of "Because You Left," and if you did, you figured out that Chang was Miles's father right away.
- You can tell there's a sense of pride when Sawyer brags to Kate, "In case you hadn't noticed, I'm head of security." It's a great moment, though we can't

help but miss the swagger and arrogance that once accompanied Sawyer everywhere.

- When punk Miles goes to see his dying mother, there's a portrait of two horses on the wall. One is brown, like the one Widmore rides into camp at the beginning of "Dead Is Dead," and the other is black, like the one Kate sees in "What Kate Did."
- His mother is still living in the apartment she was renting in the beginning of the episode.
- Miles has two white stripes in his hair when it's spiked up, and he seems to be going prematurely gray on the show. This might be a subtle nod to *The Sixth Sense*, where characters who could see and hear dead people have a streak of white hair on the back of their head.
- Hurley proves that he's paid no attention to Miles's explanation of the limits of time travel not only in the scene where he's rewriting *The Empire Strikes Back*, but when he first insists they carpool to help prevent global warming, and then asks Miles why he doesn't try to warn his parents about what's going to happen in the Purge. You can just *feel* Miles giving up.
- When Roger comes into the infirmary, Juliet is dressed all in black. Previously she'd been all in white. She had been his angel of mercy, but now she's lost his son.
- Both Mr. Vonner and Alvarez were thinking of women before they died.
- You can tell that Miles is faking it about contacting Russell; the screen always jumps and there's a whooshing sound when he's actually sensing the dead.
- Chang tells Hurley that if he breathes a word to anyone about the body bag, he'll have him shipped to the Hydra island where he can weigh polar bear feces "for their ridiculous experiments." What are they testing on the Hydra island? Why is Chang so dismissive of it? Is it just a decoy from the more important work being done on electromagnetism, or are physicists just naturally dismissive of biologists?
- Naomi is clearly wearing a wig. The actress has probably cut her hair short since season 4.
- In "Eggtown," Miles confronts Ben and tells him he's on the island to find him and deliver him to Widmore, but he'll tell them all that he found him dead if he gives him $3.2 million. Ben looks at him and asks why he wants that particular number. Now we know the number is double what

Widmore is paying him to find Ben. (This is the same number he asks Bram for.)

- The classroom where Jack is cleaning the boards appears to be the same one we saw in "The Man Behind the Curtain." In that scene, Olivia was teaching the class about volcanoes. In this episode, you can see one of the papier-mâché volcanoes she was using.
- On the chalkboard, Jack is erasing a lesson about the language and hieroglyphics of Ancient Egyptians. On the far left, there are various hieroglyphics at the top with the line "Writing the words of God" written underneath. In the middle, the language of the Ancient Egyptians is subdivided into three distinct eras: "Old Egyptian: 2600 BC to 2000 BC, Tripling ideograms, phonograms, and determinatives; Middle Egyptian: 2000 BC to 1300 BC, Classic stage of language; Late Egyptian: 1300 BC to 700 BC, From synthetic to ana___ language."
- There's a child's picture of a butterfly on the classroom wall, just like there were butterflies at Hurley's mental hospital.
- Just before Miles is pulled into the van, he's at a taco stand called La Vida, which means life in Spanish. Next to it is Angela's hair salon; "Angela" is derived from "angel" and means "messenger of God."
- Bram, the man who talks to Miles in the van and tells him to work for another group, is the man who is with Ilana in "Dead Is Dead" as Ilana asks Frank what lies in the shadow of the statue.
- In the actual opening of *The Empire Strikes Back*, the "little spy robot thingy" that lands on Hoth is an Imperial probe that is searching for the rebels. It finds them, and alerts Darth Vader to their whereabouts. In Hurley's version, Chewbacca blows it up before it can detect the Rebels and report back to Vader. Which . . . would kind of end the movie right there.
- Sawyer has gone back to calling Jack "Doc." It took a few days, but now he's comfortable with referring to Jack and Kate by their regular nicknames.
- Obviously the line in "Namaste" that said Jack was most suited to janitorial work was meant as a joke, but there might be something to that. As a janitor, Jack's allowed to finally just do the job, and not take it home with him at the end of the day. There are no lives at stake, and no long-term worries or panicked phone calls in the middle of the night. It must be a relief for him to be doing a job that doesn't require the stress of being a surgeon. When he delivers the news about Kate to Juliet and Sawyer, he leaves after

Jack Bender, director extraordinaire on *Lost*. When J.J. Abrams was recently asked if he would direct the series finale of *Lost*, he said despite it being an honor, "the reason I won't do it is that Jack Bender, who is the directing producer on the show, has essentially earned the right to do whatever he wants. He should be directing the finale." (RYAN OZAWA)

telling them what he knows, and doesn't offer any sort of plan or solution, as if he really is happy just following orders and going along with the gang.

- Bram refers to Miles as "my friend," the same way Caesar addressed Locke.
- The book Chang was reading to baby Miles is called *Me and My Polar Bear*.

Interesting Facts: At the beginning of the episode, Miles is reading an issue of *Sports Illustrated* with Tommy Lasorda on the cover from March 14, 1977, with the headline, "After 23 Years, There's a New Boss in Town." Lasorda had taken over as manager of the L.A. Dodgers in 1976 after the team's only manager to that point, Walter Alston, had retired at the end of the season. Alston had managed the team since they were the Brooklyn Dodgers in 1954. The article ran at the beginning of the new season, which is why the headline refers to 23 years rather than 22.

The son of Mr. Gray, who is the man who hires Miles to tell him if his son knew he loved him, is named Russell. Originally, the producers were going to make Faraday's first name Russell, but instead changed it to Daniel.

Star Wars was released on Memorial Day, May 25, 1977, and was an instant success. If the action in Dharmaville is taking place in July 1977, the film is already making waves in the U.S. (the title of the episode refers to Hoth, the ice planet Luke is on at the beginning of the film). Wikipedia editors had to vigilantly guard the *Star Wars* article after this episode aired as *Lost* fans changed the name of the writer of *Empire Strikes Back* to "Hugo Reyes."

Sawyer is about to reference the Hans Brinker legend, the story of the little Dutch boy whose father works at the dike that keeps water from flooding the village. When the boy sees a small stream coming out of it, he stops and puts his finger in the dike to stop the water. But then he realizes he can't leave, and stays there all night, shivering with cold and wondering why no one is coming to find him. When he is found the next morning, he is proclaimed a hero. The story is part of a larger novel called *Hans Brinker and the Silver Skates* by an American author, Mary Elizabeth Mapes Dodge, and while at the time it claimed to be based on an actual Dutch folktale, the story was invented by the author. There's a bit of clever wordplay when Sawyer is interrupted, and instead he says, "Ever have one of those days where you feel like the little Dutch boy with his finger in the . . . Doc!"

In an interview with IFC, Ken Leung talked about his own superstitions and talked about a scene from season 4 that had been cut:

> I have an awareness of a spiritual realm, and I see signs that I feel speak to me — I don't know if that falls into superstition. Last season on "Lost," there was a scene that'd been cut, so nothing really came of it. My character was telling a story . . . I'm trying to negotiate this because I'm not really allowed to talk about "Lost" stuff . . . I was talking about a man who lost his family, and he had 12 kids. There was a tragic accident and they all died. I remember having trouble with it because I had to personalize the story so I'm not just spewing from a script. I don't have any kids, and beyond the obvious tragedy of a father losing 12 kids, how do I connect to this?
>
> I was walking to get dinner, maybe two nights before the scene was to be shot. I walked by what looked like a postcard on the ground. Something about it made me stop. It was a photograph of a children's party. [The girl] in the middle had a birthday hat on, and there were balloons; it was obviously her birthday. Suddenly, I had faces to go with this story. There were exactly 12 kids in the picture. Things like that happen to me a lot.

Oops: Just a small quibble with Hurley's explanation of *Empire*: Luke has his hand cut off *before* he finds out Vader is his father. Hurley says that he finds out Vader is his father, and freaks out and ends up losing a hand, which wasn't the case.

Chang says that his baby is three months old, but the events in this episode occur only a few days before the scene that opened the season in "Because You Left." In that scene, Chang goes in to get the baby in the morning, and the baby pulls himself up on the edge of his crib, almost to standing. A three-month-old baby would not be able to do that. Also, when Roger kicks the bucket across the classroom, Jack has only erased a panel and a half of the chalkboard, but when the camera goes back to him two seconds later, it's completely erased.

4 8 15 16 23 42: This episode had a lot of Hurley's numbers in it. The time on the microwave at the beginning of the episode is 3:**16** (also the Ajira flight number). The rent for the apartment is $**4**00 per month, and the landlord asks for an $**8**00 deposit. The first dead man Miles hears is in apartment **4**. The rabbit by the door under which Miles finds a key has an **8** drawn on its ear. Lara writes the landlord a check for the deposit, and the check number is 3**16**. Miles is reading a *Sports Illustrated* issue with the headline, "After **23** Years, There's a New Boss in Town." Sawyer tells Miles to destroy the tape from security monitor **4**. There are **8** televisions in the station. When Kate shows up, Roger's had **4** beers. The foreman calls out all Hurley's numbers in sequence for the door of the hatch. Miles and Hurley were in van **8**. There are **16** vans in total. Naomi offers Miles $**1.6** million.

It's Just a Flesh Wound: Alvarez succumbs to the old "dental filling through the brain" accident. Sawyer knocks Phil unconscious.

Any Questions?:

- So Miles clearly got his ability from the island, but how? Is it like Desmond, that he had some sort of exposure to the electromagnetic energy and can see dead people in the way Des can see the future? Is Miles's mother dying of cancer because of her exposure to the radiation?
- When Miles arrives at grid 334, Radzinsky jumps out, pointing a gun at his van, and then says he was expecting LaFleur. Why would he have been pointing a gun at LaFleur?
- Naomi tells Miles there are a number of deceased individuals "residing" on the island. Why does she say "residing," as if they're living there and breathing? Are you only *sort of dead* on the island, and not completely dead?

May the Island Be With You: *Star Wars* and *Lost*

Hurley wanting to reimagine *Empire Strikes Back* is not the first *Star Wars* reference on *Lost*. Darlton are huge *Star Wars* fans, and they try to inject as many references into the show as possible (for an excellent analysis of the *Star Wars* inspiration on *Lost*, check out Jon "DocArzt" Lachonis and Amy "hijinx" Johnston's book *Lost Ate My Life*). Many of the *Lost* characters seem very similar to the ones in George Lucas's films, and even some situations are familiar:

- In *Star Wars*, there is the Dark Side and the light side of the force; on *Lost*, black and white is an ongoing theme (see "The Incident, Part 1").
- In season 1's "The Moth," Charlie gets to Jack, who is trapped under the rubble in the cave, and says, "I'm here to rescue you," which is Luke's famous line to Leia. In season 4's "Confirmed Dead," Daniel says the same line to Jack and Kate.
- In season 1, Michael and Jin were set up like Han Solo and Chewbacca. Michael could understand what Jin was saying, and vice versa, even though neither one actually spoke the language of the other. In "Exodus, Part 1," when Michael and Jin were repairing the raft, Michael ran over to Jin, and yelled in an exasperated voice, "No, no! This one goes *there*, that one goes *there*." This same dialogue happens in *Star Wars*, when Han Solo is correcting Chewie when they're fixing the *Millennium Falcon*. In "Exodus, Part 2," Michael and Jin are arguing over the flare (Michael yelling in English, Jin countering in Korean) and Sawyer stops them and says, "Hey Han, you and Chewie want to slow down a second and talk to me here?"
- Sawyer is a wise-cracking, caustic hero, much like Han Solo. Damon and Carlton admitted that they named him "James Ford" after Harrison Ford. Leia has her eye on Luke for the first part of the trilogy, but ends up with Han, just as Kate moves between Jack and Sawyer. Sawyer referred to Hurley as "Jabba" in "Fire + Water," and then strangled Cooper with a chain, from behind, just like Leia strangled Jabba the Hutt.
- Locke is the wise leader, like Obi-Wan Kenobi. In season 5, Jack seems to be more like Luke, who at first resisted Obi-Wan's teachings because he couldn't give his mind over to the Force. Likewise, Jack refused to give in to Locke's faith . . . until now.
- Just as Luke and Leia don't realize they're brother and sister, Jack and Claire don't find out they're half-siblings while they're on the island.
- In season 3's "Not in Portland," Alex, Sawyer, and Kate rescue Karl from Room 23 when Sawyer marches Alex up to Aldo as if she's a prisoner and he's an Other. Sawyer refers to this as the "old Wookiee prisoner gag," after the scene where Luke and Han dress up as stormtroopers and pretend that Chewie is their prisoner.
- While it's still not clear if Ben is the good guy or the bad guy, he certainly seems to be some sort of combination of Darth Vader and the Emperor. The Emperor tells Luke to kill Darth Vader, just as Ben tries to persuade Locke to kill his own father to join the Others (in both cases, by following through they would be joining the Other side). Darth Vader helped carry out the Great Jedi Purge; Ben orchestrated the Purge of the Dharma Initiative. Darth Vader tries to lure Luke to the Dark Side; Ben tells Locke that he can teach him everything he needs to know about the island if he joins him. Later, in "The Lie," he tries to tell Hurley to join him. (Vader never had to contend with a Hot Pocket.) Will we discover Ben was always with the Dark Side? Or will he redeem himself?

- Miles says that Felix was delivering documents consisting of photos of empty open graves and a purchase order for an old plane. These would be the same documents that Tom showed Michael in "Meet Kevin Johnson." Did Tom kill Felix to get those documents from him? How did Naomi confirm that Miles was telling the truth? Did Widmore already know what was going to be delivered to him? Did he set the whole thing up?
- So who's Bram? Are the people who, for want of an actual name, I'll call the Shadow Seekers some sort of third splinter group? Are they the DI who survived? (They look a little young for that.) Are they the children of the DI? Are they the Others, just wanting to take their island back? Are they a completely different group?
- Hurley tells Miles that when his father came back, he gave him a second chance and they got to be the best of friends. When did that happen? When Hurley left for Sydney in the first place, he was angry with his father for returning, and for not believing him about the curse, and for trying to trick him with the psychic. When he returned as one of the Oceanic 6, his father gave him the Camaro as a gift, and when Hurley turned on the car he thought his father was playing a cruel trick on him because the numbers were all over the dash. He went into a mental institution and when he broke out and told his father that people were after him, his father told him he was either lying or he was crazy. So when did they become the best of friends? Has he rewritten this history in his head the same way he rewrote *Empire Strikes Back*? Or did it happen and just wasn't part of the backstory we actually saw?
- Where has Daniel been? He certainly looks a lot healthier and happier than we've seen up to this point. When LaFleur and Miles were put into security detail, was Dan given a scientist designation and shipped to Ann Arbor with the other scientists? Did he glean all of his information about the DI when he was there? Has he been time traveling at all while he was there?

Ashes to Ashes: Alvarez was a member of the Dharma Initiative, working at the Swan station and thinking about his girlfriend when he suddenly felt a filling rip out of his molar and shoot into his brain, which killed him.

Music/Bands: When Hurley and Miles are driving to the Orchid station, they listen to "It Never Rains in Southern California" by Albert Hammond and "Love Will Keep Us Together" by Captain & Tennille. Miles must be annoyed that he can't get the Sex Pistols' "God Save the Queen" on 8-track.

5.14   The Variable

Original air date: April 29, 2009
Written by: Edward Kitsis, Adam Horowitz
Directed by: Paul Edwards
Guest cast: Alice Evans (Eloise Hawking, Age 40), Sarah Farooqui (Theresa), Spencer Allyn (Young Daniel), Brad Berryhill (Anxious Guy), Todd Coolidge (Paramedic), Marvin DeFreitas (Young Charlie), Michael Dempsey (Foreman), Ariston Green (Workman), Maya Henssens (Young Charlotte), Wendy Pearson (ER Doctor), Peggy Anne Siegmund (Caretaker), Jennifer Sojot (ER Nurse)

Focus: Daniel

Daniel returns to the island to deliver some shocking news to Jack, and reveals his plans for how he's going to change the future.

"The Variable" is a fantastic episode that comes as the natural sequel to "The Constant." Once again, the theme of free will versus destiny takes center stage. A random plane filled with random people that crashes on a random island has morphed into a story about people whose lives were connected before the crash, who were somehow chosen to be put on a specific flight that would crash on a specific island where they would take part in a series of predestined events. Every season has had at least one discussion about free will versus destiny, and by season 2 free will was conflated with science (Jack) and destiny with faith (Locke). There have been several characters who believe in destiny and fate: most notably Locke, Charlie, and Desmond. All of them, interestingly, are faith-based characters who believe in a higher power controlling their lives and accept their fates have already been written. Locke does what he does because he believes it's his destiny. Charlie died after Desmond had a vision that it was supposed to happen. Desmond talks with Ms. Hawking in "Flashes Before Your Eyes" and she explains to him that things are predestined to happen a certain way. She points out a man wearing red shoes who is crushed under falling scaffolding moments later. When Desmond, shocked, asks her why she didn't do something, she says there was nothing she could do: "Had I warned him about the scaffolding, tomorrow he'd be hit by a taxi. If I warned him about the taxi, he'd fall in the shower and break his neck. The universe, unfortunately, has a way of course correcting. That man was supposed to die. That was his path just as it's your path to go to the island. You don't do it because you *choose* to, Desmond. You do it because you're *supposed* to."

Many of the other characters believe in free will: Kate, Sawyer, Sayid, and Jack all believe they made choices in their lives and have to live with the consequences. In the past, Jack has been the most open proponent of free will. He scoffs at Christian's idea of destiny — "that's why the Red Sox will never win the series" — because he thinks that if one believes everything is fated to happen, it means no one is responsible for his/her own actions. Yet, as he's mocking that belief, he's muttering his dad's phrase and thinking in his head that most of his life has been the way it was because of his father.

Most of the characters straddle both beliefs, however, showing what a fine line there is between free will and destiny. Eko, in his final words, said that he was given a certain life (destiny) but he did the best he could with what he was given (free will). He believes that destiny is made up of a series of choices that a person makes. He refuses to repent in his final moments because his life was laid out for him. Ben, in season 3, says that days after he found out he had a tumor in his spine a spinal surgeon fell from the sky, meaning Jack was fated to come to the island. (But we all know that Ben is a liar, and probably knew that plane would fall from the sky.) He seemed to believe in destiny, and thought things were supposed to play out a certain way, but Alex's death changed all of that. Now he's taken responsibility for her death by admitting that it was the choice he made not to leave the house that led to her death. In other words, she was not destined to continue living because the island had spared her by sending Ben to her "rescue" in 1988; instead she died because of his mistake — one he made of his own free will.

In "Tricia Tanaka Is Dead," Hurley decides to tempt fate; until that moment he believed that he was cursed by the numbers, and no matter what he did, those numbers would hurt everyone around him, and no matter what he did to change them, the universe would just course correct back to curse him once again. But when he decides to make his own luck, he finds that he can do it, and that there is no such thing as destiny. That is, until he leaves the island and believes he's being chased by the numbers again. Even Jack, who so resolutely believed in free will, has returned to the island a changed man, spouting the same rhetoric Locke had done years earlier, and talking about destiny and letting things happen. He stopped trying to change or fix anything, and instead figured that he would sit back and wait for fate to make the decisions for him. Sayid, who scoffed at Locke's ridiculous trek north "because of the way the sunlight hit Mr. Eko's stick," now believes he was meant to come back to the island so he can kill Ben.

In almost every case, then, the characters seem to have broken down their previously steadfast beliefs and embrace some sort of combination of the two. In "The Variable," we see how the two beliefs come together, that they were never meant to be separate, but are inextricably linked. Dan has been caught between the two beliefs his entire life. He'd come to believe in destiny because that is what his parents — Eloise Hawking and Charles Widmore — had taught him to believe. In "Because You Left," Daniel explains to Sawyer that "whatever happened, happened," and you can't change the past. When Charlotte dies, Dan vows not to tell her anything, not to try to interfere with destiny, because it only messed things up.

But just as Jack returned to the island having switched from the free will camp to the destiny camp, now Dan has realized you can't have one without the other. Armed with his notebook and years of research, he says he believes in choices, that he can change the future through a combination of letting certain things happen the way they were meant to (i.e., trying to talk Chang into ordering an evacuation of the island that he apparently always did), and manipulating other events so they happen differently (like the hydrogen bomb stopping the release of the electromagnetism). In other words, one must use free will to carve out one's destiny.

Eloise, we discover by the end of the episode, put her son on a path that she always knew would lead to his death. We've seen her ardent belief in destiny, the way things are "supposed" to be, the universe course correcting, and even how science can be used to track destiny (the pendulum in the Lamp Post station tells them where the island is supposed to be next). We can tell her heart is breaking as she sits next to Daniel when he's playing the piano, and yet she stops him from becoming the next Glenn Gould so he can instead be the next Stephen Hawking. She tells Desmond she couldn't save the man with the red shoes because the universe would course correct and kill him anyway. So, to avoid Daniel dying in a different way (like having a grand piano fall on his head?) she knew he had important work to do, and got him to the Others' camp to deliver an important message, even if it meant she was going to put a bullet in him and kill her own son. It was his destiny to walk into that camp, and Eloise believes there's nothing she could do to change that.

One of the key scenes in this episode happens in the restaurant, when Dan has just graduated from Oxford and she gives him the journal that he will later consult throughout his life. In season 4 the notebook seemed to contain a bunch of Dan's formulae, yet by looking in it he seemed to know what was going to happen next. In this episode, Daniel waits by the Orchid station for Chang to show up, as if his notebook already stated the time at which he would. How could his notebook possibly contain notes for things that hadn't yet happened?

One possibility is that he already knew about the Dharma Initiative and before he lost his memory, he'd spent years researching their work and the Incident that he refers to that will happen at the Swan station. It would explain how he knew where Chang would be, and when, and that the Orchid accident would precede the Swan one by a few hours.

It's also possible that he'd consciousness traveled the way that Desmond did in "The Constant," and that when he was testing his machines on himself before Theresa's unfortunate accident, he traveled to a moment in the future and was able to write about things that would happen later. That would explain how he knew about the Tempest station being set to emit a shot of poisonous gas, which almost happened in "The Other Woman," and how he and Charlotte knew exactly how to stop it. He could also have consciousness traveled when he got to Ann Arbor, so even if he hadn't known much about the DI prior to getting on the freighter, he learned more by going ahead to a point in time where he *would* know more.

But there's a special significance to the fact that Dan's memory is so faulty, that his mother knows that and continually reminds him of his severe short-term memory loss, and that she is the one who gives him the journal. A stronger possibility in all of this could lie in Eloise's actions after she shoots Dan in the camp. He has the journal tucked in his jumpsuit, and if she finds it, she'll see everything that will happen in her son's life, and will know exactly what path he will be on. It's through this notebook that she'll always know what's going to happen next, how she knows exactly what he needs to become and what path she needs to keep him on if he's supposed to complete his destiny the right way. Perhaps she gives him a new, crisp, clean version of the journal while keeping the old, battered one in a nightstand somewhere, consulting it over the years. And if her son has a faulty memory, what's to stop her from creating several entries in the journal? What if the coordinates of Dan's machine in "The Constant" had already been discovered by the "great man" who created the pendulum in the Lamp Post station, and she simply jotted them into his notebook so that Dan could send Desmond back in time to give them to him? He would have no memory of writing any of the entries, and he would simply chalk that up to his condition.

He would assume that he wrote those things in there, not knowing that his mother was actually manipulating him by doing it herself. At the end of "The Constant," Dan consults his journal to find the words, "If anything goes wrong, Desmond Hume will be my constant." Did Eloise write those words?

Dan and Desmond are always linked, and now it seems that it was Eloise who made that connection happen. If she'd met Desmond in 1996 and told him his destiny was to go to the island and push a button, she ensured he would be on that island, pushing that button, so when her son knocked on the hatch door when he was time-blooping, he could give Desmond the message that he would deliver to her in the Lamp Post station (it would explain her flat and unsurprised reaction to Desmond's appearance in "316"). She also needed Desmond to be on that island when the freighter arrived so Dan could lead him to 1996 again and give him the coordinates to his device. So far, it's eerily unclear why she needed Desmond to come to her in Los Angeles, unless something worse is about to happen to Desmond now that she's made contact with Penelope and has seen what Charlie looks like. When she comes to see Penny at the hospital, Eloise says that for the first time, she doesn't know what's going to happen next. If she has been relying on Dan's notebook to know what was going to happen next, then it would have ended with his death, which is happening now, and Ellie is, for the first time in a long time, uncertain of the future.

Is it possible that despite Eloise's avowed belief in destiny, she thought she could actually *change* the outcome of Dan's life somehow? Perhaps she has been following the path of his life as her own experiment, not changing things too much and keeping him doing the things he was supposed to do, but hoping that she can tweak something at the very end to prevent that catastrophic death? Maybe she pushed him into a life of science so he could find the answer himself, and make independent choices that would lead him away from the business end of her gun in 1977, and allow him to live. Notice how she's cold to Theresa at Dan's graduation and tells him to stay away from women, as if she's actually trying to prevent the accident that happened to Theresa. Or, perhaps after trying for years to change things, she gave up after the universe kept "course correcting" all of her changes, and that's why she believes in destiny the way she does now.

Charles Widmore delivers a shocking line when he says he's Daniel's father. That makes him complicit in all of this, funding all of Dan's research (something Dan apparently didn't write in the notebook, given Eloise's look of shock when he tells her) and sending him back to the island to fulfill his destiny. And with

Penny married to Desmond, it means that Dan and Desmond are not only spiritual brothers (see page 29), but half-brothers-in-law. As horrible as Eloise's actions may seem to some, the look on her face when Dan asks if she'll be proud of him if he goes back is heartbreaking. She knows exactly what she's doing by sending him back, and she can hardly bear it. Widmore, on the other hand, barely bats an eyelash sending his son back to the place where he will die. His calculated actions deserve far worse than a face slap from Eloise.

But in both cases, what Eloise and Widmore prove is that there really is no such thing as destiny. They both orchestrated the very events that led Dan to the moment when he walked into the camp. Maybe Dan did get his memory back, and in doing so, realized that the scribbling in his notebook *was* his mother's handwriting, and not his, and that's what led him back to the island and made him realize none of this was destined, but was manipulated by his parents. And if he refuses to do the things in his notebook, maybe he can actually change the future.

If Eloise really did manipulate Dan's notebook to get him back to the island, then maybe the last thing she does know is what Jack and Co. will do when they return. Jack, who used to be Mr. Free Will and has moved over to the destiny side of things, returns to the old Jack by the end of this episode. As soon as Dan tells everyone they *can* change their lives, Jack proves that as nice as sitting back and doing nothing has been, it's simply not in his nature to do that. He wants to change the future with Dan. Will he be the one to do it? Was Dan's choice to return simply a catalyst that caused Jack to wake up and start making his own decisions? Or, like Sayid shooting Ben, could Jack simply be fulfilling the destiny he was always meant to? Could his actions actually *cause* the very Incident he was trying to prevent?

Highlight: Jack to Kate: "We disappeared off a plane in mid-air and ended up in 1977. Gettin' kinda used to insane."

Did You Notice?:
- If Chang is warned about the Incident in this episode and needs to evacuate the group immediately, and Dan is already dead, many fans wondered how they could have filmed the video that was shown at the 2008 Comic-Con. Darlton confirmed that the video was only in the spirit of season 5, and wasn't meant to be part of the actual storyline or canon in any way.
- There were several references to time in this episode: when Dan is playing

piano, the metronome is keeping time, but he keeps getting ahead of it. He tells Eloise that he can "make time," and she looks at him and says, "If only you could." When they're back at the piano 30 years later, the camera holds on Dan's watch.

- When Dan is descending into the Orchid station, the page of notes he checks in his journal is about the universe expanding over time, something that Stephen Hawking talks about in *A Brief History of Time* (see *Finding Lost — Season 3*, page 69).

- When Dan meets Chang, he's wearing a Dharma construction worker outfit with the name "Joe" embroidered on it.

- After Dan tells Chang he's from the future, Chang says, "You've had your fun, congratulations." When Desmond meets with Dan in 1996 and says he's from the future, Dan has a similar reaction, believing one of his colleagues put Desmond up to it.

- In "Jughead," when Desmond visits Dan's office at Oxford, he finds Dan's graduation picture on the floor, and Dan is wearing this same outfit with Theresa at his side (though in retrospect it's unlikely that Mommy took a picture of the happy couple). Speaking of which, Dan's got on a thin black tie with a white shirt. He accomplished his signature look early on.

- When Eloise leans down to get Dan's present in the Indian restaurant, look at Dan's glass — there's an optical illusion that makes it look like a rabbit is sitting in there. Rabbits are a recurring motif on *Lost*.

- Eloise signs herself as "Mother" in the journal. How . . . warm.

- Hurley referred to fate as "luck" and he concluded you make your own luck, that you make a series of choices that become your fate, but you don't sit back and let fate happen to you. Similarly, in this episode, Dan and Eloise refer to luck and free will as linked.

- Now that we see Daniel was told the island would heal him, the scene of the memory card game with Charlotte makes more sense. She tells him his memory is improving, but he's frustrated that it's not completely better. It also explains why that memory loss of his seems to have gotten better with time.

- When Dan tries to explain his short-term memory loss to Widmore, he begins, "I have a condition that affects my memory . . ." but doesn't say anything more. The line is a reference to the excellent 2000 film *Memento*, in which a man tries to track down the person who he believes raped and killed his wife, but because he suffers from short-term memory loss, those around him keep manipulating the situation to keep him from finding out the truth. Whenever he meets a new person, he introduces himself by saying, "I have this condition . . ."

- Sawyer's face changes completely when Jack begins to take over. Just as Juliet worried about Kate getting between her and Sawyer, Sawyer seems to have expected that Jack would take over again as the leader.
- Juliet says, "It's over here for us, anyway" immediately after Sawyer refers to Kate as Freckles. The people in the room take it to mean the charade that they're from 1977 is over, but she could just as easily mean her relationship with Sawyer. Elizabeth Mitchell is amazing in that scene, flickering her eyelids with complete recognition at what is happening, but trying desperately to hold it together.
- When Dan comes up to Charlotte, she says, "I'm not allowed to have chocolate before dinner." Those were her last words to Daniel before she died, meaning the last image she had in her head before she died was her first meeting with Daniel.
- When Juliet and Sawyer ask each other if they have each other's backs, neither answers.
- When Dan is explaining the Incident at the Swan station, he says they'll have to cement the station in "like Chernobyl." When Sayid and Jack are crawling through the area underneath the hatch in season 2's "Everybody Hates Hugo," they come upon a thick wall of concrete. Sayid comments, "The last time I heard of concrete being poured over everything in this way was Chernobyl."
- Jeremy Davies is an incredible actor. I may be sadder to see him go than any other character so far, because he created such a unique person from the character sketch he was given, and truly made this part his own. Let's hope he has a future on other television shows.

Interesting Facts: This episode was celebrated by ABC because it was officially *Lost's* 100th episode. To celebrate, the *Ace of Cakes* team came to the set and presented the cast with an elaborate cake that looked like the island, with individual marzipan *Lost* characters on it. However, the fan paying close attention will have noticed that there have *not* been 100 episodes at this point: there were 24 in season 1, 23 in each of seasons 2 and 3, 14 in season 4, and "The Variable" is the 14th episode of season 5. That adds up to 98. However, in television, a show can be sold into syndication when it reaches 100 hours, and "The Variable" is the 100th hour of the series (both "Exodus, Part 2" and "Live Together, Die Alone" were two-hour episodes). But it sounds a lot nicer to call it the 100th episode, and not the 100th hour, so ABC went with that.

In the short story "A Point at Issue!" written by 19th-century American author Kate Chopin, an independent woman agrees to marry her mathematician boyfriend as long as their marriage is one of equality. As soon as they're married, she moves to France to become more cultured and he remains in the U.S. Their names? Charles and Eleanor "Nellie" Faraday. The *Lost* writers seem to be giving a subtle nod to this short story in this episode, not only because of the almost identical first names of the husband and wife in the story (who, like Widmore and Eloise, probably engaged in a marriage of the minds and then lived apart) but giving Daniel a surname that isn't that of his mother *or* his father. The fact that Daniel keeps playing a piece by Chopin could be a tip-off to the name of the author.

When Dan and Miles arrive at Chez LaFleur, Sawyer tells them to help them-

To celebrate the show's 100th episode, a fancy cake was made featuring the *Lost* island, with each of the characters fashioned in marzipan. Here Jeremy Davies chuckles as Josh Holloway pretends to drink from the cake Dharma beer can.
(© MARIO PEREZ/ABC/RETNA LTD.)

selves to the punch. He's referring to the Jonestown massacre in November 1978. Jim Jones was a cult leader who moved his group of followers, "The People's Temple," to a remote site in Guyana. After outside family members complained that their loved ones had been brainwashed by the sadistic leader, Californian Congressman Leo Ryan agreed to go the site himself and launch an investigation. When he left, despite reassuring Jones that he would speak positively of the site and the group, Jones didn't believe him, and sent some followers to accompany

Ryan's entourage to the airport, where they shot and killed Ryan in cold blood, along with three accompanying journalists and one Temple member who was defecting. Several other people were seriously wounded. Meanwhile, back at the camp, Jones lined his followers up for a mass suicide. He had staged fake mass suicides in the camp, called "White Nights" and it's assumed many people in the group thought he was just running another drill when he filled a vat with Kool-Aid and laced it with cyanide and other poisons. As Jones recorded what happened, talking the entire time from a podium and watching his followers scoop cups of the liquid, over 900 people drank the punch, and many even squirted it into their children's mouths. After the camp was covered in dead bodies, Jim Jones took his own life with one gunshot to his head. It was the single largest loss of American lives until the events of 9/11.

Nitpicks: Dan says that following the Incident, the people on the island will push a button for the next 20 years. But the plane crash will happen 27 years from this point, so it's more like 30 years. Also, if he'd figured out that the Incident was going to happen when it did, why did he show up at the last possible minute? Did he find out everything in the last few months but the sub only arrives from Ann Arbor a couple of times a year or something? And knowing everything Penny does about the island, and how long it took to get Desmond back, and how they're constantly in danger of her father, and how a man showed up that morning and tried to kill all of them . . . why does Penny leave Charlie in the waiting room with a nurse she's never met? It seems like a ridiculous thing for her to do.

Oops: This episode was filled with continuity errors, some far worse than others. First, at the end of the previous episode, it's early evening when Miles is looking through the window of Chang's house and sees him reading to baby Miles before bed. Chang gets a phone call and leaves the house immediately, asking Miles to come with him. Dan gets off the sub, and in this episode, tells Miles he needs his help. You can hear Chang in the background saying, "I wish you could all get a good night's sleep, but . . ." and the rest is unclear, and Dan tells Miles to take him to Jack's right away. They go to Jack's house, a few minutes from the dock, and it's morning. You can see the sun behind them, and they're only there for a few moments before they leave again, and Jack goes to Sawyer's house and says it's 6 A.M. Where did the entire night go?

When Daniel sees Jack, he's wearing a black jumpsuit, and he jumps into the Dharma jeep still wearing it. But when he and Miles get to the Orchid station, he's suddenly wearing a gray jumpsuit like he was in the opening of "Because You Left." It's doubtful he changed in the back of the jeep on the way there.

Dan leaves Jack's house to go to the Orchid at 6 A.M. where he'll talk to Chang. In past episodes the Orchid appears to be about 15 minutes away from Dharmaville. But in the opening of "Because You Left," we see Chang turn off the alarm, which reads 8:15, get up, feed his baby, get dressed, and *then* go to the Orchid station, so there's no way he could have been there just past 6.

Finally, there's a terrible continuity error when we see the scene from "Confirmed Dead." Dan's hair comes down just past his ears and it's slicked back. His caregiver is a young woman with a high voice. But when the scene continues, his hair is suddenly shoulder-length and no longer greasy, and his caregiver seems to have aged 20 years and is slightly heavier. He was wearing a black sweater in the earlier scene; now it's gray. If the director wasn't going to even try to create any continuity in this scene, he should have reshot the beginning of it so it wouldn't have been so jarring, and then fans would have noticed the differences only if they'd gone back and checked the earlier episode.

4 8 15 16 23 42: When Desmond is taken to the end of the hall in the hospital, a sign says there are **4** ER bays there. Daniel says the metronome has counted 864 beats since he started playing. That's 108 times **8**, with 108 being the sum of Hurley's numbers. Dan has received a £**1.5** million research grant from Widmore. Dan mentions that they were in 1954 (or "Fonzie Times," as Hurley puts it), which is **23** years before this moment. When Dan is killed, they're **4** hours from the Incident.

It's Just a Flesh Wound: A bullet grazes Dan's neck at the motor pool shootout. He shoots Radzinsky and hits him in the arm. Daniel is shot through the chest and killed by his mother.

Lost in Translation: When Hurley sees Radzinsky's men storming the village, he says, "That's not good, right?" Jin then says something in Korean that wasn't translated. It was probably an expletive.

Any Questions?:

- The sub that comes and goes from the island seems to have a weird schedule. In "LaFleur," Horace tells Sawyer that there's a sub leaving the following day, but it'll be back in two weeks. In that same episode, the doctor tells Sawyer that Amy was supposed to be on the sub the following Tuesday so she could deliver the baby off-island, and in both cases it sounds like the sub comes and goes pretty regularly. In "Namaste," Sawyer explains that the recruiting subs only come once every six months. When Ben is shot and Juliet can't help him, Kate says they could send him out on a sub, and Juliet responds that there's not another sub due for months. And yet in this episode, only two days later, a sub arrives from Ann Arbor bringing the scientists in. Why couldn't Ben have been sent out on that one? Was it a secret expedition and Juliet didn't know the sub was coming? Or did she know it was coming, and sent Ben to the Others for another reason?

- Dan tells Miles that he's just making sure Chang will do what he's supposed to do. What is that? Was Chang the one who evacuated the island?

- So why *does* the news report of the 815 plane make Daniel so upset? Is it because he's time traveled to a point where he's already been there and knows the people, as some of us have speculated before? Is it because Eloise let slip at some point that Daniel would die on an island trying to prevent that crash, assuming that he would forget it the next day anyway? Had Eloise written out all of his notes already so they'd be ready for when he had to leave, and he'd seen them and is subconsciously relating it to the news story? Or is he simply upset about the crash and the line is nothing more than a lead-in to what Widmore is about to reveal to him?

- Theresa was put into a comatose state by Daniel's experiments, and several rats died because of them. Why was Daniel afflicted with memory loss but nothing more debilitating?

- After Kate, Jack, and Daniel get away, Radzinsky yells for someone to sound the alarm. Does he honestly think that no one in Dharmaville heard the Shootout at the Motor Pool Corral — complete with *explosion* — that happened only a few feet away? How did Sawyer and Juliet not hear it?

- If Daniel's theory is actually true, is he assuming that by detonating the bomb in 1977, everyone on the island will die, thus eliminating their double selves from the timeline?

- If Ben shot Desmond early in the morning (when he calls Jack after he's been beaten in "316," he interrupts Jack and Kate at breakfast), then why is it dark outside when Penny gets him to the hospital? Right before Ben shoots Desmond, he calls Widmore in London, and it would have taken Widmore at least 11 hours to get to L.A. (a couple of hours less on a private jet) and yet he's there. Clearly at least 12 hours have passed, so why wasn't Desmond brought in for attention immediately? Did something else happen that we haven't yet seen?

- Widmore asks Eloise if Desmond is okay, yet when Ben phoned him, he was threatening to kill Penny. How did Widmore find out that Desmond was the one who was shot?

- If the surnames of Daniel's parents are Hawking and Widmore, where did the name "Faraday" come from?

Ashes to Ashes: Daniel Faraday was a brilliant scientist who devoted his life to the study of relativistic physics and, particularly, space-time. He showed amazing potential in his early career, being the youngest doctorate to graduate from Oxford and immediately winning a £1.5 million research grant, but when an accident badly injured his research assistant, he immediately left Oxford. Because he had conducted the same experiments on himself first, he suffered from short-term memory loss, which was healed when he went to the island. Throughout his life he believed in destiny, while ironically trying to create a way to go back and change the course of events. Just when he finally admitted that his free will could win out over destiny, his destiny came back and bit him in the ass. He will be remembered fondly by his friends as "Twitchy."

Music/Bands: Daniel is playing the cantabile section of Chopin's "Fantaisie-Impromptu in C-Sharp Minor," one of the composer's most famous pieces. The piece is relevant to the story: not only does Eloise believe that allowing Dan to become a pianist is just mere fantasy, but she thinks that nothing in life is impromptu: it's all been laid out there, and she must follow the path that destiny has laid out for her.

Wired Magazine: "The Super Power Issue!" (August 2003)

As Widmore sits down in Daniel's living room, he moves aside a copy of *Wired* magazine that is sitting on Daniel's couch. The cover of "The Super Power Issue" from August 2003 proclaims, "The Impossible Gets Real!" and the magazine featured a series of articles about science-fiction powers that are becoming a reality due to recent scientific breakthroughs.

The following is a summary of the articles that were part of the topic, which you can read in full here: www.wired.com/wired/archive/11.08/.

"8 Super Powers" by Brendan I. Koerner: In this list of top 8 superpowers that are actually in development, Koerner explains the science behind things we've only dreamed about, taking the "fiction" out of science-fiction:

- X-ray Vision — Clark Kent thought he had the market cornered on this one, but using ultrasound, goggles will soon be able to see through walls; the downside is they'd have to be held up against the wall. Probably more useful for elite police forces than pubescent boys.
- Regeneration — Biologists are working on techniques that would allow human beings to regrow limbs or organs just like a salamander does . . . or like Claire on *Heroes*. Well, not quite; the limbs would be regrown separately and then transplanted.
- Total Recall — Scientists have discovered that the more PPI enzyme we have in our system, the less we remember. When disabling this enzyme in mice, they've found they can find their way through a maze flawlessly and display amazing memory retention. Now scientists are trying to isolate this gene in humans. (I nominate my husband as a guinea pig for that one, if it'll help him find his wallet whenever we're leaving the house.)
- Teleportation — It's not just on *Star Trek* anymore. In 2002 a scientist successfully teleported a laser beam, and is now working on teleporting an atom or a molecule. Next step: humans, whose bodies contain 10^{27} atoms. (I don't nominate my husband for this one.)
- Weather Control — *X-Men*'s Storm probably won't have any competition any time soon. While weather scientists are looking at ways to manipulate and control weather, they are discovering that early efforts have not worked out very well. The theory is there; it's getting reality to follow that's the problem.
- Force Fields — Britain's defense department is currently developing a metal force field that could surround tanks and prevent them from being blown to bits by a simple grenade. It's not invisible or as marvelous as Violet's on *The Incredibles*, but aesthetics isn't foremost on the agenda.
- Underwater Breathing — Now we can all be Aquaman! A research team is very close to perfecting a synthetic gill that keeps out the hydrogen in H_2O, allowing only the oxygen to come through, which would allow humans to remain underwater indefinitely.
- Super Strength — Forget the steroids: scientists are currently working on a special super-suit with exomuscles that act like human muscles, but are 100

times stronger. The exomuscles would match those of the wearer, mimicking their muscle movement.

Now, if these scientists could just hurry up and perfect mind control, my plan for world domination would be complete.

"Being Invisible" by Wil McCarthy: In a fascinating article about how the power of invisibility is closer to reality than we think, McCarthy describes the crude demonstrations that have been performed to create the illusion of invisibility (and he suggests your own party trick, so you can do it at home) and then he explains what still needs to be done to achieve it. Basically, if you have six cameras pointing out from the wearer, each filming the surrounding scene and simultaneously projecting it back onto the wearer, the person will seem to disappear because all you'll see is the landscape around and behind them. But he also illustrates how difficult it is to do this practically, and how scientists are working on a solution.

"The Antigravity Underground" by Clive Thompson: In this fascinating and funny article, Thompson talks about the burgeoning underground world of "lifters." Using the work of 1920s inventor Thomas Townsend Brown, antigravity hobbyists have been springing up everywhere, trying to create their own devices that will hover in the air and defy gravity. The article describes the grassroots campaign, the homemade videos popping up on the Internet showing the latest efforts to build a lifter, and his own experience with trying one out. He goes to the home of Tim Ventura, the man who sparked the global phenomenon, and watches as he demonstrates a lifter in his garage using 50,000 volts of electricity and screaming, "Awesome!" as his lifter hovers above the ground (it's a hilarious scene). Thompson then travels to NASA to find out what strides are being made in the world of science using the findings of these antigravity nuts, only to face a wall of denial. It's a great article, and definitely one worth reading.

"A User's Guide to Time Travel" by Michio Kaku: No doubt Daniel was reading this article with a highlighter. With the tagline, "All it takes is a grasp of theoretical physics, control of the space-time continuum, and maybe a ball of cosmic string," this article is a tongue-in-cheek guide to how you can go back in time and make your life happier. (Uh-oh . . . Miles would *not* be happy about that interpretation of time travel!) Chalking up the lack of success in the area to nothing more than an "engineering problem," he talks about scientists using

Einstein's linear theories to discover a "whirlpool" where time can curve back in on itself (score one for the *Lost* writers!) and create a parallel universe. He says in recent years scientists have been taking time travel very seriously and have been creating a myriad of time machine designs. (Kaku then warns readers not to go back in time and kill their parents . . . Miles would say that's impossible, but Kaku doesn't think so.) From there the article explains humorously how to go about traveling through time, using various scientific methods that have been theorized so far, including: Throne Plates (which allow the user to zip through a wormhole without being pulled into spaghetti, as Stephen Hawking would put it); a Gott Loop (flying a spaceship through a loop of cosmic string); a Gott Shell (a large concentration of mass that slows down gravity, and therefore time, for anyone inside); a Van Stokum cylinder (a cylinder that stirs space-time and pulls in nearby objects, sending them through space-time at the speed of light); or finding a Kerr Ring (a star that hasn't quite collapsed into a black hole but possesses a strong gravitational pull). Each suggestion comes with its own pros and cons. This is a very funny article that will be enjoyed by many a *Lost* fan.

Interestingly, J.J. Abrams was the guest editor of *Wired* magazine's May 2009 issue, which had just hit stands when "The Variable" aired. Dubbed "The Mystery Issue," it featured several articles about puzzles and brain teasers. It featured a complicated puzzle by cryptographer Bruce Schneier, which, if solved, correctly identified the statue on the *Lost* island. According to Lostpedia, "After a suggestion from [writer and filmmaker] Nick Tierce that the numbers represented an alphanumeric code, Steven Bevacqua, a postproduction supervisor for the television series *Life*, who was the first to solve the issue's master puzzle, decrypted the first half of the *Lost* sub-puzzle, whereupon Boulder, Colorado, musician Jon Leyba solved the second half of the puzzle." The answer? See page 262.

5.15   Follow the Leader

Original air date: May 6, 2009
Written by: Paul Zbyszewski, Elizabeth Sarnoff
Directed by: Stephen Williams
Guest cast: Kevin Chapman (Mitch), Alice Evans (Eloise Hawking, Age 40),

David S. Lee (Widmore, Age 40), Elisabeth Blake (Vanessa), Victoria Goring (Charlotte's Mom), Maya Henssens (Young Charlotte), Leslie Ishii (Lara Chang), William Makozak (Captain Bird), Sebastian Siegel (Erik)

Focus: Everyone

As Eloise leads Jack to the hydrogen bomb in 1977, Locke is leading his own expedition 30 years later.

Just as the title suggests, this episode focuses on leaders and followers. Jack leads a suicide mission to the hydrogen bomb; Sawyer loses his spot as leader of the group when he's caught by Radzinsky; Kate refuses to follow Jack on his expedition; and Radzinsky refuses to follow Horace, whom he believes is an ineffectual leader when he's under pressure. Eloise leads Jack's group to the bomb, and Locke leads his group to Jacob, with Ben trying to undermine his leadership the entire way.

Jack used to be the leader of the survivors, but since returning to the island he's seemed happy to lie low and let Sawyer continue leading while he just lets fate take its course. But now he's found his destiny, and the chance to start over is enough incentive for him to get up and do something. In "The Variable," Daniel explained to Kate and Jack that if he can detonate the hydrogen bomb, he can prevent the cataclysmic Incident that is about to happen at the Swan station, and all of the events that will happen as a result of it: someone being forced to push a button, the plane coming down, the freighter coming to the island. Daniel's main incentive is to erase Charlotte's death and make it so she never returns to the island and she lives a happy life. Jack sees a similar kind of possibility, and now that Dan is dead, he wants to carry on his work.

In "The Little Prince," Jack asks Kate if she's with him, and she looks right at him and says, "I have *always* been with you." Well, as of this moment, Kate is no longer with him. The conversation the two of them have in the tent is brilliantly executed by both actors. Matthew Fox, in particular, is extraordinary. Fox's performances often get overshadowed by the stellar acting of Michael Emerson, Terry O'Quinn, and Jeremy Davies, but Fox has been amazing on this series from season 1. Over the past five years, he has played the character of Jack as a combination of holier-than-thou, sympathetic, infuriating, confident, and completely lost. In season 1 he calmly walked from one catastrophe to the next, keeping things together and fixing things around him. In season 2 he refused to abandon his convictions, eventually causing Locke to mistrust his own. In season 3 he had his moments of doubt, and the stress of the island was getting to him. In season

4 he went off the island, fell apart completely, and now we see a man who is a shell of his former self, desperate to hold on to any thread of hope that he can to keep going. His eyes are filled with pain, he looks like he's been through hell, and his face looks like it's aged 15 years. But that's all Matthew Fox's acting, because when they flash back, he looks as fresh and healthy as he did in the first season. Now, he faces off with Kate, and he has a wide-eyed optimism that we haven't seen in him before. He knows when they got on that plane that there were 324 people on board. When it crashed, 71 survived in the front and tail sections, and of those survivors, the only ones who remain are Kate, Jack, Sayid, Hurley, Sawyer, Locke, Jin, Sun, Walt, and Aaron (and possibly Bernard and Rose, but we haven't seen them since the flaming arrows so Jack probably presumes them to be dead, too). If the plane never goes down, all those people wouldn't die.

But on a personal level, Jack won't have to be a doctor with no equipment watching patient after patient die on the island. He won't fall in love with Kate only to see her sleep with Sawyer. He won't have to deal with monsters and secret government scientific organizations and the craziness of John Locke and Benjamin Linus. He won't be forced to question everything he's ever known. He won't be followed from the island by demons that will force him to be miserable and addicted and obsessed and depressed. If the most he has to do is face his mother's guiltmongering when he steps off the plane with his father in a coffin, that's a walk in the park compared to what Jack's been through. Maybe he can finally not only fix things for everyone else, but also for himself.

Sayid sees everything from a personal perspective as well, and needs very little convincing to join Jack's mission — if the plane never goes down, he doesn't torture and kill people on the island, he might actually find Nadia, she won't die because she won't get caught up in the war between Widmore and Ben, and he won't be turned into a mindless assassin for Ben. Though Sayid is smiling when he says it, it's a very sad moment when he says to Jack that if this doesn't work, then it'll at least put them out of their misery. Sayid no longer has any reason to live, and that's why he's going along with Jack.

Kate, on the other hand, looks at things from a completely different point of view. Locke explained to Sawyer that he wouldn't go up to his former self banging away futilely on the hatch and describe what's going to happen, because to do so would mean he wouldn't have taken the journey he was meant to. Locke would be saving himself a great deal of pain by forgoing what he is about to go through, but he says that doing all of that, keeping those memories, is what makes him who he is. Kate, similarly, wants to hold on to her memories. Life with Jack might not have been easy, but if the plane lands safely in L.A., she won't have the happy memories of being engaged to him. She won't have the memories of the fun she had with Sawyer. She won't have met Sun or Claire or any of the people whom she considers friends. She's lost people along the way, but through the pain of losing them she's come to terms with what happened with her mother, gaining the confidence to stand up to Diane when she left the island, and she's accepted what happened to her father. And . . . she would be handcuffed to a marshal who's going to try to put her away for life. She probably doesn't understand the depths of Jack's sorrow and what he's gone through, but he's not looking at it from her perspective, either: if the plane never crashes, then the last three years of her being a loving mother to Aaron would be gone. And despite the pain of giving Aaron up to Mrs. Littleton, for Kate, the thought of never having known him as her son is far, far worse.

There are pros and cons to both arguments. Jack's desire to save the people on board Oceanic Flight 815 is noble. But on the flip side, if he detonates a hydrogen bomb he will kill people. It's not clear how many, but there are dozens of Others on the island, and if the Dharma Initiative doesn't evacuate everyone, there could be dozens more. Would it be fewer people than the ones who died on 815, or would one massacre cancel out the other? Or would he save more people by trying to stop the plane crash?

Another disadvantage to a past in which the plane didn't crash is that all of the positive things that have happened as a result of the crash would be negated, and we'd be left with very bad things in their stead: Hurley would still believe he was cursed; Charlie would be a heroin addict (and while still alive, probably not for much longer); Claire would give up Aaron for adoption; Kate would be in jail; Jin would still be breaking people's legs for a living; Sun would resent her husband, who would still be treating her like she's subservient; Locke would be a paraplegic; Sawyer would continue his maniacal search for his namesake; Walt would go on mistrusting Michael, who wouldn't know the first thing about being a father; Rose would be dying of cancer; Nikki and Paulo would still be alive.

Sawyer had been the leader of the group, and had been enjoying his position without abusing it. Just as Juliet senses that things might be over between her and Sawyer when he refers to Kate as "Freckles" in "The Variable," Sawyer realizes that his days as the group leader are over when Jack takes over and devises his kamikaze mission. Though Sawyer tries to do the responsible thing in the security station, he ultimately realizes it's over for them in Dharmaville, and he agrees to leave, giving up everything he's known. Hurley still has faith in Sawyer, and even when he sees him being led away, he's insistent that Sawyer will have a plan to get them out of their mess. Juliet is desperately trying to hold on to any modicum of a relationship they might still have even though she knows that Sawyer will always be worried about having left everyone behind, but when Kate shows up at the end of the episode, you can see all hope drain right out of Juliet's face. She can't even look at Kate when she boards the sub.

Weaselly Radzinsky takes over from Horace as leader when he believes Horace is no longer up to the task, basing his idea of leadership on who's holding the biggest gun. His even greasier sidekick, Phil, is the sort of man who follows that kind of leader. A successful leadership is one based on trust, and when Chang enters the station and sees Radzinsky staging a coup, he realizes he's been trusting the wrong people, and he turns to Miles, who is the de facto leader of his tiny group.

Ben jokes about staging his own coup against Locke, but he's powerless for the first time, and knows it. Locke had his moments of flippancy in "Dead Is Dead," but in this episode he's all business, and we realize the jokes are over when he looks at Ben in the jungle and tells him he knows that he never spoke to Jacob. There had been some fan speculation that the awesome scene in "The Man Behind the Curtain" could have been staged by Ben. Perhaps he simply guessed that Jacob would be sitting in the chair, and held onto it and pretended to yell at the man sitting in it. If he really was faking that moment, then the surprise on his face when the things in the room begin swirling around and Locke claims to have heard and seen him would have been the most genuine expression Ben had in that scene. Locke is no longer guessing at the truth about Ben — he *knows* that Ben is a false prophet, and Ben knows that he knows it. Locke looks at him at the beginning of the episode and says, "I'm not afraid of anything you can do anymore, Ben," because he now sees through Ben's lies. As Locke stands before the people who were formerly Ben's, he rallies them together and tries to conjure up dissent. By refusing to enter Richard's tent to discuss things in private and instead letting everyone else in on the discussion, he turns the heretofore dictatorship with the Others into a democracy. Or, at least, it has the appearance of a democracy.

And who is Richard Alpert? In this episode, Ben finally explains that Richard is the advisor to the leader, which suddenly makes a lot of sense. Alpert has always been the guy with the knowledge, but he seems to answer to someone else. If he's in the role of permanent advisor, he would know many things, but would have no authority to act on them. He always seems amazingly calm and collected, though he's caught off-guard by certain things (notice how he drops his mug and runs to Dan's side when Eloise shoots him). He's not omniscient, and seems baffled and in awe when John Locke returns to the camp. In "Whatever Happened, Happened," Richard takes young Ben, eager to accept what he thinks might be the island's next leader, and when one of the Others says that Ellie and Charles will be upset, he mutters that he doesn't "answer" to them. So Richard advises the leader, but he answers to Jacob, it would seem. He is presumably the one who talks to Jacob, getting lists from him and passing on Jacob's advice to the leaders. Let's hope we get a Richard flashback or at least more information about him in *Lost*'s final season.

All of the leaders — and followers — have their own agendas, but it's not clear which ones are legitimate when it comes to Locke's gang. Richard says to Ben that he thinks Locke is going to be trouble. Is he truly beginning to question Locke's ability to lead, or was he simply drawing out from Ben the information that Ben killed him? At the end of the episode, Locke drops a bombshell when he tells Ben that he's going to kill Jacob, and it's a similar shock: what is his reason? The only words he's actually heard Jacob say to him were "Help me" in "The Man Behind the Curtain." Maybe he believes that by killing him he's doing Jacob a favor, releasing him from whatever prison he's in. Maybe he's hoping to resurrect Jacob as a better person, the way he's come back new and improved.

Or maybe John isn't new and improved, and has returned as a dark version of himself. By getting Richard to hand the compass to the original John Locke, he will send that Locke back to 1954, setting the whole chain of events in motion that will put John on the road to specialness and ensure his position of authority in this moment. Knowing that it's the relationship with Jacob that seems to undo every previous leader, maybe he's out to get rid of Jacob once and for all, so he can, at last, own the island.

Highlight: The entire exchange between Chang and Hurley:
Chang: What year were you born?
Hurley: Nineteen . . . thirty-one.
Chang: You're 46?
Hurley: Yes. Yes I am.
Chang: You fought in the Korean War?

Eloise (Alice Evans) and Charles (David S. Lee) have a "complicated" relationship. I would expect nothing less from them.

Hurley: There's . . . no such thing.

The only thing that topped that line was the way Miles glanced at Jin — the Korean — and Jin looked at Hurley with disdain. Clearly Hurley thought that *M*A*S*H* was pure fiction.

Did You Notice?:

- In "This Place Is Death," Charlotte says that she and her mother left the island, and she never saw her father again. Now we see it's because the women and children were evacuated first, and the men were left behind. Who was her father?
- Watch Kate when Eloise asks if Jack and Kate came there with Daniel. It looks like she's about to say no, and when Jack says yes Kate looks like she's going to punch him.
- We see how headstrong Eloise is in this episode, and she was always that way. In "Jughead," a young Eloise tells Daniel that she doesn't believe for a second that a British woman, a Chinese man, and a scientist are all working for the U.S. Army. She sees through Dan's lies in a way that Richard doesn't.
- The ship that Richard Alpert is constructing in the bottle is the *Black Rock*.

His tent on the beach is reminiscent of where Ben had breakfast with Kate on the beach in "A Tale of Two Cities."

- When Sun and Ben first walk into the camp, there's a woman standing behind them and to the right of the screen, who some fans thought resembled what Juliet would look like if she were in her 50s or 60s, and theories suddenly abounded about whether Juliet somehow got stuck on the island in 1977 and lived the rest of her life there, eventually rejoining the Others. You see her again when Locke returns from his jungle expedition; she's standing at the picnic table behind Sun. And I must admit, she really *does* look like an older version of Juliet. (She does not accompany Locke on the expedition.)
- When Phil punches Juliet, even Radzinsky looks surprised.
- In "Namaste," Hurley panics when he realizes they're in 1977 and he doesn't know any historical facts. He asks Sawyer who's president, and Sawyer tells him to relax, that this isn't a quiz show. But that same question is Hurley's undoing in this episode.
- Widmore wonders why Daniel looks familiar to him, whereas Eloise knows who he is right away. That's because in "Jughead," by the time Widmore got back to the camp, Daniel was already on his way out of the camp with Ellie at gunpoint. Widmore asked Richard about him, wanting to know why they were letting him go, but he was probably in Dan's presence for less than five minutes.
- When Eloise comes back outside and tells Richard to untie Jack and Kate, if you listen closely to the conversation she and Widmore have, he puts his hand on her belly and says, "What about your condition?" Clearly she's pregnant with Dan at that very moment. If we're in the middle of 1977 in this episode, Dan will be born in 1978, meaning he is about 29 or 30 when he dies. When he comes to the island in 2004, he's 26. When Desmond visits him at Oxford in 1996, he's 18. That seems to be a wee bit of a stretch, but it is still possible. He tells Eloise at his graduation that he's the youngest doctorate ever to graduate from Oxford. In 1989, a prodigy named Ruth Lawrence graduated from Oxford with a Ph.D. at the age of 17. In 1985, she had been the youngest undergraduate to receive a degree from Oxford, at the age of 13. So it's possible Daniel could have been roughly that age, and when Desmond meets him, it's a year after his graduation. Despite the fact that Jeremy Davies is almost 40 while portraying this character, it's actually believable that Daniel would look much older than his years, and that he'd

have graying hair and would look pale and gaunt. He's been through more in his years than just about anyone else on the show, and has had an immense amount of pressure put on him by his mother. Add to that the catastrophic nature of what happened to Theresa, and the debilitating effect his memory loss had on him, and I can entirely believe that he could look a decade older than he actually is.

- Ben doesn't serve any purpose on the trip into the jungle for Alpert to find gunshot-in-the-leg Locke. Locke clearly only wanted Ben to tag along so he could see proof of the island communicating with Locke.
- The scene of Alpert tending to Locke's wound is mostly taken from "Because You Left." The only difference was the angle from which Locke first sees Alpert approach (we only see his torso through a hole in the trees in "Because You Left") and when Alpert first gets to him in the season premiere, he stops, smiles, and calmly says, "Hey, John." They remove that line from this episode to make Alpert look a little more unsure of himself. But the rest of the scene is simply taken from that episode.
- In "The Man Behind the Curtain," Locke says to Ben, "You know what I think, Ben? I think there is no Jacob. I think your people are idiots if they believe you take orders from someone else. You are the man behind the curtain, the Wizard of Oz. And you're a liar." Ben convinced him otherwise, but Locke was on to something.
- When Locke disappears, the sound he makes is like the noise at the end of every episode when the *Lost* end title card appears.
- It's interesting that Hurley has so much faith in Sawyer. In the first couple of seasons, the characters despised one another, leading Hurley to eventually jump Sawyer in "Dave" and beat him up. Now he trusts him.
- Juliet and Sawyer are like Lot and his wife when they escape Sodom and Gomorrah, only their roles are switched. Juliet enters the sub without ever looking back, and Sawyer stands there for a moment, staring at the island (the writers clearly wanted us to think he'd get shot or would change his mind) and then he gets into the sub, looking back one more time for good measure. Perhaps in season 6 he'll turn into a pillar of salt.
- I'm kind of happy knowing that Radzinsky will eventually blow his head off with a shotgun. Does that make me a bad person?
- If the women and children were evacuated, why didn't Ethan get on the sub? Why did he become an Other instead? Did Amy also become an Other?

Interesting Facts: Sawyer jokes with Juliet that when they get to the mainland they'll bet on the Dallas Cowboys in the 1978 Super Bowl. The Cowboys won Super Bowl XII against the Denver Broncos 27 points to 10, but because the Cowboys were the favorite to win, Sawyer would have to bet on the point spread to make some serious cash.

Nitpicks: Richard pulls out the compass and says it's a little rusty, but it still points north. Yet, back in season 1's "Hearts and Minds," Locke gives Sayid a compass, and it never works properly, and Sayid realizes that's because the island's magnetic properties prevent it from properly pointing north. So why does Richard's compass point north? Also, the compass that Richard gives to Locke as he's taking the bullet out of his leg is brand new, so the compass he gives him in this episode — which should create a time loop where the compass never has an origin point — should look exactly the same. If Alpert gives Locke a rusty compass, that would actually change the events. Also, that CGI used when the sub sinks was horrible. Even the waves in the sub's wake looked fake. And Locke insists that the group immediately leave the beach and head to Jacob's, even though Richard wants to sleep on it and leave in the morning. Locke wins . . . and yet they don't trek out until the next morning. What happened?

Finally, if Radzinsky beat Sawyer to a pulp demanding to know where Kate went, and Sawyer eventually drew them a map to find the Hostiles, why would they have gotten rid of Kate so easily and stuck her on the sub the moment she returned to the village? Why wouldn't they interrogate her separately to find out if her story matched Sawyer's so they could find Jack, too? They believe she and Jack are the two traitors who have been playing both sides. They keep Sayid in a jail as a suspected Hostile, but when they get their hands on Kate they immediately get rid of her? That doesn't make any sense.

Oops: When Richard was taking the bullet out of Locke's leg in "Because You Left," he was wearing glasses, and was still wearing them when Locke blooped away. But when he turns and walks back to Locke in this episode, he's not wearing any glasses. Also, when Daniel inspected the Jughead bomb in "Jughead," it was hanging upside down and the leak was at the top of the bomb, running toward one of the seams. When they see the bomb underground, the leak has been moved to the middle of the bomb, where it's now running horizontally between two of the seams, near where the name of the bomb is written.

4 8 15 16 23 42: The hydrogen bomb is 12 feet long (**8** + **4**) and weighs 40,000 pounds.

Sawyer's Nicknames

Charlotte: Ginger, Red
Daniel: Whiz Kid, Danny Boy, Dilbert, Dr. Wizard (Miles: "I think it's *Mr.* Wizard." Sawyer: "Shut up."), Plato, The Mad Scientist, Twitchy, H.G. Wells
Neil: Frogurt
Ellie: Blondie
Locke: Johnny Boy
Amy: Sweetheart, Sister
Miles: Enos, Banzai, Mr. "I Speak to Dead People"
Horace: Our Fearless Leader, Chief, Boss, H
Richard: Your Buddy Out There with the Eyeliner, Hoss
Hurley: Kong
Jack: Doc
Radzinsky: Quick-Draw, Stu
Sayid: Chief
Kate: Freckles
Oceanic 3: Yahoos
Juliet: Sweetheart, Blondie
Mitch (sub assistant): Nemo

It's Just a Flesh Wound: Widmore clocks Jack in the face with the butt of his gun and then hits him when he's on the ground. Radzinsky punches Sawyer repeatedly, at one point knocking his chair over. Phil hits Juliet in the mouth. Erik the Hostile throws Kate onto the ground, and kicks Jack in the face.

Any Questions?:
- Was Richard telling the truth about watching everyone die? If he's referring to them dying in a nuclear detonation, why didn't he die?
- Have the Others been leaderless for the past three years, or does Richard stand in as the interim leader when the real one just disappears? Is there Other protocol for what to do in those situations?
- Ben says Richard's been the advisor for a very, very long time. *How long?*
- If Richard is the advisor, then why does he walk into Dharmaville in "LaFleur" to confront Horace about two of his men being killed? Shouldn't the leader be doing that?
- Is Ben telling Sun the truth when he talks about Richard? Was he telling

her the truth in "Dead Is Dead" when he told her that he had no idea John would resurrect?

- Did Eloise and Richard have a relationship at some point? He looks uncomfortable when he talks about her and Widmore, and when she is swimming under the water, Richard waits at the other end, staring at the water with a very concerned look on his face.
- Jack tells Eloise that if they do what Dan wrote in the journal, "none of this would have happened." But so far Dan has been following that journal religiously, doing everything in it, and he still got shot. So what does Jack mean?
- If the Swan station is some sort of top secret lab, why does Radzinsky have a Swan logo on his jumpsuit, for all the world to see?
- What is the story between Eloise and Widmore? Why is their love complicated?
- What does Sayid mean when he says to Kate and Jack, "I killed Ben Linus and we're all still here." Did he think that if Ben died they'd all just disappear or something? Or did he think they'd all been brought back so he could fulfill this destiny and then they'd all be returned to their regularly scheduled time period?
- How extensive are the tunnels under the surface? It's amazing that the island doesn't entirely fall in on itself. Jughead is currently sitting below Dharmaville, and the similar-looking place where Ben was judged was under the Temple wall, which was quite a distance away.
- Why does Locke lie to Sun? Did his sense of morality change when he was resurrected? Earlier Locke followed through on his promise to Jin, and didn't tell Sun that Jin was alive. Now he just walks right past her when he returns to the camp, and looks her in the eye and lies to her about Jacob helping them find Jin.
- Was Ben lying when he said that he tried to kill Locke because he was becoming a problem?
- Jack says he trusts Eloise because she's the one who sent them all back to the island. Sayid asks why that would make him trust her, which is an excellent question. If Dan is right in saying that she was wrong and he was not destined to come back to the island, and that it's possible she sent him back to the island knowing that she would kill him, why would Jack trust her?
- Why is Locke going to kill Jacob? Is it because he asked for help? Is it to help him resurrect as a better person, the way Locke did? Is he trapped in some way and only death can save him? Or is Locke evil?

Dharma Logos

In the past we've seen several variations of the Dharma logos, usually representing a station:

- The Swan station logo naturally has a swan in the center of the wheel of I Ching trigrams. Daniel has one on his jumpsuit.
- The logo for the Arrow (the station where the Tailies camped out) is simply an arrow pointing upwards (when we first see Horace in "The Man Behind the Curtain," he's wearing this logo, though the black and white are reversed, making it look like a negative of the original logo).
- The Hydra station on the other island (where Jack was kept prisoner) features a depiction of the mythical multi-headed creature.
- The Staff station (the medical station where Ethan took Claire after she was kidnapped) has a caduceus, the universal sign for medicine or doctors.
- The logo of the Pearl station (where Eko discovered all the televisions) simply shows a white sphere inside the wheel of trigrams.
- Mikhail worked at the Flame station, which has a logo of a flame (Radzinsky's jumpsuit has this logo on it, because that's where he works).
- The Looking Glass station features a white rabbit (à la *Alice's Adventures in Wonderland*) in the center of it. In "He's Our You," when the Dharminians take a vote on whether to kill Sayid, Rosie (the girl dancing in the security station at the beginning of "LaFleur") is sitting among the group with this logo on her jumpsuit.
- The Tempest station (where Dan and Charlotte rendered the poisonous gas inert) shows a tidal wave in its center.
- The Orchid station has a spiral into the center, where there's a tiny orchid (seen on the hard hats of the construction workers in "Because You Left").
- The Lamp Post station, in the base of a church in L.A., simply features a beaming lamp post inside the Dharma logo.

This season we see several new logos, mostly on the jumpsuits of people, each of which designates their job assignments within Dharmaville:

- Sawyer, Phil, Miles, Jin, and the one-time-only Jerry all wear jumpsuits with a sheriff logo, consisting of a star with "Dharma" written in the middle, indicating they work at the security station underneath Dharmaville.
- Hurley wears a cafeteria logo, which is a little chef hat over a crossed knife and fork (which looks suspiciously like a skull and crossbones . . . that's one cafeteria you won't catch me eating in). I *love* this logo.
- Kate and Juliet are set off by their dark blue jumpsuits, which bear the motor pool logo, with a wrench inset and angled diagonally.
- In "Some Like It Hoth," when Hurley is writing the new and improved *Empire Strikes Back*, he's writing in a notebook that has a logo for the Dharma school, which is a stack of books with an apple on top.
- In "Follow the Leader," when Juliet and Sawyer are put on the sub, the men working in the sub wear uniforms with a sub in the center of the Dharma wheel.
- The workmen, like Jack and Roger Linus, simply have a hexagram with the word "Dharma" in the middle of it. Maybe the DI figured a tiny mop and bucket would be too humiliating for the wearer.

5.16, 5.17   The Incident, Parts 1 & 2

Original air date: May 13, 2009
Written by: Damon Lindelof, Carlton Cuse
Directed by: Jack Bender
Guest cast: Kevin Chapman (Mitch), Alice Evans (Eloise Hawking, Age 40), Andrea Gabriel (Nadia), Mark Pellegrino (Jacob), Titus Welliver (Man #2), Emily Rae Argenti (Young Kate), Adam Bazzi (Taxi Driver), Keegan Boos (Young Sawyer), Sally Davis (Woman), Rylee Fansler (Young Juliet), Colby French (Uncle Doug), George Gerdes (Mr. Springer), Daniel James Kunkel (Anesthesiologist), Agnes Kwak (Aunt Soo), Savannah Lathem (Young Rachel), Tanner James Maguire (Young Tom), William Makozak (Captain Bird), Sonya Masinovsky (Russian Nurse), John Pete (Prison Clerk), Michael Trisler (Juliet's Dad), Amy Stewart (Juliet's Mom — uncredited)

Focus: Jacob

The identity of Jacob is revealed for the first time as both Locke's group and the Ajira crew head across the island to see him. Meanwhile, in 1977, Jack tries to convince Sawyer and Kate that blowing up a hydrogen bomb could save them all.

"Two players. Two sides. One is light. One is dark."

And with those words spoken by John Locke in *Lost*'s pilot episode, viewers knew this wasn't going to be an ordinary television series. Now, five years later, the season 5 finale begins with two players, two sides. One is dressed all in white, eating a white fish, wearing white rope sandals, and sitting on a white beach. The other is clothed in a black shirt, dark gray pants, and black sandals, and has salt-and-pepper hair. The conversation between them is mysterious, revealing a long and complicated history between the two men, much like the similarly intriguing conversation between Widmore and Ben at the end of "The Shape of Things to Come."

The first time Jacob's name was mentioned was in the season 3 episode "I Do," when Danny Pickett, one of the Others, said that Jack's name wasn't even on Jacob's list. Ben referred to "Him" throughout season 3 as if he were a god. When Locke finally asked Ben to take him to see Jacob in "The Man Behind the Curtain," Mikhail and Tom objected, saying that it wasn't fair that Locke got to go when they'd never seen Jacob. Ben (clearly lying) insisted that he was the only person Jacob talked to, and he and Locke went to the cabin. There was a distinct line of ash around the cabin, and it wasn't clear what it was for. Some fans believed it was keeping evil out, making the cabin a protected place; others thought it was keeping Jacob in, turning the cabin into a prison. Locke heard a voice say "Help me" and he saw an eye turn toward him, and he ran out of the cabin in terror. In "The Beginning of the End," Hurley saw the cabin, looked inside, saw Christian in the chair, and a wild eye appeared at the window. He too ran away from the cabin, tripping along the way, and when he turned around, the cabin was gone. Locke returned to the cabin in "Cabin Fever" with Ben and Hurley, and when he went inside, Christian was there with Claire, and the other man was nowhere to be seen.

Through the flashbacks in this episode, we see how Jacob already had contact with some of the future passengers of Flight 815, and maybe it's his touch that brought them to the island. One of the characters he's touched is Jack. Season 5 saw Jack make an about-face in his personal philosophy, coming around to the same viewpoint as — of all people — John Locke. Jack has always been a very complicated character. In the past he's tried to project a sense of confidence — explaining to Kate how to let the fear in for five seconds and then force it out; convincing people he was the one to lead them; always speaking with absolute confidence on everything — but through his flashbacks, we've seen that Jack is a very vulnerable person. He's spent so long convincing everyone else that there's no such thing as destiny, he's convinced himself of the very same thing. In "Exodus, Part 2," Locke told Jack they were all brought to the island for a reason, and that "the island chose you, too, Jack. It's destiny." Jack responded, "I don't believe in destiny." Locke quietly answered, "Yes, you do. You just don't know it yet." But Jack didn't listen.

He continued to ignore Locke over the next three seasons, despite being wrong about the button in season 2, the freighter folk in season 3, and leaving the island in season 4. As Jack left the Orchid at the end of "There's No Place Like Home," Locke pleaded with him to stay, saying, "You know that you're here for a reason. You *know* it. And if you leave this place, that knowledge is gonna eat you alive from the inside out . . . until you decide to come back." Jack refused to believe him, once again reiterating, "There's no such thing as miracles," and left the island. Even when Ben moved the island, Jack refused to believe what he'd just seen with his own eyes — formerly his only criterion for believing in something.

When Jack returned home, everything Locke had predicted came true. He could no longer hide his lack of confidence from everyone else, and his drinking and drug-taking got worse. He refused to admit his own mistakes, and when facing

Locke one last time, he told his nemesis that he was delusional. But when Locke mentions Christian in return, it's the final nail in the coffin of Jack's convictions.

Suddenly believing that Locke was right (only after John is too dead to apologize to, of course) Jack returns to the island, using the same rhetoric that Locke had been using. At first he sits back, assuming the way this whole destiny thing works is that you'll feel it come and then you'll act upon it, until he finally gets what he believes to be his call of destiny — finishing the mission that Daniel couldn't, and making it so none of them ever end up on the island in the first place. In this episode he manages to get Kate on board by telling her, "Nothing in my life has ever felt so right."

Sadly, those words remind us of the end of season 2, where Locke convinced Desmond to join him in not pushing the button by saying, "I'm more sure of this than anything in my entire life." And we all saw how *that* worked out.

What is important about Jacob's touch is *when* it happened, just as Jack is arguing with his father. Jack's daddy issues are immense, and we've come to believe Christian was a man who pushed him too hard, rarely encouraged him, and even came between Jack and his wife. But in this episode, we're given a different perspective. We see Jack take Christian to task for embarrassing him in front of his staff, and he tells his father to stop treating him differently just because he's his son. Christian sighs wearily, and having seen what actually happened in the operating room, we can't help but wonder if Jack has misunderstood the situation. Christian could not have stepped back and done nothing, or the girl would have been paralyzed for life. He had to calm Jack down, and frankly, he probably treated him the way he would any student in that situation. In fact, there's a good chance he wouldn't have had a student as green as Jack performing that kind of surgery yet. He gave Jack the opportunity to finish the procedure, and congratulated him when it was over. It would seem Jack wasn't looking for his father to stop treating him differently; what he wanted was *better* treatment than Christian would have given any other student. Maybe Jack is seeing something in Christian that's not actually there. Is it possible Christian has always been proud of his son, but Jack was too angry to ever notice?

Jacob touches Kate at a pivotal moment as well — when she's about to steal a lunchbox with her friend Tommy. That boy will grow up to be Tom, the man she visits in "Born to Run," and together they will dig up this very lunchbox, which they'd turned into a time capsule, shortly before he'll be shot and killed while she's driving a getaway car trying to leave the hospital. (In this episode, behind the pickup truck, Tommy is playing with the same toy airplane that Kate gets out of the briefcase in season 1's "Whatever the Case May Be.") Kate's time capsule is something that stayed in one place and is representative of who she used to be as a child, while the adult woman is constantly on the run, refusing to be rooted to a single spot. Now, she is convinced by Jack to detonate the bomb, but her heart has been wrenched out as a result. This was not a good season for fans who loved Kate. More people turned on Kate this season than ever before (one fan recap joked that when Kate thought she'd been shot in "Follow the Leader," half the audience gasped in horror, while the other half cheered). Jack is willing to vaporize an entire island to forget about the pain she's caused him, and Sawyer's relationship of three years is suddenly in jeopardy because of the way he looked at her. Sawyer has commented previously that Kate jumps from one man to the other when it's convenient for her. Is any of this Kate's fault?

In the case of this season, no. Sawyer is looking in Kate's direction, and Juliet is filled with jealousy and resignation; Jack looks at her as the one that got away. But we know why she came back to the island, and it wasn't for Sawyer or Jack. Before she returned to the island she was happier and more fulfilled than she'd ever been, and seemed to be the only one of the Oceanic 6 who wasn't filled with regret. Until she stopped lying to herself.

For even though Aaron makes her happy, fulfills her as a person, and never asks more of her than for her to love him while he loves her unconditionally in return, she is not his real mother. She realizes that if she truly loves him, she needs to find his real mother (if she's still alive) and return him to her. The scene of her leaving him behind in a hotel room is one of the most gut-wrenching of the series, and Kate returns to the island, empty and isolated from the others, refusing to say what has gone wrong. Kate has returned to find Claire, and the relation-ship problems between Juliet and Sawyer are an unfortunate side effect. She doesn't want Jack to detonate that bomb, because even if she is able to find Claire and reunite her with Aaron, she'll still have the memory of those happy three years to keep her going. If the bomb goes off, and Jack is right, those memories will be erased — but Aaron will be with his real mother, who might change her mind at the last minute and not give him up for adoption. So, Kate decides to back Jack on this one. She's a strong woman — she'd rather have loved and lost than never have loved at all.

Juliet, on the other hand, is still reeling from the freshness of her emotional wound. From her point of view, anyone who believes it's better to have loved and lost didn't have the option of detonating a hydrogen bomb to make the pain go away.

For every fan who doesn't like Kate, there's another one who doesn't like Juliet. Some people came down hard on her for her actions in the finale, saying she was whiny and acting like an idiot. The Suliet and Skate "shippers" (those who want to see Sawyer and Juliet or Sawyer and Kate together) went to war about whether Juliet was right or not. Some said Sawyer and Kate were meant to be together and Juliet needed to accept that and shut up, while others said Sawyer clearly loved her — after all, he *said* he did, didn't he? — and that she was being silly by suggesting he didn't simply because he gave an innocent glance in Kate's direction. Still others echoed Sawyer, saying, "She couldn't have mentioned this *before* Jack and Sawyer beat the crap out of each other?" (I know I, for one, am grateful that she didn't.)

However, the writers have worked hard from the beginning of season 3 to show us Juliet's side of the story (the third season opened with a sympathetic flashback to her, showing how difficult her life was in New Otherton, and we've always seen her side of the story since that moment), so it would help to look at the entire situation from her perspective. In this episode, we saw that her parents split up when she was a child. While it's a little simple to suggest that *every* child of divorce will have doomed relationships thereafter, many children with divorced parents do become jaded after watching their parents' marriage dissolve. She then has an affair with and marries grade-A jerk Edmund Burke, who continues sleeping with his research assistants and tosses her aside. When she comes to the island, she goes from playing second fiddle to another woman to *becoming* the other woman, even though she hates what she's doing. She falls in love with Goodwin, but when his wife Harper finds out and confronts Juliet, you can tell by the stricken look on Juliet's face that she understands Harper's pain and is devastated she's the one who caused it. It doesn't end the affair, however, and through that relationship she discovers that Ben hasn't just fallen for her, but believes he owns her. She's trapped.

When she escapes and follows the others to the beach, she's surrounded by Men Who Love Kate. Jack will do anything for Kate, but joins forces with Juliet and falls for her. He kisses her at the Tempest station, but Juliet knows the moment Jack kisses her that he doesn't mean it, and tells Kate as much as soon as she's done operating on Jack a few days later. Edmund vowed his life to her, and broke that vow. Jack told Juliet he had her back, but he was still in love with Kate. Juliet is starting to understand that her parents were right: just because you're in

Bonnie and Clyde time travel to the island to try to stop Jack from detonating the bomb.

(© MARIO PEREZ/ABC/RETNA LTD.)

love with someone doesn't mean you were meant to be together. And then, along came Sawyer.

Sawyer pined for Kate for a long time after she left the island. At the beginning of season 5 we see him open up to Juliet about how upset he was. In "LaFleur" we see that he had Jin searching the island grid by grid in the hopes of finding their friends, and we know the one he wants to return is Kate. His romance with Juliet probably started by her being a sounding board for him while he talked about the relationship he'd had with Kate, what had happened between them, and how he always felt like he was coming second to the doc. But after a while, he resigns himself to the fact Kate's not returning, and takes Juliet, who is, well, there. If Kate had been there, would he have been with Juliet? Probably not. And Juliet knows that.

After three years, Juliet and Sawyer have established themselves as part of the Dharma Initiative and as lovers. Kate might be a memory, but she's the one that got away. He's grown as a person, as mentioned above, and he truly does love Juliet. They're comfortable, he knows she'll stay with him, and she gives him the same sense of security that he gives the people of Dharmaville. Juliet's not worried about any other women, because she knows the only other person he'd rather be with is long gone, and therefore their relationship is safe. But when Jin tells him the Losties have returned . . . Sawyer lies to Juliet. That lie was the beginning of the end; he wouldn't have lied if he didn't think he had something to hide. He tells Juliet the news when he returns, and her whole world collapses. It's the Jack situation all over again, but it's more devastating because she truly believed she had Sawyer, and that they'd always be together, and she'd been with him for three years as opposed to Kate's three months. But now it's no different than her parents' marriage, than her marriage, than Goodwin, than Jack. She begins watching for signs.

People can criticize Juliet for being whiny despite Sawyer professing his love, but there's a reason the cliché "actions speak louder than words" is so popular: it's true. You can tell someone you love them until you're blue in the face. But if Sawyer is making ga-ga eyes at someone else, calling her "Freckles" (which, face it, is a far more endearing nickname than "Blondie"), looking in her direction when Bernard and Rose talk about true love, and following her everywhere, she knows where his heart lies. He can corner her in the jungle and profess his undying love for her, because he does love her — his anguish when she falls down that shaft is very real. But he doesn't love her the same way he loves Kate. And the problem is, even Sawyer doesn't realize this. He believes he loves Juliet, and he's trying to bury his feelings for Kate. Juliet, on the other hand, knows the truth and can see it in his eyes, and she decides it's too much to bear. When Juliet tells Sawyer it's over, she's not being whiny or annoying — she's a broken woman who's been let down too many times, and now it's happening again. Juliet's act in the final scene of the episode is not selfish, as some fans suggested afterwards (when I was watching the show, I don't recall seeing a scene where Jack and everyone else *changed their mind* about detonating the bomb), but instead she's going along with the group and doing what she believes everyone wants, most of all herself. Her heart has been freshly broken, and she can only see one option ahead.

Sawyer disagrees completely with what Jack is doing, but he begrudgingly goes along with it anyway when he finds himself outnumbered. Sawyer is the only one at the Swan site who is not on board with Jack detonating the bomb. He's accepted Dan's credo that whatever happened, happened. He had a chance to give up his search for the original Sawyer when he was a young boy, and if he'd listened to his uncle — who told him that what's done is done — he might have had a more fulfilling life. In this pivotal moment, Jacob gently steers the boy away from that advice and toward a life of hostility and rage. Yet despite everything, like Kate and Locke, he'd rather remember who he was and how far he's come than erase all of that. Unlike the others, he knows that if he ends up back on that plane landing in LAX, he'll still be the angry man he was three years earlier, still searching for the man who destroyed his life, and possibly never finding him. After he was left behind by the helicopter, he did what he's always done — he adjusted, and he found a way to live his life the best he could. He settled down with Juliet and learned to find happiness in his new situation.

If you compare season 5's Sawyer to the nasty and selfish person we saw in season 1, you can see he's grown more than any other character. Some fans would argue he's been neutered while living in Dharmaville (citing the way Juliet sometimes talks to him like he's a child) but he's also found a purpose in a way he's never had in his life. For the first time ever, people listen to him. He's not a sidekick, he's not a stupid redneck, he's not the guy making caustic comments from the sidelines — he's the head of security, in charge of a group of people and responsible for the safety of everyone in the Dharma Initiative; no longer living by the credo, "Every man for himself" now he's living with Juliet. But the moment he discovers that some of the survivors have returned, his past comes flooding back. He is overwhelmed with feelings for Kate that he thought were over. He is threatened by Jack and what he remembers as Jack's constant need to dominate and lead. He is worried Sayid will overturn everything he's built up for himself. In other words, he's come up with the perfect con, and now the very people he's been waiting for are going to screw it all up for him.

And so, in this episode, he gives in. He quietly tells Miles not to call him LaFleur — "There ain't no LaFleur anymore" — as if he's realized it was all a pipe dream. He's been living in a fantasy world, and now reality has come crashing back to him. When Juliet falls down the shaft, he loses the last tangible thing connecting him to that world. Regardless of where they end up, next season Sawyer could resent all of them for what happens to Juliet in this episode.

Like Sawyer, Miles disagrees with Dan and Jack's plan to detonate the bomb, but ends up participating in the shootout at the Swan that will enable that to happen. While he hasn't done much ghost whispering lately, he did come to terms with his parents. He realizes his mother had every reason to resent his father, thinking Chang was throwing them off the island in anger, but he also discovers she'd misunderstood his father's intentions. Maybe Miles will be a little less angry next season (but hopefully no less fun). And perhaps they can reunite him with Locke's body and we'll get some answers.

One thing Miles has been good for this season is acting as a voice for the fans. In the week leading up to this episode many fans wondered aloud if Jack would be the guy *causing* the Incident by dropping the bomb, rather than preventing it, and here Miles voices that very concern. Hurley has been the other voice throughout the season. Along with Miles, we watched him grapple with the headier concepts of time travel. In "Some Like It Hoth," he was the one who urged Miles to get to know his father, worried that he could regret it later if he didn't try now. Hurley has been a little underused this season — we saw a lot more of him when he was off the island as one of the Oceanic 6 — but because he's the only person besides Locke who has actually seen Jacob (or perhaps it was Jacob's nemesis standing in that cabin) he is still very important to the upcoming plot. He has seen Jacob more recently than anyone else, and was deemed important enough for Jacob to urge him back to the island. Hurley's the only capable person not at the Swan, so presumably he's stayed behind with Sayid.

Sayid is on Jack's side, but he might not survive to see the result of their actions. His present situation — bleeding to death from a gaping wound — is the physical embodiment of the painful emotional wounds he's suffered his entire life. Jacob touched him at the very moment his life fell apart, just as Nadia was killed by a hit-and-run driver. Sayid's life has been a twisted circle of pain: he was a torturer, then he fell in love with Nadia. They were separated, and then he was tortured by a man whose wife Sayid had hurt. He searched for Nadia before coming to the island, where he made Sawyer suffer, then fell in love with Shannon, then lost her, then tortured Henry Gale. He then left the island where he found Nadia and married her, then lost her, then killed dozens of people, tried humanitarian work, then killed more people, and returned to the island. There he was interrogated, and he attempted to kill Benjamin Linus in a moment of clarity when he believed this was his destiny, only to discover a few days later that his plan had been thwarted. And now, for his sins, he lies bleeding on the ground, his life meaningless, his destiny unfulfilled. We leave him in a tenuous situation, because if somehow the detonation of the bomb really does send everyone back to the airplane, he will continue to search for Nadia. But if, more likely, it either leaves them right where they are or causes them to travel to another time, he still has a bullet in his stomach, and Jack says the prognosis isn't good. I do think (and hope) there is more to come in Sayid's story.

Jin and Sun were sadly underused this season. Jin learns English, but otherwise moves in and out of scenes without affecting any of them. Sun, similarly, doesn't do much this season. Sun begins the season with a lot of potential, as a new mother who loves her daughter but is hell-bent on making the people responsible for Jin's death pay. But then the writers seem to have watered down Sun the moment she got on the plane. Simply stating that she must return to the island if there's even a slight chance her husband is alive, her character becomes

The scene of Nadia's death was filmed at the intersection of Auahi and Kamani Streets in Honolulu. Two stand-ins lie in position on the ground while the film crew set up the cameras (top). Then Naveen Andrews and Andrea Gabriel acted out the scene with the cameras rolling. (RYAN OZAWA)

quiet and submissive once more (save one paddle crack to Ben's head) and instead she becomes nothing more than a prompter to help explain the action. She asks John Locke how they will find her husband. She asks Richard Alpert if he's seen Jin. She asks Ben about Alpert and Locke. She asks Ben and Locke more questions while on the way to see Jacob. When they get to the statue's foot, she just sits on a log firing one question after another at Alpert. She's nothing more than a plot device that allows the other characters to give us important information. But we see in the flashback that Jacob touched her and Jin together, at their wedding, as if his touch might be the thing to keep them together. Here's hoping the inevitable reunion between the two of them next season will make up for the lack of character development in season 5.

Dan, on the other hand, is absent for a large part of the season, but when he returns, his story in "The Variable" is astounding. We find out that he's the son of Eloise and Widmore; he links the two of them, but also becomes an invaluable piece of the puzzle himself. It's not completely clear if Eloise led Daniel to the lion's den on purpose, knowing he would die, or if she put his life on a certain course because she thought maybe she could change what would happen. The sadness in her eyes suggests she knew exactly what was going to happen, but that the outcome of his death might be worth it — a sacrifice that would save many other lives. Dan was a fan favorite from the moment he appeared at the end of "The Beginning of the End," and his death was a sad one. His connection with Desmond is probably what will remain his most important link to season 6 — that and being the son of Charles Widmore.

Widmore has hovered over season 5 like a dark cloud, helping Locke (not) fulfill his mission to bring back those who had left, but more importantly, we've learned more about who he *was*. We saw a young, jumpy Widmore in the 1950s, and an older, more confident one in the 1970s. He told Locke he was the leader of the Others, but going back we see Eloise was the leader. Widmore seems to have succeeded her, but with Ben around, he only has a tenuous grasp on leadership at best. He's linked biologically to Daniel, but antagonistically to Ben.

Oh, Ben. How is one man so loathed and loved by fans all at the same time? If there was ever a character on television deserving of the title, "the guy we love to hate," it's Ben Linus. Played superbly by the inimitable Michael Emerson, Ben is a chronic liar, and admits as much to Locke in this episode. He has appeared to be a puppet master from the moment we first saw him as Henry Gale, driving Locke over the edge. He plays Sayid for a fool throughout the second season, kidnaps Hurley, Jack, Sawyer, and Kate, manipulates the latter three over a long period of time (while putting them in bear cages), and continues to toy with them long afterward. He has challenged Locke on Locke's quest to become the Chosen One, tricked him by leaving the island when Locke was supposed to, and once off the island continued to control everyone. He turned Sayid into an unequivocal killer. He helped change Jack's mind about destiny. He manipulated Kate into thinking someone was trying to take Aaron away from her. He helped put Hurley into jail and then got him out again. He convinced Sun to come back to the island with him *while she was holding a gun to his neck*, for god's sakes. And . . . he killed John Locke.

Ben has always been the guy who's in control. And yet, since the third season, he's referred to a higher power named Jacob, as if someone is actually pulling *his* strings. But in "The Man Behind the Curtain," he talked down to Jacob, scolding him like a parent would a child, and acted like he was doing his own thing. Now Ben seems to be powerless. The new and improved John Locke has seen through him, revealing that Ben has never seen or spoken to Jacob, and he lied about that just like he lied about everything else. Lying is Ben's superpower. It's the one thing Ben does better than anything else, and he keeps everyone around him constantly asking questions — "Did he just tell me the truth, or was he lying? When he told me he was a liar, was he lying about that, too? I'm confused." So when Locke pronounces once and for all that Ben was lying about Jacob, with no doubt in his voice, Ben is unnerved. The one thing he is good at has been unveiled by the man who has been his plaything since they first met in the hatch. Locke is the Chosen One in a way Ben has never been, and will never be, and it's a difficult thing for Ben to handle. As he and Locke sit together on the beach, he says, "I lied, John. It's what I do." He makes the statement matter-of-factly, but in doing so, he also does the very thing that a liar should never do: show himself for what he really is. After this moment, Ben hangs back, no longer in charge, no longer playing Richard against Locke and vice versa, no longer trying to turn the situation back to his own advantage.

At the end of the episode, he finally comes face to face with Jacob, the man he's never actually met or talked to. The only people allowed inside Jacob's sanctuary are the Chosen Ones, including John Locke. Ben was never truly one of those people. For the first time, Ben's guard goes down completely, and looking as vulnerable as he did as a child when he cowered before his abusive father, Ben looks at Jacob and pleads with him to tell him why he never paid any attention to him. The scene is astounding, and we see Ben in a light we've never seen before. Maybe, just as Sayid isn't really a killer but became one while following Ben's orders, Ben, too, thought he was just following orders for the greater good, that he was doing the right thing. The tenderness with which he looks at Alex has always given us a hint that there really is a heart inside Ben's chest, but when Jacob looks back at him and says, "What *about* you?" that heart is ripped out and stomped on, and just as Sayid realized everything was for nothing, Ben stops believing in destiny in that very moment. He stabs Jacob with the same quickness and ferocity with which he stabbed Keamy in last year's finale, filled with an unspeakable rage and yet empty at the same time, and in doing so, he resigns himself to the truth that his entire life has been a failure.

Which aligns him with the other character who has always believed himself to be a failure: John Locke, the one person who actually derived life from Jacob's touch. As outlined in "The Life and Death of Jeremy Bentham," John's story is a sad one, where every time he seems to make a definitive decision, it's the wrong one. He spent all of seasons 3 and 4 on a quest to become the leader of the Others, and held that position for about half a minute before the island flashed away from them and he was left alone. He got himself off the island but ended up in a leg cast, unable to convince a single person to return. He wasn't even able to determine his own death — Ben talks him out of committing suicide, only to choke him a few minutes later. But the sadness of Locke's death was always tempered by the fact that we knew he'd come back to life, and was alive and well on the island, just like Christian. Or . . . was he?

Since his return, Locke has been a newly confident person. Rather than guessing or hoping he's making the right decision, he's one hundred percent sure he's correct. And unlike at the end of season 2, when he was sure he was right, but was wrong, now he actually seems to know what he's doing for once. He orders Richard to take him to Jacob. He tells Ben point-blank that he's seen through him. He knows that Richard is powerless to say no to him. He *knows* once and for all that he really is the Chosen One. He strides into the base of Jacob's statue with one mission in mind, and hands Ben the knife, ordering him to kill Jacob. No longer is John Locke asking questions, or waffling at a crucial moment, or allowing others to make the decisions for him. John Locke is no longer a failure, and the transformation is remarkable.

Until . . . we find out that's not John Locke. Locke is dead, a body in a metal crate, and the man who just strode into the base of the statue appears to be the

Man in Black, looking like Locke. Jacob recognizes him immediately. What exactly happens at the end? We'll have to wait for season 6 to know definitively, but if only the Chosen One can enter Jacob's inner sanctum, and the Man in Black cannot kill Jacob, it appears that both Locke and Ben have been manipulated all their lives for this one moment: the Man in Black's loophole was to get Locke to die so he could inhabit his body, and to do that he needed Ben on board. He needed Ben to spend a life beholden to Jacob, where he would do things at the Man in Black's bidding, thinking he was working for Jacob but really working for the wrong side. Ben killed Locke, got the body back to the island, and in the end, he kills Jacob. All his life Ben thought he was one of the good guys, but he might have just been a pawn for one of the bad ones.

The Man in Black was the unexpected feature of this episode. He's never been seen or mentioned before, at least not as a man. But there's a strong suggestion that if Jacob is aligned with the beach, the sun, and the water, that the Man in Black is the jungle, darkness, and the smoke monster. Now that it appears Locke is the Man in Black, we recall that in "Dead Is Dead," when Ben came face to face with Smokey, Locke disappeared. He could also be the one manipulating the dead — just as he's currently inhabiting John Locke's body, perhaps he was the one who appeared to others as Christian, Yemi, or Alex (notice Locke wasn't around when Alex confronted Ben, either, and yet Alex is the one who tells Ben to do exactly as Locke, or the man who looks just like him, says). Perhaps the Man in Black tries on the various bodies to see which one will be the key into the statue. He tried Yemi. He tried Christian. And now he's tried Locke, and it worked, like a key fitting into a . . . well, you know. He could have used Christian's body to lead Locke to the Orchid station the first time, and to the Frozen Donkey Wheel the second. When Ilana and her crew go to the cabin in the woods, they see the line of ash has been broken. Perhaps when Hurley ran away screaming in "The Beginning of the End," and tripped, that was the Man in Black who peered at him from the window, frightening him away and causing him to break the line of ash.

When Ilana and her people go to the cabin, they appear to be looking for Jacob. When she goes inside, however, she comes out and reports that he's gone, and hasn't been there for a very long time. She adds, "Someone else has been using it." It would seem the Man in Black was the one inhabiting the cabin. He could have appeared to Locke to make him believe in Jacob, sending him on the path that would result in the Man in Black's victory. When Locke returned to the cabin in "Cabin Fever," Christian was sitting there, possibly another incarnation of the Man in Black, once again sending Locke on the goose chase he needed. It would seem the loophole that the Man in Black needed was for a body to die off the island, and somehow crash-land back on it as a corpse (like Christian, Yemi, and Locke all did). But why was John Locke's body the one he needed? What was wrong with the other ones? Is it because they didn't know someone on the island who was tied to Jacob, the way Locke knew Ben? Perhaps the Man in Black cannot physically kill Jacob, and needed a proxy, like Ben.

So is that it for John Locke? Is he really dead? Did he die by Ben's hand, feeling like a loser and a failure, just as he did his entire life before he went to the island? Was he nothing more than a pawn in the Man in Black's game? Locke has been an integral character on the show, the one who, from the first season, has seemed more important than anyone else. Maybe his importance was nothing more than just getting to where he needed to be. But I think there may be something more to John Locke. He saw his destiny in season 1. Yes, that could have been a vision given to him by the Man in Black, who had started his manipulations before John was even born, but it could be something more. He was the one who believed the island was bigger and more important than all of them. He really was the Chosen One, the one who was able to walk into Jacob's sanctuary when no one else could. He told Jack three years earlier that Jack would believe in destiny one day, and he was right. So for his life to really end once and for all in a seedy hotel seems wrong.

But not everyone gets a happy ending, and maybe John was one of the unfortunate ones. Or maybe the island has a different kind of reincarnation. The traditional sense of reincarnation is when one spirit moves to different bodies over different lifetimes. In the case of Locke, one body has housed two spirits. To everyone else's eyes, this is still John Locke. The philosopher John Locke believed that everyone was born a blank slate. Locke has been reborn, but he's certainly not a blank slate. Is it possible the John Locke we all know and love — despite his flaws — might really return?

Jacob has touched each of the ones who came back to the island, and that touch must mean something important. He hands Jack a chocolate bar in a moment when Jack was questioning his father's treatment of him. He touches Kate and pays for a lunchbox that will later play a major role in her life. He touches Jin and Sun and blesses their marriage. He appears to actually bring Locke back to life when Locke falls out of the window. He touches Sawyer at the child's most vulnerable moment, allowing him to finish the vengeful letter that will ruin his life. Interestingly, he touches Sayid and Hurley only after they've returned from the island the first time, at the lowest point in Sayid's life and the day before Hurley will return to the island. Is his touch a way to get them to the island again? Is it a mark of protection once they get there? Or is it something different, a mark that only he will see and recognize and know that these people are part of his own destiny? (In *The Wizard of Oz*, the Good Witch of the North leaves a mark on Dorothy that keeps her safe.) His touch to Kate, Jin, and Sun comes with advice. He touches Locke and Hurley with reassurance. His touch to Sayid is a distraction. He offers condolences to both Sawyer and Locke. His touch to Jack is a subliminal message: "Guess it just needed a little push."

And yet, when he visits Ilana, he wears black gloves, as if he cannot and will not touch her. Ilana, Bram, and the Shadow Seekers are a huge question mark at the end of the season. On the one hand, they claim to be the good guys, and they have knowledge of the island, of Jacob, and of the threats to Jacob. On the other, they're hostile and enigmatic, and actually played a direct role in Sayid's return to the island. Who will they turn out to be? If the two sides are Jacob's and the Man in Black's, whose side are they on?

When this episode finished, theories on Jacob and the Man in Black spread like wildfire on the Internet. People believed Jacob was good and the Man in Black evil. Some argued it was the other way around. Several fans began calling the Man in Black Esau, after Jacob's brother in the Bible (see **Interesting Facts** on page 248). Others suggested they were Cain and Abel. Some said God and Satan. It'll be interesting to see what we find out about them in season 6. Are they representative of good and evil, or is the distinction between the two of them more subtle? Could they, instead, represent destiny versus free will? And if so, which is which?

Their discussion at the beginning of the episode seems to be similar to the ones Jack and Locke had throughout the second season. The Man in Black says that everything always happens the same way, and nothing ever changes. Jacob counters that it only ends once, and everything to that point is progress. In this discussion, Jacob seems to be arguing for free will, while the Man in Black is suggesting things will never change. They appear to be making a colossal bet on humankind and what people will do when put into a certain type of situation (interestingly, the Losties seem to have done exactly what the Man in Black says they will). Later, when Jacob is talking to Hurley, he tells him that whether or not he returns is his decision, and he doesn't have to do anything he doesn't want to.

When Ben stands before him with a knife, Jacob calmly tells him, "You have a choice." Yet if Jacob believes that he and the Man in Black cannot kill one another, and the Man in Black is determined to find a loophole, it would suggest the Man in Black is using *his* free will to change their destiny.

The scene between Jack and Sawyer in the jungle mirrors the ones Jack had with Locke throughout the series (with Jack now taking Locke's role) and the one at the beginning of this episode. Sawyer tells Jack not to drop the bomb, and Jack tells him it's his destiny. Sawyer counters, "I don't speak destiny." Like Jacob, Sawyer believes in free will. But only insofar as it affects what we do with the future. He doesn't want Jack to drop that bomb because he thinks he's making a huge mistake. Yet by that same token, he refuses to go and change what happened between his parents a year ago, believing that "what's done is done." That sounds like destiny talk to Jack, so all Sawyer manages is to further convince Jack of his mission. And then they have the knock-down, drag-it-out fight we've all been waiting to see for five years.

Lost is a show about opposites, about dark and light, good and evil, and the rivalries between them. In the beginning the rivalry was between Jack and Locke. Then it was Ben and Widmore. Now it's Jacob versus the Man in Black — just when we thought it was all about Ben and Widmore's war, it seems to be much, much bigger than that.

What will conquer evil? Desmond's story always stands apart from that of the rest of the characters' arcs and his is the story of love winning out over everything. At the end of season 2 he found Penny's heartfelt note and he turned the key, sacrificing himself to save the world. He didn't die, but was given a special gift, one that eventually brought Daniel to the island. Desmond found Penny, one of the only truly happy moments in the series. In season 5 Desmond has been used more as a conduit for Daniel's story, but there's a chance something will bring him back to the island. After all, as Eloise said, "I'm sorry to have to tell you this, Desmond, but the island isn't done with you yet."

The love quadrangle of Jack/Kate/Sawyer/Juliet hasn't been there for nothing, either. Maybe in the end, all you need is love. Yes, *Lost* is a show for the thinking viewer. It forces us to analyze heady concepts, read difficult books, learn new philosophies and scientific equations. But so much of it is based on love. Jack attempts to detonate a bomb because of how strongly he loves Kate. Juliet finishes the job because of her love for Sawyer. Kate returns to the island because of her love for Aaron, and Sun because of her love for Jin. While some fans might

36 Hours Before 316

As of the finale, we know what most of the Oceanic 5 (plus Ben) were doing in the 36 hours before getting onto Ajira Flight 316.

Jack: He left the church and went to a bar, where he was interrupted by a phone call from his grandfather's retirement home saying his grandfather had escaped. He went to the home the next morning to see Ray, and while there got a pair of his father's shoes. He returned home late that night (presumably the retirement home was pretty far away from L.A.) and Kate was in his house. They slept together, and the next morning he went to the butcher shop where he put the shoes onto the feet of Locke's corpse, and then brought the body to the airport.

Kate: She stormed away from the marina and was heading home when Aaron said he wanted a drink. She stopped at the supermarket, where she almost lost him. Distraught, she strapped him into the car and drove all night to Cassidy's house in Albuquerque. She talked to Cassidy and realized her fear of someone taking Aaron stemmed from the fact she'd taken him from his mother. She drove the rest of the day and into the night back to L.A., where she gave Aaron to Claire's mother. She then drove to Jack's house, devastated about losing Aaron, and slept with him. The next morning she returned home to get changed and went to the airport.

Hurley: The day before everyone gathered in the basement of the church, Hurley had gotten himself arrested so he could escape Ben. He was there for about 36 hours before Ben's lawyer had the charges dropped. While Jack was driving to Ray's retirement home, Hurley was getting into a taxi out front and had his run-in with Jacob. He presumably went home with the guitar, probably looked to see what was inside, and was convinced to get on the plane the next day.

Sayid: Like Kate, Sayid left everyone standing at the marina. Next we saw him at a bar drinking MacCutcheon, where he met Ilana, whom he took back to her hotel room, and she overpowered him and put handcuffs on him. What is unclear is *when* he went to the bar. It's doubtful Ilana would have kept him in handcuffs for 36 hours, so what is more probable is that he left the marina and went to his hotel, slept, got changed (he's wearing a jacket, black T-shirt, and gray pants with Ben, but a purple button-up shirt over a black undershirt with black pants when he's with Ilana), did something else during the day, and then went to the bar. He was probably in handcuffs for close to 12 hours before boarding the plane.

Sun: She went to the church with Ben and Jack, and then left before Jack was finished his talk with Eloise. The next time we see her, she's at the airport 36 hours later. It's unclear what she did in that time other than struggle with the decision to either go and find Jin or stay behind to be with her daughter.

Ben: He left the church after talking with Jack and probably scoped out the marina where Desmond's boat was docked. It's unclear how he figured out what boat it was, or what he did for the next 24 hours, but the morning of the flight he went to the marina, shot Desmond, and threatened Penny. Desmond beat him up and threw him into the water. He presumably crawled out somewhere else and called Jack, who was having breakfast. He then probably went to a hospital to get the sling put on his arm. It's unclear if he made any other arrangements within that 36 hours, but no doubt he did.

want the series to end with a big scientific explanation, it could all come down to love. Love is what propels us to do things. It causes us to do insane things, it creates our greatest happiness and our deepest sorrows. Love is what drives each of the characters on the show to act, whether that love is romantic, filial, or parental. And those who don't act out of love — Ben, Locke, or Widmore — are beholden to their obsessions, and difficult to pin down.

And what happened at the end of the episode? Juliet clearly didn't kill everyone, or we won't have much of a season 6. It's unlikely that they'll remove everyone's memories and give them all a do-over, because the characters have evolved too much to erase everything that has happened over the last five seasons. And it would undermine everything the writers have taught us about time travel not affecting the future. Perhaps some memories will be lost, but the people who were touched by Jacob will retain theirs. Or maybe the bomb won't kill them or reverse anything that has happened in their lives, but instead will simply return them to the island in 2007, where they will arrive just in time to see Not-Locke emerging from the statue. Perhaps they are the ones who are "coming," as Jacob warned. Notice how, for the first time in the show's history, the show ended with the black letters of the show title over a white screen, rather than vice versa. Could this be an indication that evil was eradicated, and the future of the island is a white-filled hope? Or could it be indicating the opposite?

Whether it comes down to love, philosophy, religion, or science, season 6 promises to be epic. The most beautifully wrought exploration of good and evil and free will and destiny is in John Milton's *Paradise Lost*, and in many ways, *Lost* has been using this book as its main text right from the beginning. This show *is* the modern-day *Paradise Lost*, with mysteries and intrigue and the bad guys rising to become the protagonists (who would have thought we'd ever feel sorry for Ben Linus?) and the good guys becoming questionable. Darlton still have a long way to go until the series finale, and many questions to answer. After Juliet detonates the bomb at the end of the season, there are several possible directions they can take, but they know where the story is going to end, and they know how they're going to get there. Will good win out over evil? Will we find out there is no good or evil? Will love conquer all? It's time to brush up on your Milton. We're in for a wild final ride.

Highlight: Not-Locke to Ben: "You mind if I ask you a question?" Ben: "I'm a Pisces."

Did You Notice?:

- The title of this episode comes from the Swan orientation video, where "Marvin Candle" explains that the original purpose of the Swan station was to study the island's unique electromagnetic properties. Then he says, "Not long after the experiments began, however, there was . . . an *incident* . . ." and he explains the protocol of having to push the button every 108 minutes.

- At the beginning of "Dead Is Dead," when Widmore enters Richard's tent to see Ben lying there, there's a fire pit burning nearby that looks exactly like Jacob's in this episode.

- After Locke returns to the island, he's always staring out at the water, the same way Jacob is in this episode.

- In "The Life and Death of Jeremy Bentham," Locke eats a mango and says it's the best mango he's ever tasted. Perhaps it's because it's the only food he's tasted in a very, very long time.

- In "Follow the Leader," when Richard is helping the real Locke with his leg, Ben says to Not-Locke, "This must be quite the out-of-body experience." Locke responds, "Something like that." Now we know his strange response was referring to the fact that he's not in his own body.

- In "Dead Is Dead," the only time we see Locke lose his cool is when Ben fires questions at him, and Locke stops and says, "You don't like this, do you, having to ask questions you don't have any answers to, or blindly following someone in the hopes they're going to lead you to whatever it is you're looking for." When Ben concedes that no, he's not enjoying being in the position he's in, John says, "Well, now you know what it was like to be me." Since we now know this man is not Locke, perhaps this is a glimpse of what life was like living with Jacob. Maybe Jacob was not forthcoming with any answers, and kept the Man in the Black in the dark the same way Ben refused to give John a straight answer.

- Some fans thought that Jacob is actually cooking a red herring at the beginning of the episode (ha!) but he's not. A red herring only turns red after it's been cooked, not before.

- Right before the sub goes under, a man says to Kate, "See you on the other side." This is an ongoing motif, with variations of "See you in another life" or "the next life." In "Follow the Leader," just as Jack was about to dive underwater to swim into the cave, he says to Sayid, "If I don't see you on the other side, I won't blame you." In season 1's "Deux Ex Machina," right before Locke was going into surgery to give dear old Dad his kidney, Cooper said to him, "See you on the other side, son."

- In "The Little Prince," when Juliet asked Sawyer why he didn't go up and talk to Kate when he saw her helping Claire deliver the baby, he said, "What's done is done," the same thing his uncle told him when he was at his parents' funeral.

- Richard says he's never seen anyone come back to life, but Locke's resurrection isn't actually the first one we've seen on the show. In season 2's "?" Eko, pretending to be a priest, is asked to confirm a miracle for the Vatican. He listens to a tape of a mortician about to do an autopsy on a dead girl (who is in fact the daughter of the psychic who tells Claire to get on the plane in "Raised by Another"). As the mortician is about to make his first incision, the girl suddenly comes alive and begins screaming, "Let John Locke go!" (viewers were able to translate what she said only by isolating the audio using special equipment). Incidentally, the girl's name is Charlotte.

- Bram refers to Lapidus as a yahoo, which is what Sawyer called him when he came to the helicopter at the end of season 4.

- Locke pointed out that Caesar referred to people as his friend, but he didn't mean it. The Shadow Seekers refer to everyone as friends as well.

- Richard tells Jack that he went off the island three times to check on Locke, but that Locke never seemed particularly special to him. The first time was when Locke was a baby in the incubator, and the second time was when Locke was five years old and Richard tested him. Presumably the third time was when Locke's guidance counselor was trying to convince Locke to enter the science fair, which was being run by Mittelos, the firm name that Richard always used as a cover-up when he went off the island. Richard was probably the one who convinced the counselor to confront Locke, and Locke's refusal to fulfill his destiny must have frustrated him further.

- Watch Juliet's face as she stares longingly at the sub while Kate and Sawyer are flirting on the boat. You can just hear her thinking, "Kill me now."

- When Vincent runs up to Sawyer on the beach, there's a rainbow in the sky. It was probably just a nice occurrence, but it could also have been added digitally as a reference to the Noah's Ark story, where the rainbow signified God's promise to humanity that there would never be another apocalypse. It's an interesting sight . . . right before they're about to create their own apocalypse.

- Rose's reaction to Sawyer, Kate, and Juliet showing up was the equivalent of "You kids get off my lawn!" Her crotchety nature is a little disappointing at first, but the more you watch the episode, the funnier her reaction is: "We traveled back 30 years in time, and you're still trying to find ways to shoot each other?"
- Bernard's first words are "Son of a bitch," in homage to Sawyer.
- Rose is holding a leash in her hand that looks the same as the one Locke found on the beach after they'd been time-blooping.
- Considering Rose and Bernard are wearing the same clothes they'd been wearing when they were being shot at with flaming arrows three years earlier, they've kept those clothes *really* clean.
- Bernard says, "We just care about being together." Bernard looks at Rose. Rose looks at Bernard. Juliet looks at Sawyer. Sawyer looks at Kate. Kate looks at . . . no one — because she's probably thinking of Aaron.
- When Juliet leaves Rose and Bernard, she puts her hand on her belly, leading some fans to speculate that Juliet may have been pregnant.
- This is the first time we've seen Jacob's cabin in the daytime. The dog painting is still there, but the jars of liquid are gone, along with many other extra items that had been there before.
- The knife holding Jacob's tapestry to the wall looks like the one Jacob was using at the beginning to cut the fish.
- Ben tells Locke he's a Pisces in an effort to make him go away. But just like everything else, that's a lie. We know that Ben's birthday is December 19, which makes him a Sagittarius. The Pisces sign is for those born between February 20 and March 20. Interesting, however, that the astrological symbol for Pisces is *very* similar to the mysterious symbol that Juliet was branded with in "Stranger in a Strange Land."
- I've been waiting since "Greatest Hits" for someone to find Charlie's Drive Shaft ring that he left behind in Aaron's crib.
- When Sun puts the wedding ring on Jin's finger, you can see the watch from Paik that caused so much aggravation in season 1's "House of the Rising Sun."

- Jin's vows to Sun were: "We will never be apart. Because being apart from you would be like the sky being apart from the earth." Both Jin and Sun fell from the sky to the earth, but he remained on the earth while she took to the sky once more.

- When Jack told Kate the story about the teenager's dural sac opening at the end of his first solo procedure in the pilot episode, he said, "I just made a choice. I'd let the fear in, let it take over, let it do its thing, but only for five seconds, that's all I was going to give it." He left out the important part that he didn't make that decision at all — Christian was the one who told him to do it.

- At the end of the season 1 finale, Jack and Kate are crouched in the bushes beside the Swan hatch as they're about to blow it up with dynamite and Jack tells Kate that he needs to know she's got his back. Now, four seasons later, Jack and Kate are crouched in the same spot as Jack's about to blow up the hatch again, and she is once again vowing to support him.

- The chocolate bar that Jack was trying to get out of the vending machine was an Apollo bar, which is the kind of chocolate bar Hurley had in the hatch. It's interesting that in "Everybody Hates Hugo," Hurley says he's never heard of the chocolate bar, and he shows them to Rose and she'd never heard of them, either. Yet apparently they were popular enough to be in vending machines (*and* there's an Apollo bar ad on the side of the bus that kills Juliet's husband).

- Sawyer says it's July 1977, which is the first time we find out what month we're in.

- Jacob gives Sawyer a pen, Jack a chocolate bar, and pays for Kate's lunchbox. When Hurley is leaving the L.A. county jail, he's given a pen, a Fruit Roll-Up, and $227 in cash, all variations on the things Jacob gave to others. Also, Hurley was eating a Fruit Roll-Up when Walt came to visit him in "There's No Place Like Home, Part 2."

- Juliet quotes Jack's "Live together, die alone," but it has a different meaning coming from her. She leaves out the extra parts, "if we don't live together, we'll die alone," and instead insinuates, "We lived together, now I'll die alone."

- Not-Locke convinces Ben to kill Jacob, telling him, "Things will change once he's gone, I promise." He's probably telling the truth — he didn't say things would *improve*, which is probably how Ben interpreted it; he just said they would change.

- The structure at the Swan station collapses onto Chang's arm. In the orientation videos we've seen in past seasons, Chang has a prosthetic hand on his left arm, and it's usually held stiffly at his side. Now we see why. Also, in the Comic-Con video shown before season 5, when Chang says that terrible things are going to happen and he can do nothing to stop them, he looks down at his left arm, and clutches it with his right hand, as if Daniel told him what was going to happen to him.
- When Jack drops the bomb, Sawyer looks at Juliet, and she smiles, hoping that looking into each other's eyes will be the last thing she sees, but at the last second, he breaks eye contact and looks down, and you can tell she's shattered.
- Juliet being dragged by the chains looked a lot like when people have been dragged by the smoke monster along the ground. Interestingly, the smoke monster always has a sound like a chain, specifically the one that cranks the car up a hill on a rollercoaster.
- We've seen Sawyer cry before, but never sob the way he does when Juliet falls down the shaft. Josh Holloway's acting reaches a new height in this episode.
- The pit of fire that Locke throws Jacob into was glowing at the beginning of the episode, as if this one fire has been burning from the beginning.
- There's a lot of speculation over who is the one who lies in the shadow of the statue, but if we take "lies" to mean "not telling the truth" then the answer is clear: Ben. He lies in the shadow of the statue, in the shadow of the tree, in the shadow of the house, in the shadow of his fedora . . .
- In "The Variable," Sawyer tells Daniel, Kate, and Jack, "When you realize you've made a huge mistake, we'll be at the beach, right where we started." The detonation of the bomb could either send them safely to LAX (right where they started) or it could send them to 2007, on the beach.

Interesting Facts: Many fans referred to the Man in Black as Esau, because he was Jacob's nemesis (and brother) in the Bible. Depending on the interpretation, Jacob believed Esau wasn't responsible enough to take over as the head of the family, so he gave Esau some soup when Esau was starving, and Esau said he could have his birthright in return. Esau was a hairy man, and so Jacob put an animal pelt on his shoulders to trick their blind father into giving him the birthright. When Esau realized what he had lost, he vowed to kill Jacob, so their mother, Rebekah, sent Jacob away. Eventually the brothers were reunited, and forgave each other.

In Norse mythology, there is a character named Höðr, pronounced "Hoth" (another possible allusion in the title of "Some Like It Hoth"). He was the brother of Baldr, a great warrior. The goddess Frigg wanted to keep him safe, so she made all living things vow to never harm him. The mistletoe was too young, so she didn't get a vow from it. Loki found out about Baldr's weakness but was unable to kill Baldr himself. So he convinced Höðr to do it by making a missile out of mistletoe and shooting it at him, killing him. Like Baldr, Jacob was deemed invincible, and like Loki, the Man in Black is unable to kill him. So he recruits his own Höðr in Ben, and completes the mission.

Jacob's tapestry features a wide pair of outstretched eagle wings with the Eye of Horus in the middle. The Eye of Horus was used as a protective image in Ancient Egypt, often put in the tombs of kings to ward off evil spirits. Under this eye Jacob has woven 17 arms that radiate like sun beams, and they reach out to a line of people who are in supplication to the arms. In the row underneath, a harpist plays music while people dance. The next row is a line of Ancient Greek. Below that a row of people harvests wheat. And in the row below that a group of ships is departing an island, and the corner is missing, which is the piece containing the statue of Tawaret that was pinned to the cabin wall.

In Carlos Castaneda's *A Separate Reality* (see page 149), don Juan tricks Castaneda into attempting to kill another woman, and tells him to take the sharp bone of a wild boar in his hand and stab her quickly with it. When Castaneda fails to kill her, don Juan breaks out into laughter and tells him he'd been tricking him all along. Similarly, Not-Locke tricks Ben into killing Jacob for his own means. Castaneda later refers to his encounter with the woman as "that incident."

Nitpicks: Sayid tells Jack that they have two hours to get the bomb to the Swan site, and mentions that when Faraday had returned, he was very explicit about his timetable. How would Sayid have known that if he wasn't around to see him? Presumably he got the information from Jack, in which case . . . why is he telling Jack? Also, Chang has a *really* good point when he asks why exactly Radzinsky is so anxious to get drilling right now of all times, when he's just spent an hour beating the snot out of Sawyer to get information that he

Ben looks at Jacob's complicated tapestry, and translates it for Locke. "Trust me, John, it says I am supposed to be the leader of the Others. Now give me back my birthright!"

(© MARIO PEREZ/ABC/RETNA LTD.)

hasn't used at all. If Radzinsky was so gung-ho to find the Hostiles, why did he get the information, then immediately send Sawyer away before verifying the information, and then when he had Kate in his clutches, get rid of her immediately, too? Why hasn't he actually checked out the map to find Ben? It seemed so urgent only moments ago and now it's the last thing on his mind.

In "Follow the Leader," Jack told Eloise that they would follow every word that Daniel wrote in his journal. But after Sayid finishes removing the plutonium core, they never consult the journal again. Did Eloise take it? Also, why does Richard knock on various parts of the wall he eventually breaks through, rather than starting with the one stone that was sticking out and completely different from all the rest? And after Richard knocks Eloise unconscious, he says he's going to take her out of the tunnels the way they came in. Through the long water tunnel? With her unconscious? How does he plan to do that? Also, Sawyer asks Jack for five minutes of his time, and Jack says fine. He didn't think to mention that Sayid was quickly bleeding to death in the back of the van?

Hurley made some major strides in "Tricia Tanaka Is Dead," realizing that he needs to make his own luck (he hurtles the van down a hill and realizes he really can change things at the last minute and is not cursed, as he'd previously suspected), and yet ever since that episode, he continues to refer to the curse as if that revelation never happened.

Oops: When Vincent runs to Sawyer on the beach, you can see a dog treat in Josh Holloway's left hand. Also, in season 1's ". . . In Translation," we see Sun putting on her after-wedding dress, and it's a silk dress with a high collar and sash. Her wedding dress — which is not the strapless numbers we see in this episode — is on the dressmaker's dummy nearby. In "The Incident," her post-ceremony dress (which she's wearing to meet her well-wishers) is completely different.

4 8 15 16 23 42: The truck Kate and Tommy are standing next to has a **23** on the license plate. The bomb weighs 20 tons (**16** + **4**). On Dan's notes on how to remove the plutonium core, there is a **23** on the side of the diagram. Chang tells Radzinsky that the temperature of the drill suddenly went up 60 degrees (**15** x **4**). Juliet detonates the bomb after hitting it **8** times.

It's Just a Flesh Wound: Roger shoots Sayid in the stomach. Jack, a lousy shot, shoots back several times and misses, but he does hit another guy, and then another one after reloading. Jack and Sawyer have an epic rumble in the jungle, throwing several punches, with Sawyer nailing Jack in the crotch before choking him. At the Swan, Jack, Juliet, and Kate each shoot a guard. Sawyer hits Radzinsky on the back of the head with his gun. Phil is killed when he's impaled by several iron rebars. Jack is clocked in the back of the head by a metal toolbox. Chang's hand is crushed under the metal structure above the Swan. Juliet falls several storeys into the shaft. Jacob is stabbed by Ben.

Lost in Translation: Ilana asks Richard what lies in shadow of the statue. He answers, "*Ille qui nos omnes servabit*," which is Latin for "He who will protect [or save] us all."

There are three lines of text on the tapestry written in Ancient Greek: on the top is a quotation from Homer's *Odyssey*, "May the gods grant thee all that thy heart desires." The middle line, also from the *Odyssey*, reads, "May the gods grant thee happiness." And the bottom line reads, "Only the dead have seen the end of war."

Any Questions?:

- So was that season 5 promotional picture (see page xxi) just Photoshopped badly, or did it indeed have some significance? Both Juliet and Daniel are missing body parts, and at the end of season 5, Daniel is dead and Juliet is all but dead.
- In "Jughead," Richard says that he answers to a higher power, and that power wanted the 18 U.S. Army soldiers dead. Why did Jacob want them dead?
- Is there some significance to the fact that the Man in Black refuses to have some of Jacob's fish, instead saying he just ate? What did he eat?
- Jacob clearly called the *Black Rock* to the island. So how did it end up in the middle of the jungle? Did he will it there? Does he have that kind of power? Who has he called there before?
- How old are Jacob and the Man in Black? Where did they originate?
- What happened to the rest of the statue if it was intact in the late 19th century?
- Who is the Man in Black? Why can't he kill Jacob himself?
- When Not-Locke tells Richard that they'll have to deal with the Ajira folk, does he mean kill them?
- When Not-Locke comments on Richard's non-aging, Richard says, "I'm this way because of Jacob." What does he mean? When did Jacob make him this way? Did Jacob once inhabit Richard's body the way the Man

The Byodo-In Temple in Oahu was previous used in season 1 as the site where Jin asked Sun to marry him, and now it's where they get married. (KEVIN FRATES)

in Black is now inhabiting Locke's? Does Richard feel cursed by his eternal youth?

- What did Bram mean when he asked if Frank was a candidate? Are they looking for a body for Jacob to jump to, the way the Man in Black is using Locke's?
- The Dharma Initiative *must* have known about the tunnel network the Others had underground, especially when one of their houses' foundations is actually the wall of the tunnel. Did they ever inspect it? Is that what led to the animosity between them and the "Hostiles"?
- Richard refers to Eloise as "our leader," meaning Widmore is *not* the leader of the group. Did he become the leader after she left the island? Was he lying when he told Locke he'd been their leader? Was Ellie already the leader of the Others in "Jughead"? In that episode, Richard tells Locke that they choose their leaders at a very young age and put

them through the test. Was Ellie put through the test when she was a little girl? How could Widmore have succeeded her if he hadn't already been chosen as a young boy?

- Where have Rose and Bernard been getting food? Have they been sneaking into Dharmaville and taking it? Why have the Hostiles left them alone? Why didn't Jin find them on his grid-by-grid search of the island?
- Who broke the line of ash that surrounded the cabin?
- Is that cabin fire going to start something much bigger, or will the humidity in the jungle prevent it from spreading?
- Why didn't Not-Locke recognize Ilana and Bram as followers of Jacob?
- What happened to Ilana? Why was she in a hospital completely covered in bandages? Why doesn't she have any scars now? How do Ilana and Jacob know each other? Why does he need her help? Did he know Ben was going to stab him?
- Ben tells Locke that he's a liar, and promptly lies about his astrological sign. So what did he say in this episode that was actually true?
- Why does everyone arrive at the statue in late afternoon, but Locke doesn't enter it until nighttime?
- As mentioned, Jacob touches Sayid and Hurley after Flight 815 but before Flight 316. Back in the episode "316," Hurley and Sayid are the only two who are a complete surprise to Jack when they show up at the airport. Did Jacob know they would be the toughest people to convince? If he's in cahoots with Ilana, and she was the one who brought Sayid to the plane, was his touch something that marked them to get them on that plane?
- Not-Locke tells Richard that he thinks he's just making up the rules as he goes along. Is he?
- Richard acts like he cannot enter the statue, yet he's the one who has been delivering the messages from Jacob to Ben for so many years. Does Richard actually talk to Jacob? How long has Richard been on the island?
- Where did Miles disappear to after he told his father to run? Why isn't he there to help everyone pull Juliet up?
- Why does Ilana call Richard Ricardos? The answer to Ilana's enigmatic question is in Latin. Was Latin Ricardos's first language and he's the one who taught it to the Others? How is Ilana connected to that legacy?

- If He Who Will Protect/Save Us All lies in the shadow of the statue, who does that refer to? Jacob, who is under the statue and technically in the shadow of it (at high noon, perhaps), or the Man in Black, who is in the jungle and presumably in the shadow of the statue? Is it someone else?
- In season 1's "Hearts and Minds," Charlie says to Jack, "If there's one person on this island I would put my absolute faith in to save us all it would be John Locke." Could Locke be the one lying in the shadow of the statue?
- When Jacob says, "They're coming," who does he mean? Ilana and her people? Or is he referring to the people who are stuck in 1977? Are they on their way to 2007?
- Is the Incident the reason women can no longer have children on the island? Did Eloise leave the island to give birth to Daniel?
- If the Man in Black really is the smoke monster, did Smokey let Ben go in "Dead Is Dead" because he sensed he really would kill Jacob? Did it sense Eko wouldn't be strong enough to do so and Ben would?
- Did Chang find a way off the island? Could he still be alive and hiding somewhere on the island in 2007?
- Again, if Locke died a few weeks ago (see page 111), why is his body still so well preserved?
- Some of Jacob's touches seem to be evil (like when he distracts Sayid and Nadia is killed). Is the Man in Black making himself look like Jacob, or was that really Jacob? Why would Jacob want to keep Locke alive if Locke would eventually be the one who leads to Jacob's death?

Ashes to Ashes: Phil was a whiny little minion who worked at the Dharmaville security station. His death by multiple-rebar impalement was cheered by many fans. He had it coming. Several other Dharminians lost their lives in this episode, but . . . we won't miss them, either.

John Locke . . . no, I just can't do it. Not yet.

Music/Bands: Kate's lifelong love of Patsy Cline was perhaps sparked as a child; Patsy's "Three Cigarettes (In an Ashtray)" is playing in the loudspeaker in the store where Kate tries to steal the lunchbox. The singer sings of how happy she was until a stranger came along and then everything in her life was ruined. She says she watched as her love walked away with another woman, and now she sits watching her lover's cigarette burn idly in an ashtray.

Oh, Those Crazy Egyptian Gods

At the beginning of "The Incident," we finally get a side view of the giant ancient statue that stands above Jacob's sanctuary. When we caught a brief glimpse of the statue from behind in "LaFleur," fans immediately began theorizing who it could be. It clearly looked like a depiction of an Egyptian god, but which god would be most closely related to the island? After the finale aired, both a recap on ABC.com and the answer to a puzzle J.J. Abrams had planted in an issue of *Wired* magazine pronounced which of the gods it actually was, and it surprised some people. But before we get to the answer, let's review the possibilities that fans discussed:

Set: Also known as Seth in Greek, Set was the Egyptian god of necessary chaos. He ruled over the desert, and was thus seen as the bringer of infertility. He was depicted as a nonspecific animal (known simply as the Set animal) with square, upward-pointed ears, a curved snout, and a forked tail. Set's main rivalry was with Horus. Set was the older brother of Osiris, the god of the afterlife. Osiris ruled with his sister and wife, Isis, and Set was jealous, so he killed Osiris and spread the pieces of his body around Egypt. Isis is said to have become impregnated by Osiris's corpse, or pieces of Osiris's corpse (*ew*), and the result was Horus. Horus was worshiped as a sun god and a sky god, and Isis told him his main job was to protect the world from Set. Horus and Set endured many battles, and in one Set pulled out Horus's left eye, and Horus ripped off one of Set's testicles (thus making Set the god of infertility, as if the guy didn't have enough to contend with at that point). To determine the new ruler of Egypt after the death of Osiris, Set and Horus engaged in 80 years of fighting before finally agreeing to a boat race, which Horus won. He became the ruler, and Set remained the ruler over the areas of Egypt that were infertile desert.

Set has the muscular body and long snout of the island statue. (HARRYILLUSTRATION)

Interestingly, the meaning and importance of Egyptian deities evolved as the politics changed in Egypt. For example, if one small region worshiped a particular deity, but then they became more powerful by taking over other regions through warfare, their particular deity would also rise in importance. Often the benevolence of a god would change as well. Set, for example, was often associated with foreigners, and he was revered until Persia began encroaching on Egypt, at which point Set was regarded as evil. Horus was the ruler of Lower Egypt, and Set the Upper, and it is often believed that the reason the two gods eventually live in harmony is because Lower and Upper Egypt became unified.

Set was a possibility for the statue. He is often depicted holding an ankh (as are most Egyptian deities) and if he is the god of infertility, it would link him to the problem many women have on the island. Often people would worship a god to try to ward off what that god represented — remain deferential to the god of infertility, and he would spare you that. But if the statue were destroyed, then infertility could rule the land. Also, Set is the god of the desert, and we've seen that when characters use the Frozen Donkey Wheel, they land in the desert, the land that Set rules. However, the statue has a flat head and short ears, and Set's ears are long.

Another link to Set would be the character of Richard Alpert. Several fans have pointed out that Richard Alpert's initials are RA, which could be a subtle nod to his earlier incarnation as the sun god, Ra. Despite often being depicted as an evil god, Set was associated with Ra as his savior. The myth of Ra states that during the day, he shone brightly in the sky as the sun, but at night he was chased through the underworld by a demon god, the serpent-like Apep, while the moon rose in the sky. In one version of the myth, Set became Ra's defender, traveling in the front of Ra's boat and protecting him from Apep. Strangely, in this myth Set is depicted as having a falcon head, like Horus. Ra's name is usually pronounced "Raw," but it was also spelled "Re," pronounced "Ray," and he was said to be the grandfather of all of the other gods. Good thing there isn't a character on the show whose grandfather's name is Ray, or the fans would go nuts . . .

Anubis: In "Dead Is Dead," Ben sees a drawing on the wall above the smoke monster's abode of Anubis bowing before the smoke monster. He appears to be summoning him in the picture. Anubis was the original god of the underworld, but after Osiris, his father, became worshiped as the god of the afterlife, Anubis became the gatekeeper to the underworld and the god of mummification. He is

Anubis leads the dead to the underworld (left) and weighs their heart on the scale of judgment (right). (LENKA PEACOCK)

often associated with weighing the heart of the deceased against a feather or leading the deceased into the underworld (both shown on a page in the Book of the Dead). His wife was Kebechut (often also depicted as his daughter), who was the goddess of the purification of bodies, often shown with jars of liquids in which to place the various body parts. Anubis is largely seen as a benevolent deity, one who takes the hands of lost souls and leads them to Osiris.

Most of the characters on *Lost* are lost souls (the show's title not only refers to the fact that these people were lost to the outside world, but they were all lost emotionally and psychologically). In Jacob's cabin in "The Man Behind the Curtain," you can see several jars of fluids along the walls, similar to Kebechut's jars. If Anubis is the gatekeeper to the underworld, and leads the deceased to Osiris for judgment, he is appropriately associated with Smokey in "Dead Is Dead," as if he may be the one to summon him forth so they may be judged. However, this would make him a little less benevolent. Instead of taking people by the hand to see Osiris, he sends Smokey to them, which is more disconcerting for the "lost soul." Anubis is a jackal-headed god (a jackal is an animal that often scavenges dead flesh, and the depiction of Anubis relates to his earlier role as a god of the dead) and his long pointy ears would suggest that the statue is not Anubis. However, if the island is a sort of afterlife/underworld place that exists on earth for people who are suffering emotional deaths, if not physical ones, he would be the perfect statue to stand on the shores as the gatekeeper to the place.

Sobek: The god of the crocodiles, he is depicted as having a head of a crocodile and the strong body of a man; in his pure form, he is a large crocodile. Sobek is a god of fertility and is believed to be the creator of the Nile River, the source of fertility in Egypt. The Egyptians were dependent on the crocodile-filled Nile for business and trading, and thus prayed to Sobek to protect them from harm. Those who did not worship Sobek and saw him instead as an evil deity would hunt and kill the crocodiles. There are several temples to Sobek around Egypt, many containing the mummified remains of crocodiles that were kept inside the temples in deference to the god. Sobek is generally seen as a god that was to be feared, but he was also close to Horus, and was the god who would call upon other gods to help in certain situations.

Sobek's flat head, long crocodile snout, muscular body, and ankhs in his hand led many fans to believe the statue was a depiction of him. (GRAEME AND TAMARA ING)

Set was antagonistic to Horus, while Sobek was aligned with him. A *Lost* fan can't think of the myth of Horus without thinking of Horace Goodspeed, and whether he might have any ties to the statue. Just as Sobek was largely a catalyst who made things happen by suggesting other gods step in, Horace also acts as a catalyst in season 5, putting certain events in motion that lead to others. More importantly, Sobek, like Set, became associated with Ra, the sun god, who was the most important deity of all. In "The Incident," the statue looks most like Sobek, with its long crocodile-like nose, muscular arms, back, and legs, and an ankh in each hand.

Taweret: The final possibility is the only female option. Taweret was the Egyptian goddess of childbirth, and she protected pregnant women and mothers as well as their newborns or unborn children. She is depicted as a hippo, with a large round belly and long hanging breasts. Her arms and legs were that of a lion, and her face a combination of a hippo and a lion. She often has a crocodile on her back, which links her to Sobek, and in some depictions she is given a scaly crocodile back. Because all of her elements were of animals that could kill men, she was referred to as a demonness. She was also considered the female consort of Apep (mentioned above as the serpent who would try to consume Ra every night) and thus was associated with evil. One would think the goddess of childbirth would actually be seen as a benevolent deity, but perhaps because she empowered women, she was considered evil instead.

Taweret has a flat head, and often carries an ankh in each hand, like the statue. She's also the most fitting as a deity for the island: if she is the protector of women and childbirth, it would make sense that after a statue of Taweret was destroyed that neither the pregnant women nor the children would be protected. And, like the statue, Taweret only has four toes on each foot. However, when we see the side view of the statue in "The Incident," the snout appears to be that of a crocodile, making it more like Sobek. The back is bare and muscular, and the arms and legs look distinctly male. And most importantly, the statue does not have a rounded belly, nor is it hippo-like in any way.

While Taweret is the best symbolic candidate for the statue, her body looks the least like it. (AUDRA WOLFMANN)

And so, according to ABC.com, which god is the one standing on the beach? None other than (drum roll, please) . . . Taweret. On the one hand, the choice makes perfect sense, but from a purely visual stance, it makes very little. What would be most intriguing would be to discover that the statue was in fact some sort of combination of the gods: If Taweret is often depicted with a crocodile, and is sometimes evil, sometimes good, perhaps she could be conflated with the others, with her purpose as the protector of childbirth being her most important association and she would also possess the traits of the other characters. It could have the head of Sobek, the arms and legs of Set, the ankhs and feet of Taweret, and the gatekeeper presence of Anubis. If the writers are insistent that the statue is Taweret, perhaps they have decided to give her a reimagining and an update. I mean, what woman who's ever been pregnant wouldn't be relieved to discover that a fertility goddess doesn't have to be depicted as being hippo-like, with sagging breasts? Perhaps the island gave her a makeover.

Everything That Rises Must Converge by Flannery O'Connor (1965)

Flannery O'Connor is known as one of the masters of the short story form. Born in 1925 in Savannah, Georgia, O'Connor grew up a devout Roman Catholic. Many of her stories involve grotesque characters whose flaws are exaggerated for effect, but who usually come to a shocking moral epiphany by the end of the story, often through violence or even death. O'Connor tackles class systems, religion, and race issues throughout her fiction, and her characters are often filled with rage, with almost every parent hating their child and vice versa. Those who aren't angry are comical, often so ridiculous the reader can't attribute any sense to their thoughts.

O'Connor died of lupus at the young age of 39. She had suffered with the disease for many years (at the time there was experimental medicine that was keeping her alive, whereas her father had contracted the same disease in the 1930s and died quickly of it) and while she was going through her own personal suffering, she was writing the stories in this book. The stories were published as a posthumous collection a year after her death, and the accolades that poured in declared her one of the great writers of the 20th century. I'll talk about the first story in detail, because it's the most famous (and one that many students probably studied in school) but I'll leave the rest of them a little open-ended so readers can go and discover these stories for themselves.

The opening story sets up the style and tone that pervade the rest of the collection. "Everything That Rises Must Converge" is the story of Julian, an angry young man who is ashamed of his mother, whom he believes is an intolerant bigot. For medical reasons she is forced to go to a "reducing" class (gyms weren't exactly prevalent in those days) and because of the new desegregation laws that allow African-Americans to sit anywhere they'd like on a bus rather than being relegated to the back, Julian's mother needs him to accompany her each week so she's not stuck sitting next to one of "them." (A warning to anyone picking up this book: the n-word is quite prevalent throughout; being from the Deep South, O'Connor uses the word liberally as if it were no different from any other word, and she doesn't intend it to carry the harsh meaning that we do now.) Julian sits on the bus next to his mother, occasionally stealing a glance at the outlandish hat that she decided to wear because she figured she would be unique. He seethes with anger as she mutters to him about the dark-skinned people on the bus, and when a black businessman boards the bus and sits across from them (and a white person beside him vacates the seat because of it), Julian crosses the aisle to sit next to the man, mostly to watch bemusedly as his mother almost explodes with anger. When an African-American woman boards the bus with her young son, the boy sits next to Julian's mother, who smiles down at him (she thinks patronizingly that black children are cuter than white ones). The African-American mother immediately begins scowling in Julian's mother's direction, and he realizes they are wearing the same hat. He can barely contain his laughter, until their stop comes up and the mother also alights with her son. Julian sees his mother opening her purse, and knowing she's going to give the child a nickel, hisses at her to put her purse away. His mother refuses to listen to him, but she cannot find a nickel in her purse, so she pulls out a penny instead. Despite Julian begging her to put it away, she walks up to the boy and offers him a shiny new penny. The African-American mother, infuriated by her condescending behavior, turns and clocks Julian's mother in the head with her bag, screaming at her to keep her pennies to herself, and walks off. Julian's mother is knocked off her feet onto the sidewalk, where at first she sits dumbfounded as Julian tries to help her up while laughing and lecturing her on how she deserved the treatment for being so stupid and racist. But when she begins muttering nonsense and then collapses on the street, and he sees that one of her eyes is looking in the wrong direction, Julian's laughter turns instantly to panic, and he races down the street in search of an ambulance. It's not clear if his mother has a stroke or actually dies at the end of the story, but O'Connor's point — beyond painting a realistic portrait of the anxieties and tensions that arose out of the civil rights movement — is that Julian's mother might have been an intolerant bigot, but her son is equally intolerant of her, and just as it's too late for his mother to ever change her ways, it might be too late for him to bury his own feelings of prejudice against his mother and actually try to be accepting of her. It's a powerful story with a shocking ending, which typifies most of O'Connor's stories.

The second story, "Greenleaf," is about Mrs. May, a woman who owns a house and hires Greenleaf, a simple man with a crazy wife and two boys, to be her hired help around the property. When she discovers a bull in her garden one night, she demands that Greenleaf get rid of it. He constantly reminds her that *his* two sons would never make *their* mother go and get hired help, and would have done the work themselves. She's disgusted by him and his lower-class ways, and feels superior to him. But when we meet her sons, we realize they're a couple of layabouts who disrespect their mother and take joy in her difficulties. Meanwhile, Greenleaf's sons went to the war and came home heroes, and are living in homes given to them by the government. When one of Mrs. May's sons tells her that the bull actually belongs to one of Greenleaf's boys, she is furious, and after getting no response from the boys when she demands they come and retrieve it, she demands that Greenleaf destroy the bull. Greenleaf is mortified, and doesn't want to destroy something that belongs to one of his boys, but Mrs. May is insistent. Begrudgingly, he accompanies her to the field — where Mrs. May gets the surprise of her life.

In "A View of the Woods," a grandfather watches a bulldozer as construction begins on a section of his property, while his beloved granddaughter, Mary Fortune, watches with him. We discover that he's despised his daughter ever since she married a lout named Pitt, and thinks all of their children are idiots, except for Mary. He refuses to acknowledge that her last name is Pitt, and instead refers to her by his own surname, Fortune. He owns vast amounts of land, and allows the Pitts to live on one tiny section of it. He's selling off the rest of it, grid by grid, to various developers, and sitting on the money, which he hopes to give to Mary one day. He notices that Pitt seems to have picked up on his favoritism, and Pitt will often ask Mary to leave the dinner table with him, where he takes her into the woods and beats her with a belt (the grandfather followed one day and watched). But when the grandfather confronts Mary, asking why she would ever let such a stupid man beat her, she looks him in the face and says, "Nobody's ever beat me in my life and if anybody did, I'd kill him." Her obstinate response at once angers him and makes him happy, because he can see his own stubbornness in her. But when he announces at the dinner table one night that he's selling the grid of land directly across the house to put in a gas station, Mary Fortune becomes quiet and resentful. She argues with her grandfather that if they put in a gas station, they won't be able to see the view of the woods across the road. He thinks she's being silly, but sees her one evening on a swing, staring across the street into the woods, which he, too, begins to stare at, and notices how they seem to come alive and glow with a magnificent light. He sticks to his guns, though, and goes ahead with the agreement. In the story's final scene, Mary declares who she really is, and the epiphany both of them have in the moment is horrific and tragic.

"The Enduring Chill" is about Asbury, a sickly self-dramatizing man who believes he is dying and his artistic potential will never be realized. He comes home to stay with his mother and hateful sister in his final days, despising both of them, as he stares at the ceiling at a mark that has been there since his childhood (and one that is eerily reminiscent of the image on the front cover of the edition Jacob is holding):

Descending from the top molding, long icicle shapes had been etched by leaks and, directly over his bed on the ceiling, another leak had made a fierce bird with spread wings. It had an icicle crosswise in its beak and there were smaller icicles descending from its wings and tail. It had been there since his childhood and had always irritated him and sometimes had frightened him. He had often had the illusion that it was in motion and about to descend mysteriously and set the icicle on his head.

Asbury's mother, who is worried about how sickly he looks but unconvinced he is going to die, calls the local doctor, who begins dropping by daily and taking blood samples. Asbury fancies himself an intellectual and is resentful that he must die amidst idiots, so he asks for a Jesuit priest to drop by, thinking it will anger his mother and allow him to have a conversation with a more intelligent person. When the priest drops by, Asbury excitedly asks him about James Joyce, but the priest is hard of hearing and simply says he hasn't met him. Discovering that Asbury is an atheist, the priest begins bellowing at him that he will never be saved if he continues on like this, and finishes by says, "The Holy Ghost will not come until you see yourself as you are — a lazy ignorant conceited youth!" The mother orders the priest out of the home, and suddenly the doctor shows up with good news — Asbury isn't going to die, he just has a fever that will continue to recur throughout his life, but it can be contained using medication. The story ends with an image that would suggest Asbury has finally seen himself as a lazy, ignorant, conceited youth.

The next story, "The Comforts of Home," is about Thomas, a man who lives with his mother, a do-gooder who always tries to help people, often to her own detriment. She reads the paper one day to see that a young woman has been put in the local jail, so she takes some baking down to her. They strike up a friendship, and she manages to get her out of jail and puts her up in a house downtown, spending every day with her. When the girl gets drunk one night and is thrown out, the mother brings her home, despite Thomas saying all along that his mother needs to steer clear of the girl. He finds the girl alluring, yet hates himself for being attracted to her, and she is immediately attracted to him as well, calling him "Tomsee." She tells his mother that she was sexually abused as a child by an older stepbrother, and at various boarding schools she'd been taken advantage of several times. Now, as a teenager, she is a nymphomaniac, and when she appears naked in Thomas's doorway one night, he throws her out and locks his door, screaming at his mother to get her out of the house. He finally gives his ultimatum — that his mother get rid of the girl, or he's going. The next day his mother returns to the house with the girl in tow, and Thomas hits his breaking point. Forming a plan to get the girl back in jail and out of his life, he puts things in motion . . . but the results are not what Thomas expects, and when he realizes what he's done, it's too late to take it back.

In yet another story about a do-gooder gone wrong, "The Lame Shall Enter First" (which is in the middle of the book, and could be the story Jacob is reading in the scene where Locke becomes lame) is about Sheppard, a man who always wants to fix things without actually thinking it through first, often making things worse (sound familiar?). He works at a reformatory where he's met Rufus Johnson, an unresponsive boy with a club foot who has an IQ of 140. Eager to expand the child's intellectual pursuits — and deeming his own son Norton too much of a selfish dullard to actually appreciate them — he offers Rufus the chance to come and live with them. Rufus at first says no, but changes his mind and comes over one night when

Sheppard is out and Norton is the only one home. He bosses Norton around, demanding a sandwich and rifling through the shrine-like room of Norton's recently dead mother, and remains stubbornly quiet around Sheppard. Sheppard only sees Rufus's potential, and waves away Norton's concerns and fears and refuses to listen to his son when Norton tries to tell him about the bad things Rufus is doing. When the police come to take Rufus away after they say he was involved in a burglary, Sheppard's resolve wavers, and he's disappointed that Rufus let him down like that. But the call the next morning confirming that Rufus was indeed innocent gives Sheppard such a wave of guilt that he decides he'll step up his efforts. Sheppard gets a shoemaker to fashion a special shoe for Rufus so he can walk straighter, but Rufus refuses it after trying it on. Sheppard buys a telescope to show Rufus the stars and teach him about constellations, and

Jacob reads Flannery O'Connor's book while waiting for someone to come falling to earth. (Did Jacob weave that bookmark he's holding?)
(© MARIO PEREZ/ABC/RETNA LTD.)

when he finds Norton looking through it one night searching the skies for his dead mother, he shoves him out of the way so he can teach Rufus something real, despite Rufus having almost no interest in it. The police show up again, saying they found the distinct footprints of someone with a club foot near another house that had been broken into, and once again Rufus says it wasn't him, so Sheppard backs him up and tells the police to go away. But things continue to build, and by the end of the story, Sheppard realizes the person he should have been focusing on was there all along, getting underfoot and just wanting to talk about the mother he's lost. Will it be too late for Sheppard to make amends?

"Revelation" is another famous story in the book. Arrogant blowhard Mrs. Turpin sits in a doctor's office bragging loudly to another woman about her benevolence, all the while glancing at a "white-trash" woman and her ugly, acne-covered daughter. She thinks to herself that if God forced her to choose between being white trash or a higher-class African-American woman, she'd choose the latter. She talks to the other woman about her farm and the pigs that they keep, and the white-trash woman mutters that you'd never catch her washing pigs. Mrs. Turpin thinks disgustedly to herself that you can't talk about something you'll never have, and becomes even louder as she discusses how good she is to the black people who work on her property, and makes subtle remarks about "other" people who don't have such things. All the while the ugly girl sitting with the woman is reading a book, and her face is getting redder as her knuckles become whiter, listening to Turpin going on and on. Turpin tries to talk to the girl, Mary Grace, who just stares at her with contempt. Then she has a moment of joy when she realizes how happy she is that God made her the way He did, not black or white trash, and she says as much, raising her arms above her head and howling, "Oh thank you, Jesus, Jesus, thank you!" She suddenly feels a corner of the book hit her above her eye and just as she realizes the girl has thrown it at her, the girl is on top of her with her hands wrapped tightly around Turpin's throat. The doctors manage to subdue the girl, who looks at Mrs. Turpin and says, "Go back to hell where you came from, you old warthog." Mrs. Turpin returns home to her farm, shocked and enraged at what has happened to her, and we see the effect Mary's words had on her.

"Parker's Back" is about Obadiah Elihue Parker (O.E., as he insists on being called) who saw a fully tattooed man at a circus once as a boy, and has similarly covered his body ever since. Only the front of his body has been illustrated, because he doesn't see the point in tattooing a section of his body that he can't see. He has his way with many women, until he meets a homely girl named Sarah Ruth. He's immediately turned off, until she shows an interest (followed by disgust) in his tattoos. Something comes over him and he wants to walk away from her, but he also wants to win her over, and over time he knows that won't happen until he marries her, so he does. Now stuck in a marriage with a girl he considers ugly, who won't even look at him when his shirt is off because her religious piety is disgusted by the tattoos, and who is pregnant (and therefore unattractive to him), he doesn't know what to do. His entire life has revolved around those tattoos — every high he has experienced is due to a tattoo that makes him particularly happy, and every low is when the excitement of a new tattoo wears off and he realizes that he doesn't like how it fits into the whole picture. His various disjointed tattoos don't swirl together in one beautiful line like the man's at the circus did, and instead just look like a patchwork quilt. So, he decides he's going to get the mother of all tattoos put on his back, where Sarah will be forced to stare at it night after night. The result (surprise!) is not what Parker expected, and at the end of the story he's a man more broken and ridiculed than he'd ever been before.

The final story, "Judgement Day," is about Tanner, a man who has been brought to New York City to live with his daughter, who no longer thinks he's fit to live in his shack in the South, which he occupies with Coleman, one of his "Negro workers" that he's known for several decades. Unhappy in the big city, Tanner has decided that he's going to escape his daughter's house (he can't stand her nor she him), shuffle his way to a taxi and go to the freight yards, where he'll steal a ride on a train to the South. He knows he might die on the way, but as long as he dies in the South, that's all that matters to him. He has pinned a note to the inside pocket of his jacket telling anyone who finds him to ship his body to Coleman, and underneath that he's written instructions to Coleman to sell anything that belongs to him and keep the money. He remembers how he and Coleman were in a shack when an African-American businessman showed up one day to announce that he owned the land and had the right to throw them off. Tanner left with his daughter at that point. When a snazzy man and woman move in across the hall — both African-American — Tanner stands in the hallway to get to know them, despite his daughter warning him away. The man is jovial to him the first day, but begins avoiding him after that, until Tanner continues to talk to him and calls him "Preacher," a name that always got him on the good side of African-Americans in the South (or so he believed). The man shoves Tanner through the door back into his apartment, yelling at him that he's an actor, not a preacher. Tanner lies ill in bed for a few days, realizing his escape must be soon, even though he's sicklier than he was before. He imagines dying in New York City and his daughter listening to his wishes and sending him to the South in a pine box. He dreams of Coleman coming to pick him up at the train station, and hearing noises inside, opening the box, where Tanner would leap out and yell, "It's Judgement Day!" When his daughter leaves for the grocery store, Tanner sees his chance, but his body gives out on him just as he meets up with the other man again. Judgement Day comes for Tanner and his daughter at the same time, and she finds a way to make peace with it.

So why is Jacob reading this book? There are several possibilities, but it's important that we see him reading it moments before Locke falls from a window and is either brought back to life or to consciousness by Jacob's touch. The people in O'Connor's stories are morally broken, and they only realize the huge mistakes they've been making in their lives when something violent happens to him. Just as Locke is thrown from a window and through his paralysis finds the walkabout and then the island (which he believes is his salvation), so, too, do many of O'Connor's characters have cathartic moments that lead to enlightenment. But often that enlightenment comes in the moment before their death, and it's too late.

Essayist and writer Patrick Galloway suggested O'Connor's short stories were heavily influenced by both Martin Heidegger's idea of *Dasein*, "wherein death represents the moment when a man's existence becomes complete, for better or worse," and Søren Kierkegaard's theory that "man's attempt to replace the Absolute with himself makes him pathetic and comical but never tragic." Both of these concepts relate to Locke and the struggle on the island — Locke's existence has become meaningful in his death, because only through his death has his body been inhabited by someone who is either evil or good. It's very probable that in season 6 we'll discover Locke's entire life has been shaped just to turn him into the very person who will die so he could be used in the way the Man in Black uses him. Similarly, if Jacob is the Absolute on the island, Ben has attempted to replace him, and he becomes pathetic in the end as he stands before him, wondering why Jacob never noticed him.

Some of the circumstances and situations in the stories might seem exaggerated and over-the-top to a new reader, and the characters often behave ludicrously. But just like other writers in the Southern gothic tradition, within which O'Connor writes, like William Faulkner, Tennessee Williams, or Harper Lee, O'Connor's characters are deeply flawed but draw us in. There's usually some small thing about them that makes us sympathetic, or repulses us so much we keep reading to find out what terrible thing will happen to them. Similarly, on *Lost*, there are situations that might not seem realistic (well, unrealistic to those who *haven't* time traveled to the 1970s recently) and characters who are grotesque, but we are fascinated by the ones whose pasts point to a deeper meaning to their badness — Ben, Widmore, Roger Linus — and just hope the rest of the hopeless characters come to a tragic end — Phil, Radzinsky, Nikki and Paulo. Just as many characters seem to be hostile to their parents in O'Connor's stories, the characters on *Lost* are often crippled by their own parental issues. And yet, many of the characters, like Julian in the title story, realize that maybe they haven't been fair to their parents, and we're starting to see early signs of sympathy toward these otherwise monstrous parents (maybe Roger Linus really wanted to be a good father; maybe Christian wasn't as harsh as Jack thought he was).

Spirituality plays a huge role in O'Connor's stories, and we've seen many spiritual characters on the show as well. Charlie is religious; Desmond was a monk; Eko was a priest, and even though that was a cover, he knows his Bible; Locke's spirituality is an earthier one, more mystical than rooted in organized religion. O'Connor explores issues of bigotry and racism, much like we've seen on the show, with the Others being given derogatory names and no one wanting anything to do with them (nor do they want to be integrated with them).

Just as most of the stories end in violence, many of the characters on *Lost* have met violent ends. Shannon, Daniel, and Ana Lucia were shot. Eko succumbed to Smokey. Michael exploded with the freighter. Boone died of internal injuries. Charlie drowned. Locke was strangled. In each of these instances, the characters have come to their own deeper spiritual understanding moments before death occurs — Shannon dies knowing that someone finally loves her for who she is; Daniel has a moment of clarity in which he believes his entire destiny had been created by his mother; Ana Lucia realizes she regrets the things she's done in her life; Eko realizes he *doesn't* regret the things he's done in his; Michael atones for the sins he perpetrated against his friends; Boone discovers he no longer has to take care of Shannon; Charlie comes up with enough happy things in his life that he dies knowing it wasn't as terrible as he'd thought it was; Locke dies knowing that his efforts are starting to have an impact on those around him.

Season 6 will finally reveal if the island is a heaven or a hell, and which side is good and which side is evil. In any case, the characters of *Lost* bear strong resemblances to those in O'Connor's stories. In one of her final letters, O'Connor confessed that when she reread her own words, she realized, much like on *Lost*, that they were about "the action of grace in territory held largely by the devil."

Questions for Season 6

Every season of *Lost* has ended with more questions than answers, but next season is the final one, and therefore the writers have a *lot* of mysteries they need to wrap up. Some questions will probably go unanswered, and many fans would prefer it that way — if the writers answer absolutely everything, it leaves nothing for us to speculate about for the rest of our lives. Here are some of the remaining mysteries that many fans want resolved, although I'll admit I'm happy to see many of these remain unanswered. Can the writers do it in the final 18 hours?

The Survivors

- Was Flight 815 predestined to crash on the island? Were the people on it chosen to be on it and, if so, why? Did their paths cross by happenstance, or is there a puppet master at work?
- Why was Libby in the mental hospital with Hurley? Is her character more significant than we've been told?
- Did Richard Malkin (Claire's psychic) really see something happening to Aaron, and, if so, what was it? Was he right when he said that only she should raise him?
- What is the significance of Aaron?
- What is the deal with Christian?
- What happened to Claire? Is she alive or dead?
- What is the source of Walt's specialness? Why did the Others take him?
- Is there something supernatural about Vincent? Why does he always seem to be present when bad things happen? Why did Christian tell him to go get Jack?
- Was Locke ever special, or did he create his own specialness by informing Richard of it in 1954? Is he really dead?
- Why don't the normal rules of time travel apply to Desmond? What makes him different?
- Can Hurley really see dead people or is he just crazy? If the former, how are they appearing to him?

The Island

- What is the significance of the island? Why is it so important? How does the island heal people? Is it a supernatural force?
- Where did the electromagnetic energy come from?
- Why was the hatch quarantined? Was that word just written on the hatch to scare anyone inside? Was the vaccination required or was it just a placebo? Is there really a "sickness" on the island, as Rousseau suggests?
- What is the smoke monster? How did it form in the first place?
- When Locke saw the monster at the beginning of season 1 and said what he saw was beautiful, what did he really see?
- How are dead people appearing on the island? Is Smokey behind it?
- What are the whispers?
- Who were the original inhabitants of the island? How long ago were they there? Who built the ancient sites on the island, like the Temple or the statue? Why were they built? How was the statue destroyed?
- Who created the Frozen Donkey Wheel, and how does it send people off the island through time?
- Who are the Adam and Eve skeletons that Jack and Kate found in the caves in season 1?
- How did the *Black Rock* end up in the middle of the island? Why did Jacob bring it there?
- Why can't pregnancies come to full term on the island?

The Others

- Who is Jacob? Where did he come from? How old is he? How did he get to the island?
- What is the meaning of Jacob's touch? Why did he touch those six particular people?
- Who is the Man in Black? Why does he hate Jacob?
- How old is Richard Alpert? Why did Jacob make him immortal? What is his affiliation with Jacob?
- Who are the Others? Why were they wearing raggedy costumes in season 2?
- Why do they have superhuman strength? Why were they kidnapping children? What is their endgame?
- Are there Others who are in the group against their will? Cindy, one of the kidnapped survivors, told Jack they were there to "watch." Watch what?
- Why was Jacob choosing specific people for his lists? Were those lists really coming from Jacob?
- Is Ben special in any way? Is there any truth in what he's said? What happened to him when Richard took him to the Temple? Will he retain any memories of the time travelers being in Dharmaville in 1977 and what they did to and for him?
- Why was Ben coming and going from the island?
- What is the real story behind Eloise Hawking and Charles Widmore? How did they come to the island? Why was their relationship "complicated"? Why does Widmore want to get back to the island so badly? Why doesn't Eloise?
- What happened to Annie, Ben's childhood sweetheart?
- How wide a reach do the Others have, and how many Others are off the island? (Like Jill in the butcher shop, for example.)

The Dharma Initiative

- What was the real reason for forming the Dharma Initiative? Did the DeGroots have a more sinister motive for starting it?
- Will we hear anything more about Alvar Hanso and his connection to the island?
- Does the Dharma Initiative have any affiliation with the Others?
- How did the Dharma Initiative find the island? Why were they looking for a place with its "unique properties"?
- Eloise says that a clever man created the pendulum and the way to find the island. Will we find out who this person is?
- What happened to the Dharma Initiative between 1977 and the Purge?
- If all of the Dharma people on the island died in the Purge, why did the off-island Dharma people continue to send the food pallets?

The Rest

- What is the significance of the numbers? Why have they penetrated every element of the characters' lives? Who made the original recording of them on the island?
- Who are the Shadow Seekers? Why did Ilana and Bram come to the island? How do they know about the island?
- Who was Matthew Abaddon, and why was he associated with both Locke and Widmore?

Sources

Andreeva, Nellie. "Matthew Fox gets a raise on 'Lost'." *Hollywood Reporter*. August 15, 2008.

Ausiello, Michael. "Exclusive: Lost recruits New Amsterdam alum." EW.com. Online. September 4, 2008.

—. "'Lost' exclusive: War erupts over Charlotte's real age!" EW.com. Online. March 23, 2009.

Brown, Mick. "The sorcerer's apprentice." *The Age*. November 7, 1998. Reprinted online at www.geocities.com/skepdigest/sorcerer.html. Accessed July 10, 2009.

"Carlos Castaneda." www.kirjasto.sci.fi. Online. Accessed July 16, 2009.

"Carlos Castaneda." *Encyclopedia Britannica*. Online. Accessed July 16, 2009.

"Carlos Castaneda and the Shaman." Narr. Dilly Barlow. *Tales from the Jungle*. BBC Four. November 29, 2007.

Castaneda, Carlos. *A Separate Reality: Further Conversations with Don Juan*. New York: Washington Square Press, 1971.

Chopin, Kate. "A Point at Issue!" *The Awakening and Other Stories*. Ed. Pamela Knights. New York: Oxford University Press, 2000.

Deborah B. "Lost and Legal Procedure." Message to Author. February 6, 2009. Email.

DharmaWantsYou.com.

Ford, Lyly. "More Infos about the Screenwriting Expo." Online. Posted on Lost-media.com. November 16, 2008.

Galloway, Patrick. "The Dark Side of the Cross: Flannery O'Connor's Short Fiction." Cyberpat.com. Online. Accessed June 16, 2009.

Gordon, Stuart. *The Encyclopedia of Myths and Legends*. London: Headline, 1993.

Heffernan, Laura. *SparkNote on Ulysses*. Online. www.sparknotes.com/lit/ulysses. Accessed May–July 2009.

Hillis, Aaron. "Interview: Ken Leung on 'Year of the Fish.'" IFC.com. Online. August 27, 2008.

Jacks, Brian. "Could there be a 'Lost' movie? Creator J.J. Abrams says 'Maybe.'" MTV Movies Blog. Online. October 17, 2008.

"Journey in Time: Foucault Pendula." The Franklin Institute. Online. Accessed June 29, 2009.

Joyce, James. *Ulysses*. 1960. London: Penguin, 2000.

Kaku, Michio. "A User's Guide to Time Travel." *Wired*. August 2003. Issue 11.08.

Koerner, Brendan I. "8 Super Powers." *Wired*. August 2003. Issue 11.08.

Korda, Michael. *Another Life*. New York: Random House, 1999.

Lachonis, Jon "DocArzt" and Amy "hijinx" Johnston. *Lost Ate My Life*. Toronto: ECW Press, 2008.

Lattimore, Richmond, trans. *The Odyssey of Homer*. 1965. New York: Harper Perennial, 1991.

Lost. TV Series. Exec. Prod. Carlton Cuse, Damon Lindelof. ABC. 2004–.

Lost-media.com.

McCarthy, Wil. "Being Invisible." *Wired*. August 2003. Issue 11.08.

Nations, Gregg. Post on The Fuselage. TheFuselage.com. February 9, 2009.

O'Connor, Flannery. *Everything That Rises Must Converge*. 1956. New York: Farrar, Straus and Giroux, 1993.

"Operation Castle." The Nuclear Weapon Archive. Online. Accessed June 27, 2009.

"Operation Ivy." The Nuclear Weapon Archive. Online. Accessed June 25, 2009.

Ostrow, Joanne. "One of *Lost*'s darkest mysteries solved by an eyelash." *Denver Post*. January 20, 2009.

Rozemeyer, Karl. "The Effervescence of Evangeline Lilly." Premiere.com. Online. September 11, 2008.

Saint-Exupéry, Antoine de. *Le Petit Prince*. Paris: Gallimard, 1946.

—. *The Little Prince*. Richard Howard, trans. Orlando: Harcourt, 2000.

Sampson, Mike. "Lost Movie Not Likely." JoBlo.com. Online. October 20, 2008.

Schedeen, Jesse. "Y: The Last Man — The End of an Era." IGN.com. Online. February 1, 2008.

Seawright, Catherine. "Sobek, God of Crocodiles, Power, Protection and Fertility." Touregypt.net. Online. Accessed June 17, 2009.

"Taweret." Ancient Egypt Online. www.ancientegyptonline.co.uk/taweret.html. Accessed June 18, 2009.

Thompson, Clive. "The Antigravity Underground." *Wired*. August 2003. Issue 11.08.

Topel, Fred. "What's up with *Lost*'s Nestor Carbonell not aging? And the 'guy-liner'?" *Sci-Fi Wire*. Online. January 29, 2009.

Wikipedia.org.

Acknowledgments

· ·

Thank you once again to publishers David Caron and Jack David at ECW Press for giving me the same assurance that ABC gave Darlton, and letting me know this series would be carried out to the end without cancellation. A huge thank-you to my lovely and amazing editor, Crissy Boylan, who was always encouraging and was a great sounding board for ideas (and for being such a diehard *Lost* fan herself) and who found all of the cast photos in the book — you are the best. Thank you to Gail Nina for doing her usual wonderful job of typesetting the book, and to my publicists, Simon Ware and Sarah Dunn.

And, as always, thank you to my editrix of awesomeness, Gil Adamson, who promised to keep editing me even though she's become a huge (*huge*, I tell you!) literary star. Thank you for watching *Lost* and smoothing out my book's many rough edges.

Thank you to my dear friend, Fionna Boyle, who once again read through my draft episode guide and pointed out any inconsistencies or errors that were there.

It pays to have university professors as friends: thank you to Dr. Matthew Pateman for agreeing to read my extremely long chapter on James Joyce's *Ulysses*, and making me actually feel good about it. Big thanks to my long-time friend and one-time American lit professor, Dr. Neil Brooks, for chatting with me about Flannery O'Connor. One of these days I'll succeed in getting both of you to watch *Lost*.

As always, my undying gratitude to Ryan Ozawa, Hawaii resident extraordinaire, who always gives me the amazing behind-the-scenes photos of the production going on everywhere in Oahu. Check out his blog at www.hawaiiup.com/lost. Just one more season to go, Ryan. Time to get out your surveillance equipment. Thank you also to all of the other photographers who contributed their photos to the book: Allison Jirsa, Bill Spencer, Michael Robles, Kevin Frates, Lenka Peacock, harryillustrator, Audra Wolfmann, Ripton Scott, Graeme and Tamara Ing.

And I never say this, but I should: Thank you to the writers of *Lost*, who have crafted such an insanely wonderful show that actually allows for such in-depth discussion. I don't know what I'll do after season 6.

And now, to the people who've become like a cyber-family to me, the readers and commentators on my blog, Nik at Nite: I tried to go through the thousands of comments and write down the name of every commentator to thank each of you, and I'm hoping I didn't leave anyone out. If so, my apologies, and please know that I appreciate your comments. So, here goes: a massive thank-you to Batcabbage, SonshineMusic, humanebean, Teebore, asiancolossus, Jazzygirl, joshua, Benny, Blam, Colleen/redeem147, KeepingAwake, Don Edwards, myselfixion, DeborahB, The Question Mark, poggy, Jeff Heimbuch, Amsted, Genevieve, Hutch, Hunter, Michele, Karolyn, Ali Bags, Missing Georgia, ashlie, mgkoeln, ChrisTemple, The Shout, Roland, Saza, TV Writer, NurseBrian, LotteryTicket, Hisham, Ambivalentman, Maggie Elizabeth, M9 EGO, Gary, Azà, Chuck Power, edgeshat, Brian Douglas, theothers108, Brandon, Tim Alan, Paticus, HD, Chapati Kid, Margosita, Robbie, lefty, Perfect Timing, Jason Paul Tolmie, Doe, Scott, Enenra MacCutcheon, Karolyn, Karen, wendy, Susan, Frank, Katey, EvaHart, Jay Menard, Seabiscuit, Jeff, Adela P., maryelere, Jarrett Pressman, Mark R.Y., Leah, Mythos, Steve, Mike Cunningham, Doe, Jeremiah, cordelia, Michael, ronald, Miss Scarlett, doyousmellcarrots, thomwade, SenexMacDonald, Danny, Laurie, groovyghosthunter, Calvin, Texas Susan, JT, tsavonglah, MiaBella, DK, taitle, Angel, Kimberly, Barry, Lesley C, RSK, Word, DanM, atruebluehusker, Jouke, J. Maggio, brodal, Alicia, Ash, Kyle, swac, JenniferS, matthew, Amy, Eric, ARTAR, ODM, Tanyam, Ann, Gregg, Julie Keen, Nashville Beatle, pete, Roger, lvgirl, Grimalkin, Allegra, Vanja, Zari, Garrett, scrvet, Annie, filipe cavalanti, Ashleigh, glossing, MW, Fatty Cahill, Dave, Megan, TCK, R.S., Yussi, Zabriina, Stan, Sam, Nancy, lostie 815, LostMyMind, Black and Purple, NanX, Minna, lostieforever, LoyallyLost, Robert Kuang, cara-chan, Crackedout, James E. Powell, Quinn, Olessi, elle, Alison, Rachel, ZooBot23, Ted, Helena, Naomi, Ivgirl, Msredhd, Sparty_Cyclone, Charon, Telmo Couto, Kirathena, Will, toquesdeipod, bluelittlegirl, Jono, LemonBailey, ejbelair, Jason and Alicia Halm, Snoochie, latelylost, David, Larisa, winsmith, Gerald Orr, pattyjean, aCanadianToker, Chris in NF, Marebabe, rcullen, adc, Target-Addict, John M Osborne, Sachin, Lael Gielow, E.B., yorick28, Shoop, achinghope, Erin, and peacockblue.

And despite the repetition, an extra-special thanks to Benny for the French translation of Rousseau and her crew in "The Little Prince"; Deborah for answering my questions about California law; Barry Johnson for the cover concept (I love it so much!); Batcabbage for chatting with me while I was reading *Y: The Last Man* (and for your suggestions of what I should read next!); to Joshua, humanebean, SonshineMusic, Teebore, and fb for reading through my season 6 questions and offering suggestions; and to Blam, Teebore, and humanebean for your brilliant time travel explanations — thank you for being the kinder Mileses to my Hurley.

And thank you to everyone who wrote the blurbs at the beginning of this book. They were definitely the words I needed to help me finish those last few chapters. (And not just because my head got so big with all the praise that I couldn't get through my office door for three days. . . .) How lovely to have such wonderful readers.

To my friends and family, especially Sue, who didn't resent me for not returning emails or phone calls right away (and, when I did, for putting up with my constant *Lost* philosophizing).

Thank you and much love to my husband Robert, for taking the kids for trips on weekends while I was madly writing, and to my wonderful children, Sydney and Liam, for making me laugh so much and for being such amazing inspirations to me every day.

And, as always, my deepest thanks to Jennifer Hale: I'd time travel anywhere with you.

The essential companions to the first four seasons of LOST

Finding Lost:
The Unofficial Guide
$17.95 U.S., $19.95 Cdn

Finding Lost, Season
Three: The Unofficial Guide
$14.95 U.S., $16.95 Cdn

Finding Lost, Season Four:
The Unofficial Guide
$14.95 U.S., $16.95 Cdn

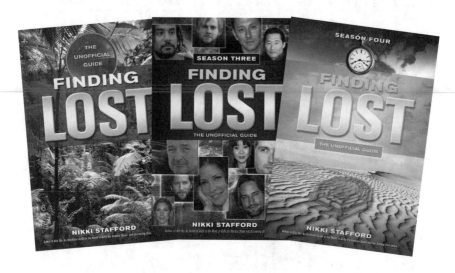

"The **Finding Lost** series is quite simply the best resource for fans. Not only is the information concise and complete, Nikki Stafford's commentary is insightful, relevant, and entertaining. No matter how well you know the show, Stafford's analysis of the themes and symbolism of **Lost** will renew your desire to go back and watch over and over again."
– Jon "DocArzt" Lachonis

"Nikki Stafford [is] . . . one of the show's leading scholars."
– *Newsday*

The *Finding Lost* series includes:

- a comprehensive episode guide and bios of all of the major actors on the show
- chapters examining major references on the show, such as the real John Locke and Jean-Jacques Rousseau (and how they compare to the fictional ones), Stephen Hawking's theories, the Lost mobisodes, and much more
- sidebars chronicling trivia such as Sawyer's nicknames for people, what Hurley's numbers could represent, comparing John Locke to Ben Linus, and what Abaddon's name really means
- summaries of the show's literary references, including *Watership Down, The Third Policeman, Our Mutual Friend, Of Mice and Men, Slaughterhouse-Five* and many more
- exclusive behind-the-scenes photos of filming in Hawaii